Frank K. Hain
and the Manhattan
Railway Company

Frank K. Hain and the Manhattan Railway Company

The Elevated Railway, 1875–1903

Peter Murray Hain

McFarland & Company, Inc., Publishers
Jefferson, North Carolina, and London

LIBRARY OF CONGRESS CATALOGUING-IN-PUBLICATION DATA

Hain, Peter Murray, 1932–
Frank K. Hain and the Manhattan Railway Company :
the elevated railway, 1875–1903 / Peter Murray Hain.
p. cm.
Includes bibliographical references and index.

ISBN 978-0-7864-6405-0
softcover : 50# alkaline paper ∞

1. Manhattan Railway Company. 2. Subways — New York (State) —
New York. 3. Street-railroads — New York (State) — New York.
4. Local transit — New York (State) — New York. 5. Hain, Frank K. I. Title.

HE4491.N63N48 2011   388.4'4097471— dc22   2011011065

BRITISH LIBRARY CATALOGUING DATA ARE AVAILABLE

© 2011 Peter Murray Hain. All rights reserved

*No part of this book may be reproduced or transmitted in any form
or by any means, electronic or mechanical, including photocopying
or recording, or by any information storage and retrieval system,
without permission in writing from the publisher.*

On the cover: *inset* Franklin K. Hain (*Biographical Directory of
Railway Officials of America*, 1889); Elevated station, Sixth Avenue
and 34th Street (Herald Square), 1880 (Library of Congress)

Manufactured in the United States of America

*McFarland & Company, Inc., Publishers
Box 611, Jefferson, North Carolina 28640
www.mcfarlandpub.com*

In Memoriam
Rebecca Mackey Hain
(1905–1962)

Table of Contents

Acknowledgments ix

Preface 1

I. The New York and Metropolitan Elevated Railroads 5

II. The Manhattan Railway Company 27

III. Colonel Frank K. Hain 37

IV. A Railroad in Flux (1880–1885) 51

V. Facing Down the Challenges (1886–1888) 67

VI. Leadership Changes (1889–1892) 91

VII. The Depression Takes Its Toll (1893–1896) 109

VIII. Steam Versus Electric Heats Up 121

IX. A Martyrdom to Duty 129

X. Electrification and the Subway 141

Appendix: A Brief Biography of Annie R. Hain (1836–1929) 161

Notes 165

Bibliography 173

Index 175

Acknowledgments

The history, organization, and operation of the Manhattan Railway Company and its principal components, the New York and Metropolitan elevated railroads, are highly complex. There are only a handful of reliable references and few current historians are fully conversant with late 19th and early 20th century rapid transit in New York City. Among the latter are Brian J. Cudahy (*Under the Sidewalks of New York*, 1979) and Joseph Brennan (*The Beach Pneumatic Transit Company*, 2005), both of whom provided thoughtful encouragement and frank advice about the scope and content of this book.

The *New York Times* and the Library of Congress online historical newspaper archives were the glue that enabled me to piece together the practical aspects of Frank K. Hain's challenges and accomplishments. Without these excellent resources, this book probably could not have been written.

My research assistant in New York City, Mary Ann DiNapoli, developed more source material than seemed possible, and her knack for always digging out "just one more" document was of great value. She was recommended to me as an excellent researcher and she was certainly that and more.

Without a trace of knowledge about the antecedents of Frank Hain's wife, Annie R. McWilliams, I turned for assistance to Cynthia Elder, president of the Montour County, Pennsylvania, Genealogical Society. She enthusiastically accepted the task and left no stone unturned as she conducted highly professional research in several archives over a period of weeks.

Coreen Hallenbeck is a well-regarded research specialist in Albany, New York, who was very helpful in following up on details about Frank Hain that only could be obtained by an experienced researcher with excellent local connections.

As was not unexpected, my wife, Pamela Chase Hain, a published author in her own right (*A Confederate Chronicle: The Life of a Civil War Survivor*, 2005), provided much needed encouragement throughout the course of this work and contributed insightful knowledge based on her own literary experiences.

Finally, a city official, several reference librarians, and research volunteers contributed their enthusiasm and expertise to this project. Chief among them were Frederick C. Sheeler, Berks County (PA), recorder of deeds; Christine Windheuser, National Museum of American History; Gretchen Feltes, New York University Law Library; Tanya Boltz, Keokuk (IA) Public Library (who came in on her day off); Susan M. Jellinger, State Historical Society of Iowa; Carol Kroeger, Rock Island County (IL) Historical Society; and the good folks at the interlibrary loan desk of the Roanoke County (VA) Public Library (HQ/419) who responded in record time to my many requests.

Peter Murray Hain • Moneta, Virginia

Preface

The Manhattan Railway Company (commonly known as the Manhattan Elevated Railway, or simply the "el") was organized originally on November 10, 1875, under the Rapid Transit Act of 1875. On May 20, 1879, the Manhattan Railway leased the two existing elevated roads, the New York Elevated Railroad and the Metropolitan Elevated Railway. However, the company was unable to meet its financial obligations and entered into receivership on July 14, 1881, only to be ordered out of receivership a little more than three months later. On August 1, 1884, after three years of litigation and behind-the-scenes maneuvering, the directors of the three companies reached a new settlement that put the Manhattan Railway Company in control of the two existing elevated roads.

The New York Elevated Railroad operated the Ninth Avenue and Third Avenue lines and was the successor organization to the West Side and Yonkers Patent Railway Company and the West Side Patented Elevated Railway Company. The Metropolitan Elevated Railway operated the Sixth Avenue and Second Avenue lines and was the successor organization to the Gilbert Elevated Railway Company.

The four lines extended the length of Manhattan Island and over the Harlem River into the Bronx with 334 steam locomotives and 1,122 passenger cars on 102 miles of track. In its heyday, the Manhattan Railway employed more than 5,000 trainmen and officials, transported 515,000 passengers per day, and enjoyed a surplus of $5.3 million on its balance sheet. About 2.5 billion passengers traveled the el from 1880 to 1895.

From its inception, however, the Manhattan Railway was an enterprise in turmoil because it was formed under questionable financial circumstances by a clique of businessmen whom the press relentlessly vilified as "robber barons." Nevertheless, the elevated roads became a stunning financial success, if not an entirely convenient and comfortable form of public conveyance.

Competing with the Manhattan Railway were 17 surface or street horse-drawn companies that had their own unique disadvantages. At this time, New York City was suffering from a population explosion that brought with it unrelenting congestion, suffocating pollution, and escalating real estate values. The enormity of the problems begged for the introduction of an underground rapid transit system. However, the company's owners were unmoved by public sentiment and adept at deferring action on issues that might cut into their short term profits.

The critics directed equal attention to conversion of the elevated roads from steam to electric motive power. Although a prototype electric locomotive was successfully demonstrated at the Chicago Railway Exhibition in 1883, and several inventors conducted trials of pneumatic and electric motors on New York's elevated tracks during the 1880s, management equivocated about introducing electricity on the el for almost two decades.

This history of the elevated railways is based partly on the experiences of Colonel Frank K. Hain (1836–1896), who served as general manager of the Manhattan Railway Company for 16 years. His experiences illustrate the challenges of operating a major railroad in the world's most important city. No recent books cover the elevated railways as extensively as this work, and much of this material has never before been published. The story is told from the practical point of view and covers the origins of rapid transit, the early elevated railroads, legislation, rolling stock, labor relations, financial results, the crusading press, accidents and the company's response thereto, the question of steam versus electric, the eventual takeover by the Interborough Rapid Transit Company, and the start up of the subway.

Frank Hain began his career at age 17 as a machinist's apprentice at the Philadelphia and Reading Railroad. In the ensuing 21 years he held positions of increasing responsibility at several railroads, including eight years as a superintendent. As a lead draftsman for the world's largest locomotive builder, he was dispatched to Russia where he introduced anthracite-burning locomotives to the Russian railways. Twice he interrupted his career to serve as an assistant engineer on federal gunboats in both the pre–Civil War and Civil War Navy. He was slightly wounded in the battle of New Orleans, and he was aboard the vessel that accepted the surrender of Baton Rouge, Louisiana, and Natchez, Mississippi.

Frank Hain was a hands-on manager and proved to be a shrewd and strong-willed negotiator in several confrontations with the trainmen's unions. Despite his reputation as a strict disciplinarian, his modest, straightforward demeanor and sense of fairness inspired the trainmen's loyalty and cooperation. He built his reputation on his concern for the safety of the traveling public and thorough knowledge of every "nut and bolt" in his steam locomotives. Colonel Hain was not immune to sniping by the railroad's critics, but he was not smeared by the financial scandals that plagued his superiors. Instead, he was highly thought of in a city that was not known for extending praise unless it was truly earned.

During his final two years at the helm, he suffered a "nervous breakdown" that was attributed to overwork. At the urging of his superiors, he admitted himself to a sanitarium for a complete rest. Although he seemed to make good progress towards complete recovery, he died suddenly, shocking the city. The *New York Times* described his passing as a martyrdom to duty.

A little over five and half years later the Manhattan Railway ran its first electric-powered train over the Second Avenue Line. On March 31, 1903, the company was taken over by the Interborough Rapid Transit Company (IRT). And, after 19 months of excavation and construction, the IRT subway opened to the public. The final act was played out at

Preface

11:59 P.M. on August 31, 1958, when a short segment of the surviving elevated line, the "Polo Grounds shuttle," closed down. From that date on, the elevated railroad system in New York City ceased to exist. But, from 1880 to 1902, the steam-powered elevated railway was an institution in the Big Apple and more passengers, satisfied or not, traveled the el than on any other rapid transit system in the world. For five cents!

I

The New York and Metropolitan Elevated Railroads

It has been said that in 1746 ox carts were the first form of street transportation in New York City, traversing Broadway from the Battery to Houston Street. If true, this form of transportation was too slow even for New Yorkers of that era.[1]

A public street transit system existed in New York City from 1827 when Abraham Brower put into service a 12-seat stagecoach, or omnibus, named "Accommodation." In 1832, John Mason organized the New York and Harlem Railroad, a street railway that used horse-drawn cars that ran on embedded metal tracks on Fourth Avenue between Prince and 14th streets. In 1852, reportedly one horse car every 15 seconds passed through the intersection of Chambers Street and Broadway. Three years later, 593 omnibuses traveled on 27 Manhattan routes and horse-drawn cars ran on street rails on Third, Fourth, Sixth, and Eighth avenues. In 1864, when the city's population was about 700,000, 12 horse car lines operated on the streets and carried about 61 million passengers. But horse-drawn vehicles were slow, had difficulty climbing hilly streets, and produced unpleasant debris. And, horses were susceptible to disease, notably equine flu, providing evidence that the public was not well-served by a single source of public transportation.[2]

By the middle of the 19th century, congestion in New York City was out of control. A means for moving the masses up and down Manhattan without adding to the gridlock was needed.[3]

> Broadway became unsafe for pedestrians [and] the rivalry between omnibus drivers was so great that they recklessly drove over men, women, and children in their haste to beat their nearest competitors to waiting passengers. The newspapers ... denounced the conditions and scored omnibus and car companies. Reckless driving and crowded omnibuses were not the only grievances. The drivers were accused of swearing at passengers and giving them bad money or tickets in change. The *New York Herald* savagely attacked the omnibus nuisance, and called upon the capitalists of the city to establish cab lines to relieve the suffering citizens.[4]

The successful introduction of the London subway in 1863 inspired proposals for an underground railway in New York City, and in early 1864 the first rapid transit bill was introduced in the state legislature. The Metropolitan Railway Company filed articles of incorporation and sought the rights to build an underground railroad in Broadway from the Battery to 34th Street and then under Sixth Avenue to Central Park. The promoter of this plan was Hugh B. Willson, a Michigan railroad man, who had been impressed with the London subway. The company was incorporated under the general railroad law of 1850 for a period of 100 years and $5 million in capital stock was issued, divided into $50 shares. However, despite the support of several well-known investors, "the Willson project was not received with enthusiasm" in the legislature.[5]

The elevated railroads proved to be the first viable means of rapid transit. Henry Sargent obtained the first patent for an elevated railroad in New York City in 1825. Several other individuals obtained subsequent patents for various types of one-, two-, and three-deck structures, but most never advanced beyond the planning stages. Pneumatic propulsion, steam, and cables were the most popular means of motive power, and the many devices patented were limited only by the ingenuity of the inventors. For instance, one plan envisioned "aerial transit cars" suspended by cables and attached to towers or tall buildings.[6]

While several underground railway proposals were advanced during the late 1860s,

Proposed Arcade Railway, Wall Street, 1869 (Library of Congress).

I. The New York and Metropolitan Elevated Railroads

the Arcade Railway and Beach Pneumatic plans stood out. The Arcade plan originally envisioned a six-track railway but was amended to four tracks in 1870. This plan proposed to "excavate Broadway from house to house, to the depth of twenty-five feet…. The cellars of the buildings thus exposed, to be finished architecturally, and furnished with sidewalks, so as to give a new range of stores below the present ones." Four arched tunnels were planned below the railway to provide for horsecars and roadways.[7.]

Alfred Ely Beach's plan was for a huge forced air blower to propel a railway passenger car inside a tube under Broadway. In 1868, he received permission to build a pneumatic tube to transport small packages inside two tubes, each 54 inches in diameter. Construction began in 1869, but instead of moving forward with the approved project, Beach covertly constructed a tube nine feet in diameter and 312 feet long that ran under Broadway for about one city block from Warren to Murray Street. The tunnel opened to the public on February 26, 1870, and it featured an elegant underground station with a goldfish pond and grand piano. A cylindrical car about 18 feet long and 8 feet in diameter was designed to transport 18–22 passengers. Beach's subway reportedly transported 400,000 people over his short stretch of track.[8]

The Arcade Railway and Beach Pneumatic plans were introduced to the legislature

Station view of Alfred Ely Beach's pneumatic railroad, 1870 (*Appleton's Journal of Literature, Science, and Art*, June 25, 1870).

almost simultaneously. While the Arcade bill was "the most popular scheme ... ever introduced for a steam railroad in New York City," the Beach project apparently diverted attention from what many considered a better plan. A leading opponent of the Arcade Railway was A. T. Stewart who had "for years opposed any and every project for a railroad in Broadway, either underground, elevated, or surface." However, on April 25, 1870, the Pneumatic bill was voted down, while the Arcade bill passed. According to the *Times*, a vocal opponent of the Arcade bill: "As there was money in the Arcade Railroad bill, the Legislature could not of course adjourn without its passage...."[9]

On May 5, A. T. Stewart and a group of his followers met with Governor Hoffman to speak "at length about the damage to their businesses that would be caused by construction" of the Arcade Railway. And, on May 15, Hoffman vetoed the bill. It was "the last gasp of the Arcade plan — or so it seemed" at the time, because the Arcade Railway was similar to what was eventually built. But, despite considerable initiative and accomplishment, Beach's "pneumatic system ran into both political and practical problems and never progressed past the demonstration stage." Regardless of the details, however, the point was that "no subway line could get financing and the elevated with its lower capital cost was built."[10]

Meanwhile, Tammany Hall's William M. "Boss" Tweed (1823–1878) countered with

Charles T. Harvey's trial run of his cable car, Greenwich Street, December 7, 1867 (Joseph Brennan Collection).

his Viaduct Plan—a series of elevated lines running above the street on 40-foot high stone arches. His plan was approved but it was slow to develop because of vigorous press attacks on corruption at Tammany Hall. Boss Tweed was indicted on December 15, 1871, and convicted in 1873, effectively bringing his political career to an end.[11]

The New York Elevated Railroad

The New York Elevated Railroad operated the Ninth Avenue and Third Avenue lines and was the successor organization to the West Side and Yonkers Patent Railway Company and the West Side Patented Elevated Railway Company.

Under laws of 1850 and 1866, the West Side and Yonkers Patent Railway Company was awarded a 999-year franchise for the purpose of "constructing, maintaining, and operating an elevated railway in the City of New York, devoted to public use, for the conveyance of persons and property by means of a propelling rope or cable attached to stationary power." The sponsor of this rapid transit bill was Charles T. Harvey. The elevated road was to begin near the southern tip of Manhattan Island and "extend northward with branches parallel or lateral to the main line" to Yonkers, a distance of about 25 miles. In 1867, the legislature authorized the West Side and Yonkers Patent Railway Company to construct the first half-mile of elevated railroad in New York City.[12]

The initial quarter mile of the authorized half mile was built "on the easterly curb line of Greenwich Street, between Battery Place and Morris Street, and afterward extended to Cortlandt Street." Work was begun on July 1, 1867, and the first column was erected on October 7, 1867.

> And so, block by painful block the thirty-foot high, one-legged elevated superstructure crept up Greenwich Street, past the second floor windows of banks, hotels, saloons, stores, warehouses, and dwellings. Since the columns supporting the track were set in the sidewalk just inches from the curb, the cars would run very close to the building facades along the route; in fact it would be nearly possible for someone living in a second floor room to reach out and touch a passing cable car.[13]

"The method of operation was by an endless chain or cable wound around a drum a couple of times, to prevent slipping, and then passing overhead to the level of the structure. The drum was driven by stationary steam engines, placed in vaults at intervals of about 1,500 feet beneath the sidewalk under the elevated structure."[14] On December 7, 1867, Charles T. Harvey drove a car truck on this single-column structure over Greenwich Street. The railroad's board of directors was pleased with the demonstration and authorized Harvey to proceed with construction of the second quarter mile to Cortlandt Street, which was then built in March and April 1868. On July 3, 1868, Harvey took the directors on a trial ride, and according to the *Times* (July 4), "the car ran easily from the Battery to Cortlandt Street, starting at the rate of five miles an hour and increasing to a speed of ten miles. The company does not pretend with its present machinery to run the cars faster than fifteen miles an hour; but during the next two months will make arrangement for much more rapid motion."[15]

From 1868 to 1870, the West Side and Yonkers Patent Railway Company and its successor, the West Side Patented Elevated Railway Company, extended the road on a single-column structure to 30th Street and Ninth Avenue. When the structure was complete to 29th and 30th streets, mechanical troubles, legal issues, and financial difficulties caused the "impractical cable operation" to be abandoned. The West Side Patented Elevated Company, then in control, could do no better than the original company and shut down. The railroad remained in limbo until November 15, 1870, when the entire railroad — rolling stock, patents, etc. — were disposed of for $960 at a sheriff's sale. Francis H. Tows was the purchaser on behalf of the bondholders of the two defunct companies.[16]

The rejuvenated West Side Patented Elevated Railway discarded the cables, stationary engines, "and all equipment and machinery in connection therewith." After some structural repairs, the company began operations as a steam railroad on April 20, 1871. A new and ornate dummy engine was introduced to "eliminate cinders, noises, and the scaring of horses" on a single track structure on Greenwich Street and Ninth Avenue, from Battery Place to 30th Street, a distance of about three and one-half miles. Two stations, one at Dey and Greenwich streets and the other at 29th Street and Ninth Avenue, served both north and southbound trains and were connected by a bridge at track level.[17]

In the summer of 1871, three mortgages against the West Side Patented Elevated Company became due and were foreclosed. The company was purchased by the New York Elevated Railroad Company and its articles of association were filed on October 27, 1871, with a capital stock of $10 million. It immediately acquired "all franchises and properties of the defunct companies" for about $801,000 by issuing stock, a part of its $10 million capitalization. On May 24, 1876, the Rapid Transit Commission approved the New York Elevated Railroad Company's use of "locomotive dummy steam engines, of the size, plan and structure, as are now in use, and such similar new and improved engines as they hereafter construct and desire to use, in place of stationary steam power in the propelling of cars."[18]

In May 1877, Cyrus W. Field purchased a controlling interest in the New York Elevated and became its president. On November 1, 1877, the New York Elevated Railroad Company began construction of the Third Avenue Line from South Ferry to the Harlem River. Construction began at Whitehall Street, and Chatham Square, and proceeded north along the Battery and Third Avenue to 42nd Street. After a few trial runs, the Third Avenue Line opened to the public from South Ferry to Grand Central Depot on August 26, 1878.[19]

In 1881, the New York el operated 108 locomotives, 271 passenger cars, two supply cars, and eight gondola cars. Sixteen stations were on the Ninth Avenue Line and 25 on the Third Avenue Line. The daily average (1880) of paying passengers on the Ninth Avenue and Third Avenue lines was 14,500 and 80,000, respectively. By 1883, the New York el operated over 32.755 miles of single and double track, including sidings and turnouts.[20]

Construction of the road developed as follows:

Ninth Avenue Line

Single track extended to 34th Street and Ninth Avenue, July 30, 1873.
Single track extended to 42nd Street and Ninth Avenue, November 6, 1875.
Single track extended to 61st Street and Ninth Avenue, January 18, 1876.
Double track extended to South Ferry, April 5, 1877.
Double track completed to 61st Street and Ninth Avenue, June 2, 1878.
Double track extended to 83rd Street and Ninth Avenue, June 9, 1879.
Rebuilding of the old track in Greenwich Street and Ninth Avenue was completed May 2, 1880.[21]

Third Avenue Line

Double track line extended from South Ferry to 42nd Street and Third Avenue, August 26, 1878.
Double track line extended from 42nd Street and Third Avenue to 67th Street and Third Avenue, September 16, 1878.
Double track line extended from 67th Street and Third Avenue to 89th Street and Third Avenue, December 9, 1878.
Double track line extended from 89th Street and Third Avenue to 129th Street and Third Avenue, December 30, 1878.[22]

Branches

42nd Street branch, Third to Fourth avenues, August 26, 1878.
City Hall branch, City Hall to Chatham Square, March 17, 1879.
34th Street branch, Third Avenue to East River, July 1, 1881.[23]

The Metropolitan Elevated Railway

The Metropolitan Elevated Railway operated the Sixth and Second Avenue lines. It was the successor organization to the Gilbert Elevated Railway Company.

On June 17, 1872, under Chapter 885, Laws of 1872, the legislature chartered Dr. Rufus H. Gilbert's plan to "construct, maintain, and operate" a "tubular" road propelled by "atmospheric pressure, compressed air or other power" to "operate over the streets, avenues, and thoroughfares of New York City supported by gigantic Gothic arches springing from curb to curb." However, Gilbert's plan proved impracticable, as well as "extravagantly expensive," and the Rapid Transit Commission compelled him to adopt "simpler and more economical plans of construction." Moreover, the Panic of 1873 prevented the company from obtaining capital and, in any case, found it impossible to build the proposed lines within the prescribed time limit, even with an extension.[24]

After several concessions, including a change to steam motive power, the company set about "devising ways and means for development." The instrument was the New York Loan and Improvement Company and a contract was signed on March 13, 1876, in which the latter agreed to construct and equip the road in response to the requirements of the Rapid Transit Commission — essentially a line from Morris Street to 83rd Street, over a

Dr. Rufus H. Gilbert's tubular pneumatic road, 1871 (Library of Congress).

distance of 6.12 miles on double-tracked road, and including 17 stations. But, on August 3, 1876, property owners and a surface car company succeeded in gaining an injunction and the work was halted. However, in November 1877, a court of appeals removed the injunction and work resumed. By the spring of 1878, the line was complete as planned, from Morris Street to Sixth Avenue and 59th Street. On May 29, 1878, a trial run of one engine and four cars was successfully completed and, on June 5, 1878, the Sixth Avenue Line opened for business.[25]

On the next day, June 6, the Supreme Court ordered the name of the Gilbert Elevated Railway Company changed to the Metropolitan Elevated Railway Company. Two days later, the new company continued construction of the next section of road on 53rd Street, between Sixth and Ninth avenues, and from there north on Ninth Avenue to 59th Street, which was already under subcontracts from the former Gilbert Company. This line was to continue north of Ninth Avenue to 110th Street, then to Eighth Avenue and the Harlem River. However, a portion of this route, on Ninth Avenue from 53rd to 83rd streets, was part of the franchise route of the New York Elevated Railroad. Thus, joint agreements were executed between all companies to enable construction to proceed.[26]

The last of the four elevated lines to be built on Manhattan Island was the Second Avenue Line. Its routing was fixed by the Rapid Transit Commissioners under Chapter 606, Laws of 1875, and was part of the route granted to the Gilbert Company and its successor, the Metropolitan Elevated Railway Company. However, the Second Avenue Line overlapped part of the routes originally granted to the New York Elevated Railroad Company. The railroad companies and the Rapid Transit Commissioners agreed that where routes of the two companies coincided, "those portions could be built by either company and the cost divided in some equitable way." And, "after the section had been put in operation, the expense of maintenance should be divided under separate agreements."[27]

The Metropolitan Elevated Railway Company began construction of the Second Avenue Line on February 24, 1879. By the fall, all foundations had been "practically completed" as far as 127th Street and the iron work erected near 65th Street. Under the Tripartite Agreement between the Metropolitan and New York els and the Manhattan Railway Company, the latter took over construction and "completed all the sub-contracts previously made with the other companies and finished the Second Avenue structures in the time prescribed." The first trial run over the section from South Ferry to Second Avenue and 65th Street took place on January 15, 1880, and the line was ready for regular operations on March 1, 1880. "By August 16, 1880, all structures and tracks were ready for operation, and trains were operated from South Ferry to 127th Street, then the extreme north limit."[28]

In 1881, the Metropolitan Elevated operated 95 locomotives, 316 passenger cars, and 6 gondola cars. Twenty-six stations were on the Sixth Avenue Line and 23 on the Second Avenue Line. The daily average (1880) of paying passengers on the Sixth Avenue and Second Avenue lines was 68,500 and 24,500, respectively. By 1883, the Metropolitan el operated over 39.585 miles of single and double track, including sidings and turnouts.[29]

Construction of the road developed as follows:

Sixth Avenue Line
From Rector Street to 8th Street, opened June 6, 1878.
First train to 53rd Street and Eighth Avenue, January 9, 1879.
First train to 104th Street and Ninth Avenue, June 7, 1879.
First train to 125th Street and Eighth Avenue, September 17, 1879.
First train to 135th Street and Eighth Avenue, September 27, 1879.
First train to 155th Street and Eighth Avenue, December 1, 1879.

Second Avenue Line
First train to 65th Street and Second Avenue, March 1, 1890.
First train to 127th Street and Second Avenue, August 16, 1880.[30]

Construction

A simple recitation of history does not do justice to the tremendous engineering effort that went into construction of the elevated roads. *Scientific American* put matters into perspective in discussing construction of the Second Avenue Line in early 1879:

> In all nearly a thousand tons of iron are said to have been required in arching over pipes in the 2,400 foundations for piers. In making these foundations 60,000 cubic yards of rock had to be blasted and removed under the most exacting conditions, and 80,000 cubic yards of earth. Five steam pile drivers were employed in driving 300,000 lineal feet of piles for foundations in marshy places. The engineer in charge gives the amount of lumber used in the piers at 800,000 feet board measure, in addition to 50,000 cubic yards of sand for mortar, 80,000 cubic yards of broken stone for concrete, 70,000 barrels of cement, and 21,000,000 bricks. One contract for iron for the superstructure called for 80,000,000 pounds.[31]

Various styles of superstructure were used in construction of the elevated railroads, and no one company was consistent in applying a uniform style. The final choice depended on a number of factors, including preferences of the engineers and contractors, the width of the streets, the nature of the nearby inhabitants and adjacent structures. On narrow streets, the tracks were laid on trestles over the middle of the street with the columns set along the curb lines. In these cases, the roads beneath the superstructure would be partially covered, but the sidewalks would be uncovered. On wide streets, the tracks could be placed close together over the center of the street or run along each side of the street. Along the Bowery, for instance, the New York Elevated placed the columns along the curbs and ran the tracks on each side of the street. On Third Avenue, however, it was thought best to run the tracks on two lines of columns in the center of the street so as to distance the tracks from the adjacent buildings. Among the prominent contractors were New York Loan and Improvement; Clark, Reeves; Passaic Rolling Mill; A. R. Whitney; Edge Moor Iron; Keystone Bridge; and Mills & Ambrose.[32]

As seen above in the quote from *Scientific American*, a project of these dimensions presented surveyors and site engineers with many complicated challenges, including sewer basins, hydrants, manholes, lamp posts, gas and water mains, or storage vaults. Generally, the plan called for the elevated tracks to be placed 20 feet over the street and level with the second story of adjacent buildings. However, the track levels had to be adjusted for existing geographical conditions, such as hollows and, for example, the hilly areas west of Central Park where the trestles had to be placed more than 60 feet high.[33]

The foundation stage of construction began with workers excavating pits in the street about seven feet deep and nine feet square. The relative quality of the soil and any subterranean obstacles determined the further design and depth of the foundation and piers. For instance, on the Sixth Avenue Line along West Broadway, the soft subsoil required more extensive work than a solid soil situation to ensure a secure foundation, requiring piles driven to a depth of 25 feet.[34]

Once the foundation was secured, the columns of the superstructure were set on the base casting and filled with cast iron cement. This procedure was first done by a construction crane, wagon, and horses and later by a steam-operated moving crane located on the superstructure. Seven men and a team of horses could set up ten to forty columns in a day.[35]

After iron workers erected the superstructure, construction crews laid the track foundations and rails. In so doing, crossties of yellow pine were placed ten inches apart except on curves, crossings, and turnouts, where heavier white oak was used. Heavy 5 × 8 inch and 5 × 10 inch guard rail timbers were bolted to the ties on each side of the rails to prevent trains from falling to the street in case of accidents.[36]

The final step involved painting all surfaces of the elevated structure. After experimenting with a metallic base coat and white lead second coat, olive drab became the color of choice.[37]

The potential for structural disaster involving the vertical columns and horizontal girders of these great iron bridges was ever present and required the company to put in place a rigidly enforced program of inspection and maintenance. The Engineering Department of the Manhattan Railway was ultimately responsible, but the Roadmaster's Department did the work. Teams of specialists — riveters, cleaners, painters, etc. — had specific responsibilities to patrol and examine structural elements along clearly defined sections of track. Especially high sections of the road, such as the 110th Street "suicide" curve, were inspected daily. Repair and maintenance work was facilitated by a numbering system on the columns that enabled workers to locate the defects quickly.[38]

Obviously, the costs were enormous for a construction project of this magnitude. "According to Russell Sage ... the total cost of building the four elevated lines when they were just completed about 1881 was $4,535,754.70" and the project employed some six thousand workers during the peak construction period in 1879.[39]

Rolling Stock

Locomotives

The first generation of locomotives on the New York el were light, 0-4-0 engines with 30-inch drivers known as "dummies," so called because they were disguised to appear as little like steam engines as possible to make them more acceptable to opponents of steam. They were "very quaintly camouflaged little vehicles with windows all around, and like the doll houses they were, the exteriors were nicely lacquered, scrolled, striped, and gilded in the prevailing taste of the time." Moreover, the noise was muffled so as not to scare the horses on the streets below.[40]

The New York el's dummies were designed by the road's superintendent and master mechanic, David W. Wyman. His emphasis was on construction of very small and light engines that could be run on the single column elevated structures built for Charles T. Harvey's cable car. The first dummy locomotive, named the *Pioneer*, was built in April 1871 by the Albany Street Iron Works. However, *Pioneer* proved to be too small and underpowered and it was taken out of service after three years. Wyman went on to design improved, heavier versions for service on the more substantial elevated structures that were being extended north on Manhattan Island. While the improved structures were more stable, the cars still traveled on a single row of columns that inspired a sense of uneasiness among the passengers. Whether their fears were realistic or not, the fact remained that a serious street accident involving a single support column could more easily bring down the road than if the cars were traveling on a row of double columns supported by horizontal girders.[41]

From 1872 to 1877, 21 dummies were built for the New York el by several locomotive manufacturers and they were given names such as the *Spuyten Duyvel, Kingsbridge, Greenwich*, etc. They weighed in at 8,000 pounds (nos. 1–8), 12,000 pounds (nos. 9–13), 15,000 pounds (nos. 14–15), and 14,000 pounds (nos. 16–21).[42]

Expert opinion was divided on the next generation of locomotives for the New York el. One group favored simple four-wheel tank engines (0-4-0T) and another group favored an eight-wheeler (0-4-4T) designed by Matthias N. Forney. In 1866, Forney had patented the small, light 0-4-4 tank locomotive for frequent service over lightly traveled roads. The Forney was designed with the boiler located over the driving wheels for maximum traction, and the water and coal supply were over a four-wheeled truck at the rear of the locomotive. The New York el's experts equivocated about the two designs, but Director David Dows decided to order an equal number of both locomotives and "whichever proved best would become the road's standard."[43]

Spuyten Duyvel, 0-4-0 dummy, built for the New York Elevated Railroad by Brooks, May 1875 (Joseph Brennan Collection).

The New York el purchased three sizes of 0-4-0T

and two sizes of 0-4-4T from Baldwin and Rhode Island between June and December 1878. "The Forneys proved superior and became the standard on the elevated railways."[44]

Meanwhile, the Gilbert/Metropolitan management decided on 2-4-2 tank dummies, manufactured by the Grant Locomotive Works of Paterson, New Jersey. Sixteen of these engines were delivered in April 1878. While larger and more elegant than Wyman's dummy designs, the Grant dummies were underpowered and no more effective than the smaller Wymans. Nevertheless, the Metropolitan continued to order an additional thirteen 2-4-2 engines from the Grant works through October 1878. Soon after, the Metropolitan el abandoned the dummies and began ordering 2-4-2ST engines, of which 51 were acquired from the Grant, Danforth, and Rhode Island works between October 1878 and June 1880.[45]

The first Forney engines came to the New York Elevated's Third Avenue Line in June 1878 with a delivery of five Class B 0-4-4Ts (nos. 36–40) from the Baldwin Locomotive Works. Between August and December 1878, the New York el acquired 15 more Forney Class B (nos. 41–45 and 56–65) and 19 Class C (nos. 66–84) from Rhode Island and Baldwin. [Engines nos. 36–45 and 56–65 were the engines in competition with the 0-4-0T's]. Procurement carried over into March 1879, during which time the company acquired six more Forney 0-4-4T Class C (nos. 85–90) and 35 Class D (nos. 97–131) engines from the same manufacturers. The Class B motors weighed 33,000 pounds (nos. 36–45) and 29,880 pounds (nos. 56–65). Class C: 36,000 pounds (all). Class D: 37,900 pounds (all).[46]

The first Forney tank engines came to the Metropolitan Elevated Railway in February 1881 when the company acquired from Baldwin six Class E 0-4-4T (nos. 281–286). Baldwin delivered another seventeen Class E (nos. 287–303) between February and May 1881. All of the Class E motors weighed 40,300 pounds.[47]

Forney engine no. 39, class B 0-4-4T, built for the New York Elevated Railroad by Baldwin, June 1878. Typical of the Forney engines that became standard on the Manhattan lines (Joseph Brennan Collection).

The Forneys could operate in both forward and reverse with equal ability. The Second and Third Avenue engines faced downtown, although in at least one case, engines on the Second Avenue Line faced uptown. On the Sixth Avenue and Ninth Avenue lines, the engines faced uptown. Five cars was the maximum train length. "The Forneys negotiated curves as sharp as 56 feet and had an average speed of 15 mph. Maximum speeds were 45 mph on the express lines and 25 mph on the local lines."[48]

The size of the Forneys essentially was determined by the structural limitations of the trestles, i.e., no more than 24 tons as compared with passenger and freight locomotives on the mainline railroads that weighed 40 tons and 100 tons respectively. Because of the weight limitations, design engineers turned to developing lighter, thinner materials in their efforts to increase horsepower. Eleven classes of Forney engines evolved over the years — classes A to K — and the several major engine builders were expected to build to these standards.[49]

Situated on the roofs of Forney cabs were a pair of colored discs in the daylight hours and a lantern at night. Before trains entered a station, passengers could tell from color codes about a train's destination and whether it was a local or express.[50]

Beginning in early 1881, the Forney tank engines became standard on all Manhattan lines. The engines showed "superior hauling capacity, tracking ability, and reduced cost of maintenance." As many as 16 types of Forneys were used to meet varying operating conditions. When the Manhattan Railway Company converted to electric motive power in 1902, the company had 334 Forney locomotives on hand that were abandoned or sold.[51]

During the course of their operational life, the little red Forneys had their work cut out for them, and they did it well. The elevated system served a large and expanding population in a condensed and congested area. Experienced railroad men, such as Frank K. Hain, were required to manage and operate the 3,600 trains a day that were running on tight schedules. It was a "task for true professionals and it was a task that broke many a man. Being the General Manager just about insured a nervous breakdown."[52]

Passenger Cars

The evolution of passenger cars on the elevated roads passed through several stages from basic rustic designs to luxurious parlor cars, until the directors finally settled on a standard model about 1880. For the most part, the elevated cars were miniature versions of the standard railway coach, scaled down to reduce size and weight in order to meet limitations of the superstructure. Standard railway coaches were designed with all cross seats, but the elevated cars had about two-thirds of their seating aligned bench-like along the sides to accommodate standing room and to facilitate passengers getting on and off at the ends of the cars. Elevated cars weighed from 16,000 to 22,000 pounds, while standard railroad passenger cars weighed from 30,000 to 40,000 pounds.[53]

Management of the elevated roads originally gravitated to the idea that many of their traveling public would welcome extra-fare, lavishly accommodated Pullman Palace cars, such as were available on the mainline steam railroads. However, the expense of

I. The New York and Metropolitan Elevated Railroads

Engine no. 10_, class D 0-4-4T, built for the New York Elevated Railroad by Baldwin, March 1879 (Joseph Brennan Collection).

running two classes of cars proved to be their undoing, because even the well-heeled passengers evidently decided that the extra fare was not worth the cost for the short distances traveled.[54]

Once the standard model was adopted, elevated passenger cars changed little over the years. Aside from minor differences in detail and color, the cars were "characterized by batten-board side paneling, arched or pointed windows in a variety of arrangements, open platforms with iron gates, clerestory roofs, truss rods for bracing beneath the floors, and wooden construction." From the time it gained control of the elevated lines in 1879, the Manhattan Railway retained the color scheme of the New York Elevated Railroad: dark red car bodies, black striping, and MANHATTAN in gold leaf on the sides. These colors remained in effect until about 1909 when the road's new owner, the Interborough Rapid Transit Company (IRT), "adopted standard railroad Pullman green with decorative striping."[55]

Lighting in elevated cars evolved in much the same way as in the surface steam railways. Little attention was paid to lighting in the beginning of passenger travel because trains seldom ran at night and trips were usually of short duration and required only minimal illumination. A pale lamp at either end of the cars assisted passengers in entry/exit, but reading was next to impossible. However, as time went on and longer journeys became more common, passengers began to expect greater comforts. The addition of more oil lamps and candles was helpful, but they had limitations. Thus, overcoming illumination deficiencies was born of frustration with existing conditions and came to fruition when German manufacturer Julius Pintsch (1815–1884) invented a fixed gas manufactured from distilled naphtha. Known as Pintsch gas, it was compressed into storage tanks and then drawn off through a regulator that reduced the pressure and enabled its use in burners. As for the elevated passenger cars, originally all cars were lighted with sperm oil candles mounted on wall brackets. However, when Pintsch gas was introduced into the United States in 1883, the elevated roads were among the first railroads to adopt it. The gas was manufactured at the rail yards and transferred to tanks underneath the cars. Pintsch gas burned brighter and longer than the oil lamps and could withstand vibration and rough usage without extinguishing the light, but the gas added fuel to any fire in a railroad accident. While electric lights were finding great demand during the early elevated era, electricity was expensive, and the Manhattan Railway's management equivocated on adopting electric lighting until the lines converted to electric motive power.[56]

Steam-heated railway cars were certainly a reasonable expectation, but in the early days of railroading it was not that simple. One writer researched burned mainline railway trains dating back to 1864 and discovered 24 such accidents in which 92 people were injured and 40 killed. And he felt that those figures represented only about half the accidents and deaths that actually took place because of fires.

It had been the practice to position coal burning stoves at both ends of railway cars, which tended to overheat passengers nearest the stoves, but rendered the middle sections of the cars uncomfortable. Several steam heating systems were put into place to remedy the problem, but none were entirely successful for technical reasons. It fell upon Edward E. Gold of New York City to supply a viable technique to heat trains with steam radiators. Gold was a nephew of the late Stephen J. Gold, a pioneer in steam heating who received a patent in 1854 for "improvement in warming houses by steam." Gold's low pressure heating system for passenger cars was adopted by the Manhattan Railway's elevated roads and other lines in and around New York City and New Jersey. After electrification, the el converted to electric heat with coils under the seats.[57]

The Eames vacuum brake, largely abandoned in the United States by 1890, was the standard braking system for the elevated lines from the 1870s until the lines were electrified and re-equipped with the Westinghouse air brake. The air brake was more powerful than the vacuum brake, but the latter was less costly and proved to be dependable and effective for the elevated lines' short, light trains.[58]

New York Elevated Railroad

The first passenger cars (nos. 1–3) were placed on the elevated structure in May 1878 for cable car operations on the Greenwich Street and Ninth Avenue lines for the West Side and Patented Elevated Railway. These cars, of rustic wooden construction with bench seats, were 30 feet long to the ends of their platforms and 8½ feet wide. Regular passenger service began on February 14, 1870, between Dey Street and 29th Street, but by November the line was closed down because of technical problems and financial difficulties and the

I. The New York and Metropolitan Elevated Railroads

Cable car no. 1, built for the West Side Patented Elevated Railway Company, 1868. The lettering over the windows reads "Greenwich St. and Ninth Avenue" (Joseph Brennan Collection).

line was sold. Operations under new ownership resumed on April 20, 1871, but this time steam dummies pulled the cars. Cars nos. 1–3 were retired from service in 1872 when new cars were delivered to the New York Elevated Railroad.[59]

Cars nos. 1–16 were the first passenger cars built for the New York Elevated Railroad by Jackson & Sharp (nos. 1–8) and Cummings (nos. 9–16) in 1872, 1873 and 1875. These cars were distinguished by a low center of gravity and were known as "shad belly" or "drop center" cars, so constructed to soothe passengers' concerns about the height of the cars above the streets and the possibility of trains falling off the trestle. The cars accommodated between 40 and 44 passengers along the sides. These cars were 35 feet long to the ends of their platforms and 6 feet 10 inches wide, with 9-foot 6-inch high ceilings. Entry and exit were via swing doors on the end platforms. Light weight 12,600 pounds (Jackson & Sharp) and 14,000 pounds (Cummings), respectively. Cars nos. 1–16 were sold or scrapped by 1885.[60]

The shad belly design with the high ceilings created a sense of spaciousness. Also, with a double row of windows in the dropped center, the cars had ample light and provided passengers with good "view." The cars were painted a light yellow or "straw." While the interiors of the cars were said to be nicely finished, the ventilation system was limited to emitting air from within but failed to circulate fresh air into the cars from the outside.[61]

"Shad belly" cars on both ends flank a newer side door car (Joseph Brennan Collection).

Between 1875 and 1877 the New York Elevated took delivery of 23 cars (nos. 17–39) that were designed by Gilbert & Bush and Jackson & Sharp and featured a door on each side of the car in addition to the end platforms. These cars were of wood construction and seated 44–46 passengers. They were 5 feet 6 inches longer than cars nos. 1–16 and light weight: 14,330 pounds (Jackson & Sharp) and 16,000 pounds (Gilbert & Bush). All cars were eventually sold or scrapped. In addition, Jackson & Sharp delivered two slightly longer (41 feet) luxury experimental demonstrators (nos. 40 and 41) in 1877. These cars were of wood construction and featured perforated veneer seats that were arranged along the sides and curved near the car ends. They had large plate glass windows and were painted dark claret or maroon. These were center door cars without end platforms. These cars were believed returned to the builder and scrapped. The car numbers were reassigned to the next car purchases.[62]

The next series of distinctive designs delivered to the New York Elevated were 14-window coaches delivered by Gilbert & Bush (nos. 40–119 and 150–205, except that nos. 150–167 had 13 side windows) and Wason (nos. 120–149 and 206–242) in 1878 and 1879. They came in Gothic-style pointed windows (Gilbert & Bush) and rounded-style (Wason). Both car designs were of wood construction and seated 46–48 passengers. They were approximately 44 feet 10 inches in length to the ends of the platforms and about 8 feet 3 inches wide. Light weight (Gilbert cars) was 22,620 pounds (nos. 40–119; 168–205) and 21,080 pounds (nos. 150–167). The Wasons weighed 27,000 pounds. All of the cars were illuminated by oil lamp and heated by steam. Several of the Gilberts were converted to other uses throughout the years, and the remainder were sold or scrapped before 1928. All of the Wasons were sold or scrapped before 1921.[63]

A third, more basic design—an open air line—nos. 243–292—was delivered by

Gilbert in 1879. The cars were of wood construction, and the seats were arranged along the sides with individual cushions on rattan seats. Standing capacity was 79 passengers. These cars were 44 feet 10½ inches to the ends of the platforms and were 8 feet 10 inches wide. They light weighed 29,040 pounds. This design was electrified in 1907, and all cars were sold or scrapped by the end of 1946.[64]

Metropolitan Elevated Railway

The first passenger car deliveries to the Metropolitan Elevated took place from 1878 to 1880 from Barney & Smith and Pullman (20 from each) and consisted of two types. Car nos. 501–540 had 18 windows on each side and were known as second-class cars.

The seats were individual cushions on rattan, and standing capacity was 77. These cars were 44 feet 9 inches in length from the end of the passenger platforms and 8 feet 10 inches wide and light weight at 34,280 pounds. All cars were sold or scrapped in the 1930s and 1940s.

The next 40 cars (nos. 541–580) were built by Pullman and were first class wood construction cars with a combination of seven large and ten small windows alternating on each side. The seats were individual cushions on rattan, and the cars had standing capacity of 81 passengers. The cars were almost the exact dimensions and weight of the previous cars.

In 1879, Pullman again delivered the next 20 wood construction cars (nos. 581–600) that reverted to the 18-window design (two types of window posts and frames). The seats were individual cushion on rattan, and standing capacity was 77 passengers. The cars were 46 feet 1½ inches long from the end of the platforms and 8 feet 9½ inches wide and light weight 34,280 pounds. All cars were sold or scrapped in the 1930s and 1940s.

The most significant deliveries (nos. 601–699) took place beginning in 1879 and introduced the 6-4-6 window style. This design continued as the regular window style of the Metropolitan Elevated and became the standard for the Manhattan Railway Company beginning with car no. 688. These cars, built by Pullman, were of wood construction with individual cushions on rattan. The seats were arranged lengthwise except for four cross seats on each side of the aisle in the center of the car, two of which faced each other. Standing capacity was 77 passengers. These cars measured 46 feet 1½ inches in length from the ends of the passenger platforms and were 8 feet 9½ inches wide. They were light weight at 34,300 pounds and cost an average of $3,500. The cars were electrified in 1902 and 1903 and were sold or scrapped in the 1930s and 1940s.[65]

The last delivery of the 6-4-6 cars was in 1893 when Wason delivered car nos. 1020–1094 to the Manhattan Railway. In all, a total of 728 6-4-6 designs were delivered from 1879 to 1893 by Bowers, Dure & Co., Gilbert & Bush, Pullman, and Wason. The cars were virtually identical to the original Metropolitan designs. "The only visible changes were the railroad clerestory-style roof and the simplified window frame and post design. The more ornate and simplified window frames and posts were used concurrently for a short time on 6-4-6 cars starting in 1879." Car nos. 791–825 were built by Pullman in

1881 at an average cost of $3,200; nos. 826–919 built by Gilbert & Bush, 1887, $2,830; nos. 920–1094 by Wason between 1890 and 1893 at an average cost of about $2,900; nos. 1095–1098 by Pullman in 1885 at about $3,016; and nos. 1099–1120 by Gilbert & Bush between 1886 and 1889 at a cost of about $2,800. The latter 26 cars (nos. 1095–1120) were originally operated by Suburban Rapid Transit as car nos. 1–26. Many of the 6-4-6 cars continued in service until subway unification in 1940.[66]

STATIONS

The stations along the el were located at the top of three flights of stairs and were reached by passengers after what one author referred to as a "cardiac climb." The standard practice was to build separate stations at each stop along the line at intervals of about five blocks on the west side of the street on the downtown lines and about half mile intervals on the east side of the street on the uptown lines where fewer people lived. The stations were located over the street crossings and the stairs led down in pairs to cross streets. Where there was insufficient space for two separate stations, as in the lower East Side, a single island station was built between the tracks. Single island stations required fewer employees, but the need for wider track right-of-way interfered with the possibility of separate express tracks.[67]

The stations built from 1878 to 1882 were an improvement over the primitive wooden

Elevated station, Sixth Avenue and 34th Street (Herald Square), c. 1880 (Library of Congress).

sheds that were prevalent in the early days. The Manhattan Railway Company introduced standardization in the stations, so that they lost their individuality and took on an "elevated railroad character." They were all painted apple green outside with hunter green and maroon trim, a color scheme that continued until the 1920s. The stations were reminiscent of mainline railroad depots, but more elegant and distinctive because of their unique placement above the streets. "Quintessentially Victorian, the general design of the station exteriors might be classed as Hudson River Gothic."[68]

A well-known landscape painter of the time, Jasper Cropsey, was the architect of the stations along the Sixth Avenue Line. His artistic flair contributed to "New York street architecture [and] did much to eclipse the dark intrusion of the el in the streets."[69]

> From the pedestrian walkways the el stations looked incredibly rich and inviting in their pretty, ornamental gingerbread, romantic peaked gables, lacy iron balustrades, fancy eaves, quaint cupolas topped with finials, and Corinthian capitals on iron pillars. Unlike most railroad depots of the age, the new stations were built almost entirely of iron, a requirement of the Rapid Transit Commission, presumably as an effort toward fireproofing. Yet the buildings were so light and delicate architecturally that few people would fail to think of them as rustic wooden cottages.
>
> Passengers reached the station platforms from street level via light, iron stairways enclosed on the side and covered by fancy pavilion roofs. The stairs were particularly graceful, some with elaborate iron work and sculptural decorations in a lion's head motif. At the top of the stairs was a balcony from which passengers entered the ticket office and waiting rooms, one each for men and women. The waiting rooms, according to *Leslie's Illustrated*, were done in the Eastlake style with black walnut paneling and pine benches stained and grained in various hues.[70]

The Eastlake style of architecture is frequently referred to in discussions of the elevated stations. According to one knowledgeable source, the Victorian era English architect, Charles L. Eastlake, wrote about furniture and other interior design details. The Eastlake style in architecture uses the type of brackets, scrolls, spindles, and other elaborate woodwork he described. Hallmarks of the style are beaded spindles, jigsaw wooden forms, and massive lathe-formed columns and balustrades.[71]

However, time marched on, and as millions of passengers rushed for their trains, the stations became symbols of grit and grime. A necessary convenience just the same, but in modern times, the elegance and nostalgia of bygone days were way past their prime.

II

The Manhattan Railway Company

This fraudulent aggregation of stock ... is only a pyramid of water, on a pedestal of transparent fraud. A healthy breeze of public sentiment would dissipate it as the spray of a waterfall, and an honest administration of law send its architects to the State prison or penitentiary [Annual Report of the Board of Railroad Commissioners, 1883].

The Manhattan Railway Company (commonly known as the Manhattan Elevated Railway, or simply the "el") was organized originally on November 10, 1875, under the Rapid Transit Act of 1875. The company was capitalized with $2 million in stock, divided into 20,000 shares of $1,000 each. The company adopted the routes determined by the Rapid Transit Commissioners, which were substantially the routes occupied by the New York and Metropolitan elevated railroad companies. Thus, the Manhattan had "nothing to do unless one of the companies faltered in its mission."[1]

However, "a curious mistake by the Rapid Transit Commissioners in 1875 drove these competitors into a hasty alliance." It was a matter of the New York and Metropolitan roads crossing each other's lines at various points, and, because of the great volume of traffic, the situation became increasingly dangerous to the traveling public. Management of the two roads, reacting to prodding from the commissioners, was said to conclude that, "after much consideration," the only way to guarantee public safety was to place both lines under a single management.[2] Thus, under terms of a lease agreement dated May 20, 1879, the Manhattan Railway Company leased the roads of the New York Elevated and the Metropolitan railway companies. The 13 articles of the agreement were registered with the New York State Legislature in a lengthy document and required the Manhattan Railway Company to perform the following services:

- Operate the New York and Metropolitan roads and receive all of their earnings in return for payment of principal and interest on their bonded indebtedness of $8,500,000 ($17,000,000 total) at seven and six percent respectively.
- Pay each company an annual rental of $10,000 ($20,000 total) for 999 years.
- Guarantee each road an annual dividend of ten percent on capital stock of $6,500,000 ($13,000,000 total).

As a further consideration of the leases, the Manhattan company issued its last-named bonds ($6,500,000/$13,000,000) payable on demand to a trustee named for the stockholders of the New York and Metropolitan elevated roads, with authority to use the bonds in payment for stock of the Manhattan company at par. The bonds were so exchanged for stock and divided equally share for share among the stockholders of each of the other elevated roads, making the entire capital of stock and bonds $43,000.000.

The officers of the road asserted in a sworn statement: "The capital actually expended by the Manhattan company is $13,000,000, for the leases of the other roads." [However, the Board of Railroad Commissioners concluded that]: "There was not a dollar of capital expended by the Manhattan company. The whole transaction was a gigantic fraudulent scheme to issue and divide $13,000,000 of stock among a few stockholders, who, controlling all three of the roads, had secretly conspired to perpetrate this fraud."[3]

The crux of this scheme was that the directors of the Manhattan company issued $13 million in bonds backed up by only $100,000 in capital. In other words, the bonds were scarcely worth the paper they were printed on. The State Board of Railroad Commissioners offered this perspective:

> [The Manhattan company was organized ostensibly to deal with the problem of tracks crossing or tracks used in common. However,] The real motive was selfish greed, disregarding the public who had surrendered the streets and avenues of the city to these roads…. Here we have a railroad company — on paper — with but $100,000 capital, not a dollar of which has ever been used in building a road, suddenly, by the magic touch of a pen, with $13,000,000 of "capital actually expended," although not a dollar of this vast amount was ever paid into the treasury…. This fraudulent aggregation of millions of stock is not in any sense the capital referred to in the general railroad act of 1850. On the contrary, it is only a pyramid of water, on a pedestal of transparent fraud. A healthy breeze of public sentiment would dissipate it as the spray of a waterfall, and an honest administration of law send its architects to the State prison or penitentiary.[4]

This is the atmosphere that Colonel Frank K. Hain entered in March 1880 when he resigned as superintendent and purchasing agent of the Keokuk and Des Moines Division of the Chicago, Rock Island and Pacific Railroad and accepted the position of general manager of the newly-formed Manhattan Railway Company. He succeeded Brevet Brigadier General Edward F. Winslow (1837–1914) who held the position of vice president and general manager of the Manhattan Railway from November 1, 1879, to March 31, 1880.[5]

By now, Frank Hain had 21 years of significant railroad positions under his belt, including almost eight years as a superintendent and seven and a half years as a lead draftsman for the world's largest locomotive builder. At just under 5 feet 6 inches tall and slight of build, he was not a physically imposing individual. Yet his experience spoke for itself at a time when the railroad was "king."

In 1850, Congress began granting federal land to develop steam railroads. The roads expanded and played a major role in the Civil War, particularly in the North, by moving troops and supplies. But the roads really took off after May 10, 1869, when the Central Pacific and Union Pacific railroads were joined at Promontory, Utah, to form the nation's first transcontinental link.[6]

About the same time, several engineering improvements gradually increased the power and speed of steam locomotives and improved safety. Many surface locomotives reached speeds of 50 to 60 mph. Steel rails replaced iron rails and lasted 20 times longer. George Westinghouse patented the railroad air brake, enabling mainline trains to slow down more quickly than with hand brakes. Eli Janney patented an automatic coupler and, in doing so, spared brakemen and switchmen of the surface roads mutilated or lost appendages that were an ever-present grisly possibility with manual coupling. George Pullman organized a company to manufacture sleeping cars, and by 1875, 700 Pullman sleeping cars were in service. Railroads also introduced luxurious parlor cars and elegant dining service for wealthy travelers. The net result was more and more people traveling by train.[7]

When Frank Hain joined the Manhattan Elevated Railway, the nation's 631 railroad corporations had 17,412 locomotives in service, as well as 12,330 passenger cars, and 375,312 freight cars operating on 87,833 miles of track. The corporations had invested $4,112,367,175 on construction of the roads and owned equipment valued at $418,045,458.[8] Clearly, a lot of money was involved, and the era's free-wheeling economic environment enabled unscrupulous "entrepreneurs" and "financiers," of whom there were no shortage, to capture substantial profits.

In the bigger picture, the Manhattan Elevated was but one company in the rapidly expanding national railroad system, but it dominated transit in the nation's largest city, where the potential to reap profits was at least as great as in the hinterlands. More specifically, the Manhattan company was controlled by owners who owned leases on the Metropolitan and New York elevated roads that were achieved under circumstances that were reviled as "stock jobbing." It was, therefore, a wonder that Frank Hain chose to leave the relative tranquility of the Midwest to operate an elevated system that was in constant turmoil and under vigorous attack. For example, the *New York Times*, in particular, was an energetic defender of the public interest and took every opportunity, and then some, to berate the Manhattan company's management.

However, Frank Hain's job was to keep the trains running. He did so by being a "hands on" manager whose visibility opened him up to the hard questions about operational deficiencies within his domain. Reduction of costs, accidents, passenger complaints, and the perception that a railroad born as a public convenience operated with blatant disregard for the public's interest were the nagging issues on General Manager Hain's plate. Personnel matters were not the least of his challenges because the trains were run by an energetic group of engineers, firemen, brakemen, conductors, ticket sellers, and telegraphers, etc., who constantly sought improvement in their working environment. But, despite the confrontations, Frank Hain was applauded for his fair dealing, sense of responsibility, and practical knowledge of all aspects of railroading.

A lengthy biographical sketch of Col. F. K. Hain appeared in the *Elevated Railway Journal* on December 4, 1880. A short excerpt is captured here in the flowery language of the era:

> He laid the foundation of his future success [by his early apprenticeship with the Philadelphia and Reading Railroad], for, not content with learning the trade in the common acceptation

of the phrase, he applied the whole power of his mind to the mastery of the varied and intricate details of engine building, and by constant attention, unwearied application, and close observation thoroughly grounded himself in the great fundamental principles of mathematics and mechanics which thus early fitted him for the enviable position among American engineers, which he has since maintained with marked credit and growing distinction.[9]

General Manager Hain's sharply focused and increasingly important experience eminently qualified him to manage a major railroad. Hitting the ground running, he took over 72.34 miles of single and double track, sidings and turnouts, 203 locomotives, 588 passenger cars, and 90 stations, and he employed more than 3,000 trainmen with a payroll of over $120,000 per month.[10]

The Manhattan Elevated, despite its shortcomings, was the most reliable and heavily traveled rapid transit system in the world. However, General Manager Hain inherited operational management of a company that was sorely in need of positive numbers on its financial balance sheet. For, not long after his arrival, the company was headed toward receivership because it could not make payments on its obligations. He immediately put into place several cost-reduction schemes, but to no avail, because on July 14, 1881, the Manhattan company entered into receivership.

This action resulted in depressing the price of the Manhattan Railway's stock. The "Gould, Sage, Field clique" was generally credited with buying up the majority of the depressed stock from timid stockholders. However, on October 25, 1881, after months of complex maneuvering by the clique, Judge Westbrook ordered the Manhattan company out of the hands of the receivers. And, at the Manhattan's November annual meeting, an election of officers was held wherein Jay Gould was named president and his allies, Sage and Field, directors of the company.[11]

The *Times* was enraged at these developments and closed out 1881 with a vigorous attack on the company and its protectors in Albany. A poignant excerpt:

> There is no more disgraceful chapter in the history of stock-jobbing than that which records the operations of Jay Gould, Russell Sage, Cyrus W. Field and their associates in securing control of the system of elevated railroads in this city.... We have never been led to expect that they would have a fastidious regard either for the rights of other men or the interests of the public where an opportunity was presented for putting millions of dollars into their own pockets.[12]

The years from 1881 to 1884 were marked by uncertainty. Gould and Field pursued full control over the less than prosperous Metropolitan and its reluctant majority owner, Sylvester H. Kneeland. It became a war of attrition and litigation. On May 6, 1884, Gould's maneuvering paid off when the court invalidated the lease agreement of May 20, 1879.[13]

"Surprisingly," on July 1 and August 1, 1884, the directors of the three companies reached a settlement, then ratified by the stockholders, to convert the shares of all three companies into one class of stock. Thus, a "new Manhattan was born with Gould firmly in control."[14]

> The three year contest was at an end ... [Gould] enlisted the support of his former antagonist [Field] to aid him in acquiring a monopoly of the city's rapid transit system ... and

when he appeared to be on the brink of financial disaster, he succeeded in eliminating all opposition. He was now master of the rapid transit lines of New York City.[15]

The Tripartite Agreement required the Manhattan to pay taxes applicable to the three roads. However, from the beginning, the Manhattan company was delinquent on the taxes, citing the city's over-assessment of its properties and financial losses in the operation of the roads that prevented them from paying the taxes. The lawyers on both sides no doubt became wealthy litigating the issues until, finally, the city and the Manhattan company reached an agreement.

On December 6, 1884, R. M. Gallaway, acting in his capacity as president of the Manhattan Railway Company, accompanied by Jay Gould and Cyrus W. Field, presented a check on the Mercantile Trust Company to the city controller in the amount of $1,285,533.51. "There. That settles it," said Gallaway. "I think it does," said the controller. The check was for the city's claims for the years 1879 through 1884 and represented the amount that the city was entitled to claim from the elevated railroads and the interest on the taxes for each of the years in dispute.[16]

By 1885, consolidation of the roads was complete. The Manhattan Railway Company was re-capitalized with $26 million, and 730 shareholders received a six percent dividend totaling $1,560,000.[17] With the new merger agreement in force, and taxes now accounted for, the company's long range prospects were stable for the first time and more than encouraging.

Yet, there continued to be a dark side. The company was under relentless attack from the *Times* and senior management was vilified regularly. Public demand for improved passenger comforts and convenience was beginning to take shape. An integrated rapid transit system that included a subway was talked about, but far from a reality. Electric motive power was the wave of the future, but the Manhattan Railway's management paid lip service and stared down the issues.

Jason "Jay" Gould, Russell Sage, and Cyrus W. Field were highly successful, ambitious businessmen who had amassed enormous wealth in their other business and financial ventures. They were widely known as shrewd operators and their acquisition and control of the Manhattan Railway Company was their *pièce de résistance*.

Jayson "Jay" Gould was born on May 27, 1836, at Roxbury, New York, the son of a farmer. He taught himself surveying and mathematics and prepared maps of southern New York. At age 21, Jay Gould entered into part-

Jayson "Jay" Gould (1836–1892) (Wikimedia)

nership with an elderly, experienced leather tanner, and they formed a tanning business in the Scranton–Wilkes Barre area of eastern Pennsylvania. This business employed 250 men and became quite successful — so successful that the town of Gouldsboro, Luzerne County, was named after him.[18]

In 1860, Jay Gould moved to New York City where he became a leather merchant. But the leather business was not Jay Gould's long term calling. An extraordinarily creative and shrewd businessman, even at a young age, Jay Gould turned to the world of finance where he displayed the full range of his talents as a ruthless, devious manipulator. However, he did not burst upon the scene overnight and turn the financial world upside down. Instead, he laid low, learned the business thoroughly and essentially came from nowhere to build his empire. "In an age when most business was done through personal contact and the rules were at best slippery, nothing was more important than knowing who could be trusted how far. Jay revealed an uncanny instinct for discerning a man's true colors, for knowing who would fight and who would not, and adapting his tactics to each temperament." In 1863, he married Helen Day Miller, the daughter of a prominent merchant and patriarch of a conservative family steeped in New York City's Murray Hill society. Their children were George Jay (1864), Edwin (1866), Helen (1870), Howard (1871), and Frank Jay (1877).[19]

Finally emerging from the shadows of his financial apprenticeship, he had mastered the art of speculation, stock trading and manipulation. In the years between 1867 and 1872 Jay Gould traded in stock of his own companies and used banks he was associated with to finance his dealings. While his activities were not invisible to legislative and judicial oversight, he skillfully went about influencing authorities who threatened to derail his plans. In 1867, he became a member of the board of directors of the Erie Railroad and by age 32 he emerged as its president.

The Erie was only the beginning of Jay Gould's railroad career. One by one, he gained control of the Union Pacific, the Wabash, the Texas and Pacific, and the Missouri Pacific. In the case of the Wabash, a primarily wheat-carrying railroad, he secretly bought gold on the free market, thereby pushing up the price of gold and driving down the value of the U.S. dollar abroad. This maneuver made wheat more affordable for foreign buyers and resulted in more business for the Wabash. However, a disastrous side effect that became known as Black Friday — September 24, 1869 — had more far-reaching consequences. Gould and others, principally James Fisk who represented a syndicate of gold investors, began buying up gold in volume, thereby driving up the price even more. Unexpectedly, however, the federal government intervened and flooded the market with $4 million in gold, causing a sharp decline in the gold price. Fortunes were lost, investors were ruined, and the nation's business was paralyzed, but Gould escaped his gold-market creditors through clever political maneuvering.

Jay Gould's expansion westward was highly profitable and continued until his death in 1892. His involvement with the Erie Railroad and the Keokuk and Des Moines (later taken over by the Chicago, Rock Island & Pacific, of which Jay Gould was a director) no doubt brought steam motive specialist Frank K. Hain to his attention as a capable operations manager ... a technocrat whom he may have known from his early days as a leather tanner.

With these business enterprises on his plate, Jay Gould turned his attention to New York City's rapid transit system. At the same time, he purchased the American Union Telegraph Company and merged it with Western Union in 1881. Jay Gould also owned the *New York World*, enabling him to float rumors in the financial markets for the purpose of manipulating stock prices of the Manhattan company to his advantage. And, on November 9, 1881, Gould was elected president of the Manhattan. "The next few years would fulfill the *Times*' prophecy that the elevateds 'are likely to prove a mine of wealth to the lawyers.' By the end of 1881 Gould sat firmly astride what would be the three pillars of his business empire: the Missouri Pacific, Western Union, and the Manhattan Elevated."[20]

Russell Sage was born to a farming family on August 4, 1816, in Oneida County, New York. He had a public school education and worked in the grocery business while growing up. At an early age he showed an interest in public affairs, serving in several local offices until he was elected to the U.S. Congress for two terms between 1853 and 1857. In 1869, Russell Sage was arrested for violating New York State's usury laws and received a small fine and a five-day prison sentence that was later suspended.

In 1874, he settled in New York City and purchased a seat on the New York Stock Exchange, thereafter becoming known as a financier and the "father" of "puts and calls." He became interested in the railroads and purchased stocks in several western roads where he was often in partnership with Jay Gould. As the smaller roads were absorbed by the larger roads Russell Sage became wealthy. Over the course of his career, he became president of companies, a member of boards of directors, and a large stockholder in banks, railroads, utilities, and telegraph companies.

He was a director of the Manhattan Railway Company. While details of his participation in this get-rich enterprise are not always clear, there is little doubt that he was one of the three principal members of the clique, if not *the* mastermind. It went this way.

Sage was on the receiving end of a large bloc of stock when the Manhattan company was formed. Coincidentally, skillful media agitation touted the Manhattan company as a growth stock resulting in a surge of buyers and causing the share price to rise rapidly during the winter of 1879. However, in the spring of 1880, after the principal stockholders — Sage, Field, and Gould — had unloaded their shares at inflated prices, the stock price depressed rapidly and was appraised by the experts as "utterly worthless." As a result, the public frantically unloaded their shares of Manhattan at, say, $20 a share after having bought at $50. Adding further fuel to the panic was the Manhattan company's announcement that the company could not meet its quarterly dividend. Subsequently, the attorney general petitioned the New York City district court to place the company in bankruptcy and appoint a receiver. When the petition became known, Manhattan's stockholders could not sell their shares fast enough.

Who were the buyers? It was widely believed that Sage, Field, and others were the ones who manipulated the stock price. And that they sold at the market highs and bought at the lows, thereby reaping millions on the stock's decline. However, in the face of this adversity, the price of Manhattan's shares "mysteriously" firmed and then began to rise. Out of the blue, an unknown "bull clique" with deep pockets began buying up the shares and withdrew them from general circulation. This action was not without danger to the clique, however, because the company was in imminent danger of being dissolved by court order before profits could be taken.

Influence came into play. According to one account, Sage persuaded the New York district judge to drop the matter before his court and transfer the Manhattan case to the Albany District and Judge Theodoric Westbrook. It was a master stroke, because Judge Westbrook was closely associated with Sage and Jay Gould, and the case was supposedly heard in Gould's office in the Manhattan company's building. Two receivers were appointed, but they were both associated, in one way or another, with Gould-controlled railroads. As part of the deal, Sage devised a plan to raise the fare on the elevated roads from five cent to ten cents in order to extricate the roads from their financial obligations.[21]

The press and public fury exploded on the Sage, Gould, Field clique. After all, the elevated system served the public interest, went the reasoning, and now the fare had been doubled. Sage and Gould were unconcerned about public opinion, but Field was "appalled" at the *Times*' attack and, as a person more thoughtful about his image, he restored the former five cent fare.[22]

Little did Field know that his simple act of "public service" would alienate Jay Gould and Russell Sage and ultimately result in his financial ruin a few years later. But, at this time, his view of the future was rosy—the railroad was on solid footing, and his personal worth was estimated to be $6 million.[23]

On December 4, 1891, an individual identifying himself as H. D. Wilson entered Russell Sage's office at the headquarters of the Manhattan Railway Company to seek an interview. Coming face to face with Sage, the man demanded $1.2 million in cash. Sage of course refused, at which time Wilson detonated a bomb that he pulled from a satchel. The explosion "blew the bomber to bits" and wounded Sage and several others in his office, as well as mortally wounding a clerk and destroying portions of adjoining offices. The assailant was later identified as Henry C. Norcross, a Boston stockbroker. The motive for the attack was not entirely clear.

Initial versions of the incident reported that Sage was partially shielded by a partition but was thrown down by the force of the explosion and received several superficial cuts and bruises. However, later versions suggested that Sage used another individual as a human shield to protect himself. The individual, William R. Laidlaw, Jr., received disabling injuries from the blast and sued Sage for compensation. Sage refused to pay damages, but after four trials he was ordered to pay more than $40,000 to Laidlaw. Surprisingly, a court of appeals later reversed the judgment and Laidlaw received no compensation. The scandalous incident served to reinforce the public's already negative impression of Russell Sage as a "skin flint, miser, and heartless millionaire."[24]

Russell Sage died on July 22, 1906, at age 89 at his summer home on Long Island. He left a vast fortune reputed to be worth more than $70 million, which he left to his widow who devoted a major portion of her inheritance to philanthropy. She established the Russell Sage Foundation for "the improvement of social and living conditions in the United States," founded Russell Sage College, and donated extensively to Rensselaer Polytechnic Institute, the Emma Willard School, and several benevolent organizations and societies.[25]

Cyrus W. Field was born on November 30, 1819, at Stockbridge, Massachusetts, son of a clergyman. At age 15 he went to work as a clerk for a mercantile firm in New York City. For the next several years he moved from one company to another, but by age 34 he had accumulated sufficient money to retire. He traveled abroad for a while and then became attracted to the idea of a trans-Atlantic telegraph cable. By December 1856 he formed the necessary corporate entities on both sides of the Atlantic and secured funding from the American and British governments.

After early unsuccessful attempts to lay a cable, the complete cable was laid in the summer of 1858. Transmission of telegraphic messages was successful for a few months, but the system soon failed for technical reasons. Another attempt in 1865 also failed. However, in July 1866 Cyrus W. Field and his associates successfully laid a trans-Atlantic cable and put it into operational use. The U.S. Congress awarded him a gold medal for this technological achievement.

In May 1877, Cyrus W. Field purchased a controlling interest in the New York Elevated Railroad Company and became its president. He also worked with Jay Gould on the Wabash Railroad, became president of the Wabash, and purchased two New York City newspapers, the *Daily Mail* and the *Express*, which merged into the *Mail and Express*.[26]

Field's New York Elevated was a profitable road, while its competitor, the Metropolitan road, was on shaky financial ground. Sizing up Field as "gullible and subject to persuasion," Jay Gould and Russell Sage proposed a merger of the two roads which would establish a single coordinated system, under a holding company — the Manhattan Railway Company — that would serve to eliminate competition. But by 1881, the Manhattan company was unable to make good on its obligations and entered into receivership.[27]

However, Jay Gould then went to work. Using his *New York World* as the instrument, he undermined faith in the Manhattan's stock, causing it to decline in price. All the while he purchased the company's stock secretly until, by October 1881, he had attained control with 48,000 shares, and the district court released the company from the threat of receivership. Now, a triumvirate controlled and operated the elevated roads: Jay Gould, head of the Manhattan; Field remained as president of the New York; and Russell Sage became president of the Metropolitan. The *Times* described the maneuvering as a "disgraceful chapter in the history of stock jobbing."

In 1885 stories began to surface that Field planned to invest heavily in Manhattan stock. By January 1886, propelled by Field's support, Manhattan's stock rose from the 70s to 128 and then to 164, and on to 175, causing him to boast that the Manhattan was worth $50 million at about $200 a share. His holdings increased from 10,000 to 70,000, and at $200 a share, would have been worth $14 million.

But now the time was ripe for Gould and Sage to exact revenge on Field for lowering the railway fare six years earlier. In early 1887, they began unloading their Manhattan stock and Field bought them at the inflated price. But unprecedented downward swings of the stock market and his miscalculations in the speculative markets required Field to borrow money to retain the shares he purchased on margin. At the same time, Jay Gould withdrew funds from the banks that loaned Field money and the banks began calling in Field's loans. By June 24, 1887, Field was finished. In a deal that became known as the

"Manhattan Squeeze," Field offered Jay Gould 75,000 shares of Manhattan for $120 a share that he bought for $175. This was followed by an additional 10,000 shares sold to Gould for about $90. With the repayment of his loans, his 24-hour loss came close to $6 million, about equal to his net worth.[28]

Now "Gould had become the undisputed master of an enterprise which had a monopoly of the rapid-transit facilities in the largest city of the country, and he never surrendered its control. Its earning power increased … its financial position was strengthened … its credit was enhanced … and the property proved to be … the basis of Gould's business empire in his lifetime and one of the prime pillars of his estate after his death."[29]

Cyrus W. Field died at age 72 on July 12, 1892, in New York City. He was said to be worth less than $100.[30]

III

Colonel Frank K. Hain

Franklin Kintzel Hain, commonly known as Frank K. Hain, and by the honorary title of Colonel Hain, was chief operating officer of the Manhattan Railway Company from 1880 to 1896. He was the first of five children of Samuel Hain (1809–1884) and Margaret Fitzenberger Kintzel (1813–1887), and he was born July 22, 1836, at Stouchsburg in western Berks County, Pennsylvania.

Samuel Hain was a fourth generation descendant of Palatine Germans who emigrated to New York in 1710 and migrated to Pennsylvania in 1723. He owned a farm at Stouchsburg and kept a general store. Later, he worked for a saw and cement mill along the Union Canal.[1] Compared to other nearby towns, Stouchsburg was "characterized by less progress, less wealth, less variety, and less change." The nineteenth-century people of Stouchsburg symbolized the tastes of the common man — tradespersons, storekeepers, and factory workers. They built sturdy houses with plain features similar to homes on rural Pennsylvania German farmsteads. Frank Hain was schooled at Tulpehocken Academy, which was founded as a private school and converted to a township free school in 1840.[2]

Frank Hain's siblings were Lydena aka Lydia Hain (1838–1863), ladies' hat maker; William Theirwechter Hain (1841–1922), self-employed metal cornice manufacturer; George Meily Hain (1845–1883), machinist and master mechanic, Pennsylvania Railroad; and Charles Henry Hain (1855–1941), chief clerk, passenger office, Union Pacific Railroad, Kansas City.

About 1850, sensing canal traffic dwindling, Samuel Hain and his family moved from Stouchsburg to Reading, Berks County, where he worked in a hardware store. By then, Reading had become a thriving city with a population of about 16,000, and the discovery of coal fields, the steam railroad, and iron manufacturing contributed largely to the city's rapid development. Among the industrial firms gathering momentum in the city, the Reading Railroad's coal transportation business was the dominant industry.[3]

The Hain family lived at 105 South Fourth Street in Reading, an unpretentious two-story, red brick "row house" on about 1,500 square feet of land that Frank Hain's mother purchased for $1,100. Many of these types of dwellings were built by owners of local industries for their workers and were one room wide and shared common walls.[4]

Philadelphia and Reading (1853–1857)

Frank K. Hain began his railroad career as an apprentice machinist for the Philadelphia and Reading Railroad in 1853 when he was seventeen years old.[5] "The Reading," as it was called, was prominent as a coal transporter from the anthracite fields of Schuylkill Valley. Although corporate management was located in Philadelphia, the car shops were based in Reading on a 36-acre facility in the heart of downtown. "At its height in the 1870s, The Reading was one of the richest corporations in the world — not only running trains, but operating an empire of Pennsylvania coal mines, canals, and ocean-going vessels."[6]

The Reading hired from wherever it could find qualified employees rather than rely exclusively on local workers with no technical background. The company paid top wages to mechanics, which enabled recruitment of top talent. One of the superintendents of the car shops instituted a "highly developed and jealously preserved" apprenticeship system. "Competition for jobs in The Reading shops was fierce" and apprentices "must be of good character, ... able to pass an examination in reading, writing, and arithmetic ... and were required to attend evening classes to learn drawing or mechanical physics." The men and some women who worked in the shops were "stubbornly proud of their national reputation for innovation and craftsmanship" and considered the Pennsylvania Railroad's famous Altoona works "johnny-come-latelies" due to the Reading's 23-year head start.[7]

Frank K. Hain's family home, 1855–1857; 105 South Fourth Street, Reading, Pennsylvania. Modern facing replaced original red brick (photograph by the author, 2007).

Service Aboard the USS *Colorado* (1857–1858)

However, after four years in the Reading's machine shops, rapid expansion of the U.S. Navy's engineer corps offered Frank Hain professional experience and challenges that the railroad could not match. On November 21, 1857, he was appointed Acting Third Assistant Engineer, and on January 15, 1858, he was ordered to the USS *Colorado*.[8]

> It has been written that it is difficult to become sentimental about the [naval] engineer. This idea is born of the belief that he deals only with material things and takes no part in the glories of war or in the victories that are won from storms. This theory is absolutely false; his post of duty is as dangerous, as responsible, and as romantic as any in a ship. The man of the engine and boiler rooms faces dangers of another kind and performs his duty in another atmosphere, though equally exposed to the dangers that are peculiar to a life afloat. The naval engineer and his men toil in darkness in the depths of the ship, knowing full well that much of what they do will be unknown and unnoticed, however important it may be; and they often meet emergencies so bravely that their ships are saved from destruction or disablement, both in peace and war, by a few noble instances of duty well done.[9]

Engineers operated the engines and were not expected to perform military duties because those were the responsibility of the line officers, traditionally the elite of the navy. This sharply defined division of labor created a cultural chasm between the engineers and line officers. In fact, the line officers detested the greasy engineers and their smoking boilers, and the engineers resented the "aristocratic" line officers because their work, while unsung, was no less heroic.[10]

During Frank Hain's service aboard the *Colorado*, the ship patrolled the waters around Cuba to deter British naval vessels from searching and seizing American ships suspected of illicit slave trading.[11] The *Colorado*'s deck logs describe in detail the ship's 3,789-mile journey from Norfolk to the Caribbean to Boston from May 12 to August 6, 1858, all of which time Frank Hain was aboard. In brief, however, *Colorado* was anchored off Haiti for much of the time where the blacks and mulattoes competed for political control. From there, she sailed to Panama, then cruised off Cuba, and finally anchored at Key West for more than three weeks. A few days shy of three months on station in the Caribbean, the *Colorado* returned to Boston and was placed on "ordinary."[12] Frank K. Hain's resignation was accepted on August 9, 1858.[13]

Danville, Pennsylvania (1858–1861)

After his service aboard the *Colorado*, Frank Hain next turned up in Danville, Montour County, Pennsylvania, where he was in the leather business, "belts, etc.," and used his expertise with steam engines to operate machinery employed in the tanning process.[14] He probably became acquainted with his future employer, Jay Gould, at this time because Gould operated a leather tannery in nearby Luzerne County.

During this period, Frank Hain met Annie Rebecca McWilliams of nearby Mooresburg. Her father was a large landowner and former treasurer and postmaster of Montour

County, and the family was among the most respected families in central Pennsylvania. On January 23, 1861, Frank Hain and Annie McWilliams were married at the Mooresburg Presbyterian Church.[15]

Service Aboard the USS *Iroquois* (1861–1862)

The Civil War began on April 12, 1861, and finding the leather business a bit tame under the circumstances, Frank K. Hain again answered the call of duty. On May 23, 1861, four months after his marriage, Frank Hain re-enrolled in the Union Navy as Acting Third Assistant Engineer. On June 15, he reported to the USS *Iroquois* after she returned to New York from patrol in the Mediterranean.[16]

On July 6, 1861, *Iroquois* was ordered to join the Atlantic Blockading Squadron. For the next month, the vessel sailed off New England in search of the Confederate privateer *Jeff Davis* and later took part in the blockade of Savannah.[17]

On August 20, Third Assistant Engineer Frank Hain was admitted to sick bay for five days suffering from adynamia (lack of physical strength due to a pathological condition).[18]

In the fall of 1861, *Iroquois* was in active pursuit of the CSS *Sumter*, commanded by Admiral Raphael Semmes, that had captured several ships near Cuba and off the South American coast.[19] *Iroquois* found the *Sumter* in mid–November while she was anchored and re-coaling in Martinique harbor, but on the first dark night the *Sumter* slipped out of the harbor and escaped without a shot being fired.[20]

On January 14, 1862, *Iroquois* stopped the British sloop *Rinaldo*. On board were Confederate ministers James Mason of Virginia and John Slidell of Louisiana, who were captured earlier by a Union ship, but released. This brief naval operation had a dangerous political antecedent that was known as the "Trent Affair." On this day, the *Iroquois*' commander decided that discretion was the better part of valor and allowed the *Rinaldo* to proceed under surveillance.[21]

USS *Iroquois* (Navy Historical Center).

Two days later, Frank Hain's only child, Rebecca McWilliams Hain, was born in Montour County, Pennsylvania. He had been married less than five months, and his wife was about three months pregnant, when he shipped out to sea. *Iroquois* was on constant patrol and the official record indicates very little possibility of a reunion with his wife taking place during her pregnancy or at birth. Thus, it would not be until October 1862 that Frank Hain was able to greet his daughter, then about ten months old.

In March, *Iroquois* was ordered to join Flag Officer David G. Farragut's West Gulf Blockading Squadron in preparation for the attack on New Orleans, the south's largest city and a major international port, located about 90 miles up river from the mouth of the Mississippi. New Orlean's defenses were concentrated about 70 miles downriver at Fort Jackson and Fort St. Philip, which were situated directly opposite each other.[22]

On March 30, *Iroquois* met up with Farragut's fleet, but it was not until April 18 that preparations for the attack on New Orleans began in earnest.[23] On April 24, *Iroquois* moved abreast of the forts but ran into trouble with the CSS *McRae*. A Confederate officer aboard the *McRae* reported: "We sheered to port, and delivered our starboard broadside." Grape and slugs swept the *Iroquois*, wounding 24 men and killing eight in the gun fight. Nevertheless, *Iroquois* continued to sail upriver, and, as one officer reported, the *Iroquois* was "badly injured in her hull ... all our boats are smashed, and most of them are not worth repairs."[24]

The CSS *Louisiana* might have posed a serious threat to the Union fleet, but the ironclad was moored and largely immobile. At one point, *Iroquois* delivered a broadside attack on the *Louisiana* from a few feet away, but did very little serious damage while "she herself was riddled by *Louisiana*'s fire."[25]

Flag Officer Farragut's report: "Eleven of the enemy's steamers were destroyed during the morning fight, which practically annihilated their fleet. Casualties in the [Union] fleet amounted to 37 killed and 147 wounded. Two officers, both midshipmen, were killed and eleven were wounded; three of the latter ... [including] Acting Third Assistant Frank Hain, were of the engineer corps, all injured by gunshot wounds."[26]

Farragut's fleet reached New Orleans on April 25 and found the city largely undefended because the troops had been diverted to defend Tennessee in the battle of Shiloh (April 6–7, 1862). Farragut sent a small force ashore on April 29 to hoist the stars and stripes, but the city was not secured until May 1 when General Butler's army arrived and took control.[27]

After the capture of New Orleans, Flag Officer Farragut sent seven vessels up the Mississippi "to keep up the panic as far as possible." He planned for *Iroquois*, *Richmond*, and *Oneida* to proceed to Baton Rouge, while the others were to sail as far as Vicksburg in order to cut off the South's supply lines from the west.[28]

Surrender of Baton Rouge and Natchez

Capt. James S. Palmer, commanding the *Iroquois*, sent a landing party ashore at Baton Rouge and secured the city on May 8.[29] Five days later *Iroquois*, along with *Oneida*, took possession of Natchez.

On May 20, Frank K. Hain was admitted to sick bay for 10 days because of a case of diarrhea.[30]

Iroquois remained in the Vicksburg area throughout the month of June and into late July. Beginning July 8, Frank K. Hain was twice admitted to sick bay for a total of 10 days because of "intermittent fever" (malaria).[31]

On September 1, 1862, *Iroquois* re-entered the Gulf of Mexico to take part in the blockade of Southern commerce, but on September 21, Farragut ordered *Iroquois* to "proceed to New York ... for repairs to your vessel." The USS *Iroquois* arrived at New York on October 2 and decommissioned on October 6, 1862.[32]

The capture of New Orleans was one of the most significant episodes of the Civil War. The Confederacy lost its largest city and main port, an important ship building center, and control of the Mississippi River. Union naval vessels were able to patrol all but 200 miles of the river. And New Orleans went on to become an important center for northern commerce.[33]

On October 20, 1862, Frank K. Hain was detached from *Iroquois* and awaiting orders. On October 29, he was appointed Acting 2nd Assistant Engineer, and on November 4 he was ordered to the USS *Sangamon*, a *Passaic* class monitor. Owing to ill-health contracted in the line of duty, he never sailed on the *Sangamon* and his resignation from the navy was accepted on January 24, 1863.[34]

Delaware, Lackawanna and Western (1863–1864)

In February 1863, shortly after his resignation from the Navy, Frank Hain signed on as a draftsman with the Delaware, Lackawanna and Western Railroad in Scranton.[35] Scranton was the third largest city in Pennsylvania and the center of the anthracite coal industry in the northeastern part of the state. It became the hub for the steam railroads that hauled anthracite to New England and Canada.[36]

41st Regiment, Pennsylvania Infantry Militia (1863)

However, the Civil War was beginning to take a critical turn and the threat of invasion of Pennsylvania was more real than imagined. Frank Hain once more answered the call of duty, and on June 30, 1863, he enlisted as captain of Company "C," 41st Regiment, Pennsylvania Infantry Militia. He commanded 102 officers and men, organized at Reading within the Department of the Susquehanna, which was created to protect Harrisburg and southern Pennsylvania, and to deny Lee's armies passage across the Susquehanna River.[37]

Throughout Frank Hain's railroad career brief news items refer to his prior "gallant" army service. However, his official military file does not reflect that description, which was probably in a generic sense because he, like many of his fellow citizens in the militia, suspended their personal and business lives to defend the Commonwealth in the face of great peril and uncertainty. Most likely, the 41st was held in reserve to support the Army of the Potomac if needed and deployed to defend the city of Reading, thereby relieving the regular army of the responsibility.

Many of the officers and men of Company "C," 28 by rough count, but probably many more, had ties with Scranton and its environs. Frank Hain evidently used his position at the Delaware, Lackawanna and Western to recruit a company of soldiers from among his acquaintances and fellow railroad employees.

By the time many of Pennsylvania's emergency militia units were mustered in, the rebel invasion had been beaten back. After one month of service to his state and the Union, Captain Frank Hain was discharged from the army on August 3, 1863, and resumed his employment as a draftsman with the DL&W.

Philadelphia and Erie (1864–1867)

In March 1864, Frank Hain was appointed master mechanic of the eastern division of the Philadelphia and Erie Railroad at Lock Haven, Clinton County, Pennsylvania. Federal tax lists place him in Renovo, where the machine shops were located, about 30 miles northwest of Lock Haven. He worked as master mechanic until January 1, 1865, at which time he was promoted to superintendent of motive power and served until January 1867.[38]

Frank and Annie Hain's only child, Rebecca McWilliams Hain, died at Renovo on August 28, 1866. She was a little more than four and a half years old. No information is available about the daughter's death, but at her tender age she would have been susceptible to prevailing epidemics, especially if she was not physically strong to begin with. Both parents were about 30 years old at the time and presumably could have had more children if they desired. However, living in a small, rustic railroad town where contagious diseases would have spread rapidly could not have been conducive to a long and healthy life.

> Early in 1864 the Philadelphia and Erie Land Company offered lots for sale on easy terms so that almost every man could establish a home for himself and his family. Lots were eagerly bought and houses big and small sprung up side by side with the workshops. Boarding houses were erected and at once filled a little fuller than capacity. Almost every house in town was a boarding house in late 1865; about this time the U.S. Hotel was built — here many of the mechanics and roadmen were accommodated with board and lodging. The following year [the company] put up a number of fine and commodious dwellings for the officers and foremen, north of the railroad at the base of the mountain, beside the still waters of "Swamppoodle."[39]

However, the prospect of more unhealthy railroad towns, amid crowded boarding houses and belching steam locomotives, may have convinced Frank and Annie Hain that a railroad career in the hinterlands was not the place for children. Another possibility, albeit highly speculative, is that the health problems Frank Hain contracted aboard the USS *Iroquois* affected his ability to father children. Malaria can be a cause of infertility, and while Frank Hain's civilian medical records are not available, it is a condition that could have impacted their family planning decisions.

Baldwin Locomotive Works (1867–1874)

In January 1867, Frank K. Hain joined the major locomotive builder, Baldwin Locomotive Works of Philadelphia, as a lead draughtsman.[40] (Here it should be noted that several news items place Frank Hain "in charge" of the BLW design department. However, his entries in the Biographical Directory of Railroad Officials do not reflect that description. Nevertheless, it is evident that he held a responsible position in the design department, and for that reason he is herein referred to as "a lead draughtsman.")[41]

Frank Hain lived in company housing together with his brother, George Meily Hain, a foreman and machinist at Baldwin.[42]

The Baldwin Locomotive Works was the most successful locomotive builder in the world. The company was founded in 1831 by Matthias W. Baldwin, a former jeweler.[43] Baldwin was at the forefront of creating custom designs for its customers and aggressively responded to market demands and opportunities. In 1860, the company produced a total of 80 engines to 18 different designs. However, as design diversity increased, by 1890 Baldwin constructed 946 locomotives in 316 varieties.[44]

Matthias Baldwin had been "lukewarm ... to the necessity of a Draughting Room," and he employed only three draftsmen in 1860, but sixteen were employed by 1878.[45] Because of relatively small production before 1850, many components were built without drawings. But as the product line expanded, systematic production and interchangeability of parts became more important. Thus, to manage the increasing variety of custom designs, in 1854 the firm instituted a record known as the Specification Book for systematizing drafting practices and coordinating work among departments. Essentially, the Specification Book spelled out the customers' exact requirements, while Card Books allowed them to be met wherever possible by standard drawings, and Law Books ensured that all card drawings conformed to production practices.[46]

Baldwin cultivated the export market after 1870 and made inroads by offering pricing, delivery, or technical advantages. The firm employed traditional marketing techniques and advertised in foreign trade publications.[47]

Most foreign customers required modifications from the U.S. practice because the locomotives of nearly every country had national characteristics. "As a result, Baldwin designers had to create hybrid engines that generally had the basic attributes of American design traditions with graftings from the technology of the recipient country."[48]

Baldwin in Russia

In 1871 the Baldwin Locomotive Works dispatched Frank Hain to Russia where he introduced the government to anthracite coal burning locomotives. He departed New York City on July 1, 1871, with the SS *Atlantic* for Liverpool, England, and returned aboard the same steamer on November 9, 1871. His passport application was endorsed by George Burnham (1816–1912), one of the owners of Baldwin.[49]

№ 13,279   *Iss'd June 26th 1871*

United States of America.

Be it Known, That on the day of the date hereof, before me Daniel H. Buck, Notary Public for the Commonwealth of Pennsylvania, by lawful authority duly commissioned and sworn, residing in the _____ of Philadelphia, and by law authorized to administer oaths and affirmations, personally appeared

Frank K. Hain

Aged 35 years.
Stature, 5 feet 9 inches, Eng'h.
Forehead: High
Eyes: Hazel
Nose: Straight
Mouth: —
Chin: Bearded
Hair: Brown
Complexion: Fair
Face: Thin

Who being by me duly affirmed according to law, did declare and say, That he is a Native of Berks County, Pennsylvania, and is a Citizen of the United States.

Frank K. Hain

And *George Burnham* being by me also duly affirmed did declare and say, that the facts above stated are true to the best of his knowledge and belief.

Geo Burnham

In testimony whereof, I have hereunto set my hand, and affixed my Notarial Seal, this 22d day of June 1871.

Daniel H. Buck

Notary Public.

Frank K. Hain's passport application for travel to Russia, June 26, 1871. Application certified by George Burnham, one of the owners of the Baldwin Locomotive Works (Ancestry.com).

The small locomotives heretofore built in Russia ... were all built for consumption of wood for fuel, till the agent of the Philadelphia firm [Baldwin] had brought the attention of the consuming departments [in Russia] to the fact that anthracite coal of the best quality can be found around the town of Worenish [Voronezh] in southern Russia. The American locomotives finally accepted and introduced here [are] being expressly built for coal consumption — have led Russian capital to the development of the now quite numerous coal mines in the district named.[50]

The above news item touches on Frank Hain's visit to Russia and amplifies assertions in railroad biographical directories that he introduced the Russians to anthracite-fueled locomotives that he designed.[51] It is apparent that his travel to Russia was to acquire first-

Register of engines designed for Russia by Frank K. Hain, 1874 (Baldwin Locomotive Works Collection, Archives Center, National Museum of American History, Smithsonian Institution).

hand knowledge of the terrain, environment, and the Russians' requirements to enable him to modify Baldwin's existing designs for application to their situation. Thus, it is significant that Baldwin shipped two "sample locomotives for burning anthracite" to the Technical Department of the Russian government in 1874. One of these was a passenger locomotive and the other a "Mogul" freight locomotive that was heavily used for freight service in the United States.[52]

By 1872, 60 percent of locomotives constructed by Baldwin were American standard 4-4-0 and 85 percent of all locomotives in the United States were 4-4-0s. Frank Hain's designs for Russia were simply take-offs of existing specifications. 4-4-0 refers to four guiding or "pilot" wheels up front, mounted on a swiveling bogie or "truck" to guide the locomotive through curves and over rough track. The four larger "driving wheels" propel the engine.

The sample passenger locomotive for Russia, construction no. 3558, completed its trials on March 28, 1874. It was an American standard 4-4-0, class 8/26 C 62, designed for five-foot gauge rails, with 67-inch drivers, 2,400-gallon capacity water tank, 16 × 24-inch cylinders, iron flues, and steel furnace, and it was the 53rd engine ordered from Baldwin in 1874, the 40th constructed, and the 62nd of all engines built in its class. It weighed about 12 tons. The cost was 3,200 pounds sterling and it was deliverable FOB Cronstadt (Port of St. Petersburg) in August 1874.[53]

The sample freight locomotive for Russia, construction no. 3559, was tested on March 31, 1874. It was also an American standard 4-4-0, class 8/30 D 20, five-foot gauge, with 54½-inch drivers, 2,400 gallon tank, 18 × 24-inch cylinders, iron flues, and steel furnace. It was the 54th engine ordered in 1874, the 41st constructed, and the 20th of all engines in its class. This engine also weighed about 12 tons, cost 3,400 pounds sterling, and was deliverable in August 1874 at Cronstadt.[54]

The class numbers of the engines have the following meanings:

8/26 C 62 (passenger): 8 = number of wheels; 26 = cylinder diameter in inches; C = two pairs of coupled driving wheels; 62 = sixty-second locomotive in its class.

8/30 D 20 (freight): 8 = number of wheels; 30 = cylinder diameter in inches; D = three pairs of coupled driving wheels; 20 = twentieth locomotive in its class.[55]

Baldwin's "Glory Days" Fade Temporarily in the 1870s

Baldwin's engine production increased every year from 1868 (124 engines) to 1873 (437 engines).[56] In September 1873, just before the Great Panic of 1873 set in, Baldwin employed 2,800 men full time with an average weekly wage of $14.57. However, a major financial firm declared bankruptcy on September 18, and years of abnormal economic growth, overbuilding on railroads, and the collapse of the Vienna, Austria, stock exchange marked the beginning of the Long Depression. Eight months later only 1,400 Baldwin men had jobs, they were working three-quarter time at an average wage of $9.47 per week. In a short time, the firm cut employment, wages, and hours further. Orders for new engines for American roads came to a standstill, and production was reduced from

40 finished engines to 16 or 17 per month. The Great Panic of 1873 continued for five years during which time as many as 89 railroads went bankrupt, 18,000 businesses failed, and unemployment reached 14 percent.[57] In June 1874, Frank Hain, whether released by Baldwin because of economic necessity, or voluntarily, left his employment with the Baldwin Locomotive Works.[58]

The Erie (1874–1876)

However it developed, Frank Hain landed on his feet and was appointed superintendent of motive power for the Susquehanna Depot of the Erie Railroad. He served in this position from June 1874 to August 1876.[59]

Jay Gould was president of the Erie Railroad from July 1868 to May 1872 when he was forced out of office by other members of the Erie's board of directors. However, he was enamored with Susquehanna Depot, which in its heyday was the operating headquarters of the road and one of its most important stops for all trains.[60] In 1870 he sent a correspondent from the *New York Herald* to the Erie to write a series of articles on the condition of the property. "The company's large works at Susquehanna excited his especial admiration."

However, the labor situation at Susquehanna Depot in early 1874 mirrored developments that were taking place at the Baldwin Locomotive Works and within the general economy as well. On March 31, 1874, about 1,300 men went on strike at the Erie because they were not being paid. Negotiations between the strikers and the Erie Company went on for several days until a compromise solution to the problems was worked out. Meanwhile, the company's finances had been going from bad to worse. The Erie was in receivership from 1875 and eventually reorganized.[61]

Frank Hain's secretary at Susquehanna Depot was George Adams Post, a young man of 20, who was to play an important role in his and his wife's lives in subsequent years.[62]

Keokuk & Des Moines (1876–1880)

With the Erie's future prospects somewhat cloudy, Frank K. Hain moved on, and in August 1876, he was appointed general superintendent and purchasing agent for the Keokuk & Des Moines Railroad.[61] During his three-plus year residence in Keokuk, he boarded at the Patterson House along with his brother, Charles H. Hain, station cashier and assistant ticket agent for the K&DM.[63]

Keokuk, Iowa, current population about 11,000, is one of four gateways on the Mississippi River and is located at the foot of the Lower Rapids where the Des Moines River meets the Mississippi. The city is named for the chief of the Sacs and Foxes.

The Keokuk and Des Moines Railroad was born as the Keokuk, Fort Des Moines and Minnesota Railroad Company in 1853. The road became immersed in financial difficulties and portions of the road were sold. Out of the various transactions, the Keokuk and Des Moines Railroad was incorporated on January 6, 1874.[64]

On May 14, 1878, apparently impressed with the potential importance of the Keokuk-Des Moines territory, the Rock Island Railroad Company entered into a 50-year lease agreement with the Keokuk & Des Moines. On October 1, 1878, Frank K. Hain was appointed superintendent of the K&DM division of the Rock Island Railroad.[65]

By 1880, the Rock Island's management decided to consolidate its holdings and, on June 2, filed paperwork with the State of Illinois that resulted in a change of the corporate name to the Chicago, Rock Island, and Pacific Railroad Company.[66]

Perhaps sensing bureaucratic uncertainty, and a lessening of his position within the CRI&P's new corporate structure, Frank Hain was offered and accepted the position of general manager of the Manhattan Elevated Railway. Here it is noteworthy that his future employer, Jay Gould, served on the Rock Island Board of Directors from 1877 to 1884.

IV

A Railroad in Flux (1880–1885)

I am not going to have any volcanoes lying around loose; every man who belongs to the [union] will be made to walk the plank [Col. Hain; *NYT*, March 29, 1882].

Col. Hain once confided to a friend that on foggy nights, when he thought of the trains chasing each other up and down the island, he couldn't sleep and was often found after midnight on the road assuring himself that everything was in order [*NYT*, May 12, 1896].

General Manager Hain's first significant challenge when he took over operational management of the road was bringing costs under control. Also, problems with the railway union and the threat of a strike tested his negotiating skills. In the bigger picture, he enabled several inventors to conduct tests of their experimental pneumatic and electric-powered cars on the elevated tracks.

In April 1880, the Manhattan Elevated carried 187,500 passengers per day; 238,000 daily passengers were required to enable the company to pay interest on the outstanding debt of the York and Metropolitan roads, and, moreover, the company required savings of about $1,000 per day in order to meet its tax obligations to the city.[1]

Colonel Hain enacted changes that resulted in a $300 per day reduction in expenses by discharging two superintendents, two station inspectors, and 200 other employees. He assumed some of the supervisory duties himself without reducing compensation of the employees who were retained. Nevertheless, he did not find an immediate way to secure the necessary reductions that would meet his board of directors' requirements. One of his ideas was gradually to elevate the standards of efficiency. Another was to ignore recommendations of politicians who were desirous of obtaining employment for their constituents and accept only such applicants who, in his judgment, were qualified for the available positions. He also planned to discontinue some of the trains that operated after 8 P.M.[2] Nevertheless, despite the cost-cutting, the company went into receivership on July 14, 1881, and more than three years elapsed before the company got on its financial feet.

Every large enterprise is ultimately dependent upon its work force for the relative success of its business. The Manhattan Railway Company was no different than any other company in this respect. With about 3,000 trainmen on its payroll, disagreements between management and workers were inevitable, especially since the economy had been in a deflationary spiral since 1865. The post–Civil War deflation was a result of increased productivity and downward pressure on prices exacerbated by an inflexible monetary policy, namely the gold standard. With an over abundance of goods, prices fell. And, when prices fell, wages followed suit.[3]

In 1882, General Manager Hain encountered his first significant test from the trainmen. It began with them meeting to discuss the merits of applying to the board of directors for an increase in pay after Col. Hain had already refused their request. The trainmen's representatives felt that the success of the elevated roads was largely due to the "faithfulness, intelligence, and sobriety" of their brethren and, as a result, the employees were not adequately compensated. The first meeting was adjourned and discussion postponed without action taken on the matter.[4]

However, despite their initial indecisiveness, the trainmen were only getting started. Next came an assemblage of the Amalgamated Society of Engineers, Firemen, Conductors, and Brakemen of the Manhattan Elevated Railway to prepare for an "uprising" against Col. F. K. Hain or "against his ways." The society complained that within a week Col. Hain had discharged 11 conductors and five brakemen, allegedly because they belonged to the Manhattan Railway Trainmen's Mutual Aid and Protective Association, which, they claimed, was a benevolent and social organization. Fueling the fire was an alleged boast by one of the discharged employees who claimed that the Trainmen's Association would bring the Manhattan's officers to "terms." To which Col. Hain was said to reply, "I am not going to have any volcanoes lying around loose, and every man who belongs to the Association will be made to walk the plank."

Amidst the chest-thumping, the Society of Engineers decided to demand reinstatement of the men and obtain the company's pledge not to retaliate against employees who belonged to the society. The trainmen also considered asking for a wage increase, and while they did not expect to secure the removal of Col. Hain, they "anticipated bringing about a new order of things."[5]

A four-man committee from the Society of Engineers called on Col. Hain and demanded reinstatement of the discharged men and a 10-percent increase in pay for all hands. However, Col. Hain rejected both demands and refused to negotiate, saying that he would "entertain no overtures that came from a secret organization or a committee composed of members of it." Col. Hain's decision was passed along to the society's rank and file who expressed "considerable indignation." At this moment the possibility of a strike raised its ugly head. The trainmen planned to meet with Col. Hain once more to express their demands and, if he again refused, "he might be told that the trains would stop running at a certain hour at whatever stations they chanced to be."

However, the "throngs" of trainmen did not act immediately but continued deliberation of their "seemingly hopeless prospects" and considered submitting their grievances to arbitration. For the moment, the word "strike" was tabooed and would be resorted to only if all efforts to secure a settlement failed. Their next step was to appoint a joint committee of the Society of Engineers to call on Col. Hain again and determine whether he would accede to their grievances.[6]

Meanwhile, the society learned that Col. Hain had not revealed the true cause of discharging the employees. He had given three or four reasons, but the real reason, in the minds of the trainmen, was that experienced employees were not necessary on the elevated roads. Men who were receiving the highest wages were discharged and inexperienced men were hired in their places. All of this, they reasoned, was intended to save the company money while the public suffered. It was said that placing green hands in important positions resulted in killing a passenger a few months earlier and a little girl more recently. What's more, the road was employing 17- to 19-year-old boys in violation of the law. Col. Hain was contacted in reference to these issues and he had nothing to say in regard to "probabilities or possibilities."[7]

Although Col. Hain had "nothing to say," he was not wilting under the trainmen's pressure. To the contrary, he called their bluff by sending out to all train stations large signs that bore the inscription: "MANHATTAN RAILWAY LINE BLOCKED TRAINS NOT RUNNING." The signs, according to Col. Hain, were for use in case an engine broke down or an accident blocked the tracks. The discontented trainmen, who had risen against Col. Hain, contended that the company feared a strike and issued the signs pending an emergency. Many rumors floated during the day, one of which was that the trainmen would abandon their trains at 10:00 unless Col. Hain acceded to their demands. However, the day ended as before, with more discussion about sending another committee to confer with Col. Hain.[8]

As they deliberated endlessly, two camps emerged: one group preferring arbitration, the other calling for a strike. However, "wiser counsels prevailed," and they continued to "waffle" as they deliberated about how best to approach Col. Hain. Meanwhile, the *Times* learned that a conductor on the Sixth Avenue Line, who had been discharged, received a letter of commendation from Col. Hain and was reinstated to duty. It also was reported that four others would be reinstated.

The trainmen once more mustered their resolve and formed a large committee to meet with Col. Hain against the advice of their leaders who thought that the prospects of a strike were waning because of Col. Hain's positive actions. In any case, the "strikers" were in a minority now because, even if Col. Hain gave them no satisfaction, it was not certain that the men would desert their trains. They charged that Col. Hain had been unfair, and they could never again regard him with respect.

Superintendent Green (Charles L. Green [1836–1884]) was also under attack for being a "tool of Col. Hain," and "unjust," because he filled the best positions with his brothers-in-law, "of whom there seemed to be almost no end." "Some day," a conductor said, "the hands would rise and demand the removal of both Col. Hain and Superintendent Green." Yet, it was the general impression among the men that Col. Hain would instruct Green to reinstate most of the men except for three "turbulent spirits." Col. Hain, the men concluded, had taken an "adroit course" and it looked as if his strategy would forestall a strike. Eventually, after all the bravado and turmoil, not to mention their incredible lack of resolve, the trainmen backed down and a strike did not take place. What is more,

Col. Hain must have been feeling rather good about his performance because he was obliged to do no more than return several of the discharged trainmen to duty.[9]

Threats of strike and insurrection from among the men were not the only sticky problems faced by General Manager Hain. The elevated roads were a public conveyance and the public sought to get their share of the action. In late 1882, a book dealer brought a case against the Manhattan Elevated Railway because the elevated road refused, "in violation of the law," to carry a package of printing on the Sixth Avenue Line between 23rd Street and Park Place. In response, the Manhattan's attorney sought to prove through Col. Hain that the road did not usually carry freight and could not carry it except at great inconvenience. The suit was to recover $100 in damages. In response to questions from the plaintiffs, an agent for the elevated road stated that Col. Hain had issued orders forbidding transportation of bulky articles. Other defendants testified that trains were run at so frequent intervals that any attempt to carry freight would be an annoyance to passengers, tend to block the business of transporting passengers, make transportation dangerous, and put an end to rapid transit for which the elevated system was primarily established.

However, Col. Hain testified that the company already carried baggage over the Sixth Avenue Line between the two depots of the New York City & Northern Railroad Company located at 53rd Street and 155th Street. He also said that bundles of newspapers and periodicals for a news company were carried when in the custody of one of the news company's employees for delivery at stations where news stands were located. As for transporting freight at night, Col. Hain said it was not possible because the roads were fully occupied at night with extra trains put on to carry coal and ashes. It should be noted here that the company had a contract with the U.S. government for $5,000 per annum to transport the mail over all lines operated by the company.[10]

After each side's positions were aired, the case went to jury. The judge cautioned the jury to purge their minds of prejudices against the elevated roads. "Though they have great powers," he said, "they are necessary and a great benefit to the city. If they have earned large sums, they have enriched the city." Furthermore, "under their charters it is the duty of the roads to carry freight if possible."

The jury consulted for only five minutes and returned with a verdict for the plaintiff to recover the "time honored" six cents [sic] damages. Attorney for the defense allowed as how the road would "probably" pay the damages imposed, despite the fact that it established precedent and would enable anyone to recover a like amount if the company refused to transport their baggage.[11]

Despite the slings and arrows inherent in day-to-day operations, General Manager Hain had a railroad to run, and he was under orders from the owners to bring costs under control. But cutting back was easier said than done when the press had an axe to grind. For instance, Colonel Hain issued an order discontinuing trains running at 20 minute intervals on the Sixth Avenue Line from midnight to 5:30 A.M. because it was not cost-effective. "We have tried the experiment for a year," he explained, "in response to the demands of the press and the public, and the year's experiment has resulted in a great loss. I advised Mr. Gould [about the potential losses] some time before we started such trains, and now, for lack of patronage, and against his judgment, we are compelled to discontinue the trains or else continue them at a very considerable daily loss."[12]

The *New York Times* could not agree less with General Manager Hain's rationale:

> The idea that a corporation, after obtaining for nothing a valuable franchise on the ground that was designed to be a public convenience, should adopt the policy of serving the public only in such hours of the day as were profitable is a revelation to many who have not fully comprehended the greed, arrogance, and assurance of the elevated railroad managers. "They do not pay," was the reason General Manager Hain gave ... [However], the profits of the elevated railroads in this city are certainly large enough in the aggregate to enable them to accommodate a good-sized portion of the public for a few hours at a loss, that, comparatively, can only be trifling.[13]

Late night workers also chipped in with their indignation:

> "This is the last straw on the camel's back," said one. "Yes," said another, "and it will lead to legislative action that will teach the elevated roads the duty they owe to the public." A third night owl asserted: "We must have a law defining the duties of the elevated road companies more clearly. There should be cheaper fares, better service, less carelessness, and more civility."[14]

The storm continued to gather as the *Times* quoted unnamed "prominent" citizens:

> A "banker": "The fact is that this corporation is so grasping that it is unwilling to accommodate the public at all, unless it can see an immediate money return of 100 or 200 percent."
>
> A "gentleman": "It is no longer possible now to go visiting in Brooklyn, take supper after the theatre, or spend an evening at the club without incurring heavy expense for cab hire. When Gould says that he is not making money out of this road he willfully lies."[15]

But management of the Manhattan Elevated fought back, taking the high road, perhaps, with tongue-in-cheek responses. Under the heading of "The Withdrawal of Night Trains to Improve Public Morals," the *Times* quoted Jay Gould as saying that taking off the late night trains would "improve the morals of the community because they are conducive to late hours and dissipation." Russell Sage was more down to earth, but no less insincere: "If people can afford to stay out at night, they can afford to take a carriage home."[16]

Seeing no end to this craziness, Col. Hain implemented a plan. He issued orders to run hourly trains that departed either end of the road from midnight until 5:30 A.M. These trains replaced the "emigrant" or "owl" trains that started at 1:00 A.M. to pick up company employees leaving work and started out again at 4:30 A.M. to drop off employees heading to work. Thus, the "emigrants" and "owls" now rode with the normal late-night public, killing two birds with one stone.[17]

Solving one problem, however, was merely a drop in the bucket because public inconvenience and exasperation took many forms. Steam was a noisy, dirty means of motive power. For instance, the Sixth Avenue Line was a nuisance to nearby residents from Rector Street to Harlem because of "the pungent odor of the coal-gas emitted by the locomotives" and the "snorting and puffing of the machines" that disturbed sleep. One passenger reported that he never attempted to sleep until the final trains passed over the road.

Getting up steam set a fan in motion and "a rumbling like a small earthquake, only more steady and more prolonged, jars the nerves." When too much steam was produced, "the safety valve hisses and sings like a huge tea kettle." Col. Hain put a number of new engines on the Sixth Avenue Line, but they were no better because they introduced a new noise that "penetrates the ear like a steam whistle." A passenger asked an engineer of the road whether it was possible to prevent this shriek. And, typical of the elevated roads' perceived indifference to public opinion, the engineer responded: "Maybe it might."[18]

Lack of heat in the passenger cars during the winter months was another complaint that cropped up from time to time. For instance, a passenger complained that on January 5 he rode an elevated train at 155th Street in company of his wife and the car was not heated. It was a day when the outside temperature averaged about 11 degrees and, as a result, his wife took sick.

Col. Hain had no knowledge of the allegation and replied that if the car was not heated, it was only a temporary inconvenience. He argued that elevated railroad employees spent a lot of time ensuring adequate heating in the cars during the winter and the passengers were apparently satisfied because complaints were very few. The Board of Railroad Commissioners investigated the incident and determined that the company showed "due effort" to heat the cars properly.[19]

Another common issue was light, or lack thereof, on the streets beneath the elevated roads. The bulky trestles, train stations, and long flights of stairs leading to the platforms blocked sunlight from shining on the businesses below and greeted potential street-side customers with a dingy, uninviting appearance. Also, customers and shop owners alike were not immune to hot cinders, oil, and dust escaping through the tracks each time a train passed overhead.

In one of several such cases, a business owner sued the Manhattan Railway Company for damages because of deterioration of his property values due to a nearby elevated railway structure. At issue was how much the value of the building had depreciated by the partial exclusion of light. The judge reasoned that the street was opened under the Act of 1813, for general street purposes, which did not include the passage of elevated railways. "I am neither prepared to accept the plaintiff's extreme estimate of his damage nor the defendant's optimistic views of the blessings cast with the shadows of its structure," said the judge. Thus, he took a middle ground and awarded the plaintiff damages amounting to $2,500 "by reason of the defendant's appropriation of his light."[20]

In another case, a private citizen whose property was "destroyed by the encroachment of the Manhattan company's elevated structures" gave notice that he intended to test the company in the courts. The citizen referred to his misfortune to own property on a part of Rector Street that the Manhattan Elevated was using so as to connect two lines of roads and facilitate transfer of passengers from one line to the other. However, Vice President Gallaway responded that the "Manhattan company had the legislature on its side, and the courts on its side, and paid for its law by the year." Therefore, the company took the position that it was within its rights to occupy the entire width of the street to the housefronts on either side and build whatever structures it required without regard to the "exclusion of light and air from the adjacent buildings." As a result of the company actions, the citizen's property was said to depreciate "enormously" in value, he was not offered compensation, and his complaints to the company were "treated with scorn." A resolution of the issue was not reported in the press.[21]

The *Times* was critical of almost all aspects of the elevated roads and their attacks were born of frustration. The independent conglomeration of steam-driven elevated trains, horse-drawn surface vehicles, and a smattering of cable cars did not fit into an integrated grand plan that would best serve the public's interest, in the *Times* opinion. Each company fiercely promoted its own interests, and the prospects of working together in the common good did not have a snowball's chance. A subway? Not likely in the immediate future. But the owners of the Manhattan Railway were by no means naive. They had made a lot of money from other railroad enterprises, and they saw integrated rapid transit as a viable proposition only so long as they were in charge of it. Yet, technological advances, primitive though they were, forced their hand and required them to pay more than lip service to the public's long range goals.

One of the early technological experiments was a 2-4-0 cab-in-front, compressed air locomotive built by Baldwin for the Pneumatic Tramway Engine Company after a design by a Scottish engineer, Robert Hardie.[22] Pneumatic engines had been under development for some time because they were thought to be suitable for use in the confines of subways and not release noxious fumes that threatened the health of railroad employees and passengers alike. The Pneumatic Company's vehicle was taken for a test run in late 1881 on the Second Avenue Line from the 127th Street station to South Ferry. The engine pulled a four-car train filled with passengers. It had four steel cylindrical tanks that contained compressed air, and a cab, like any ordinary motor, but without a tender. There was no smoke stack, no steam pipe, no bell to the engine. On board were the inventor, the regular engineer, and the general foreman of the Manhattan's 98th Street repair shops. Col. Hain and several stockholders and owners of the Pneumatic Company were in the forward passenger car.

The stops were made as easily and the starts as smoothly as those made with a steam engine. There was no puffing sound and no escape of steam. South Ferry was reached in 42½ minutes in comparison with a regular locomotive running time of 40 minutes. The tracks were slippery because of a recent rain, so the extra running time was, as Col. Hain put it: "Quite excusable, for many of the [steam] locomotives could do no better on such a day." Moreover, Col. Hain judged the experiment to be "quite satisfactory," but he was unable to comment about whether pneumatic engines had a future on the elevated roads until the system was perfected.[23]

In late 1884, representatives of five companies met to discuss the advisability and practicability of organizing a business company to produce an electric motor for the elevated railways that would combine features of several known systems. By pulling together various technologies into a single company, the representatives hoped to produce the best system for electric railroading and prevent "suicidal competition." It was opined that the elevated roads would have saved twice the cost of their plant if they had an electric motor system from the beginning.

Attending the meeting were four members of the Field family, including Cyrus W. Field and Stephen D. Field, representing the Field motor; a representative of Drexel, Morgan & Company, representing the Edison motor; and representatives of the Daft motor, Brush motor, and Siemens motor. They were joined by General Manager Frank Hain of the Manhattan Railway, as well as by a noted patent attorney.[24]

Col. Hain offered his Second Avenue Line for testing and said he would lay a center-of-the-track third rail to furnish power for the dynamos. At this meeting and five others, it was decided to test each system on the elevated road. However, only the Daft Electric Light Company and the combined Edison-Field interests actually participated in the trials.[25]

The new company would be capitalized with stock of $1 million, one-half to be paid in cash and the other half to be apportioned among the owners of the five different motors according to their relative values. The question of "relative value" would be submitted to a distinguished commission of railroad men and academicians. Tests of the Daft and Field motors took place as outlined in the following paragraphs. However, despite the energy directed toward forming a joint company and building a successful motor, the plan did not materialize.[26]

The following year, Stephen D. Field, a nephew of Cyrus W. Field, visited New York City from the West Coast where he had worked as an electrical engineer and conceived the idea of operating electrically powered railways in San Francisco. Stephen Field, along with Thomas Edison, just the year before had successfully exhibited a three-ton electric locomotive at the Chicago Railway Exhibition. Cyrus W. Field supposedly became enthusiastic about electric motive power and spoke encouragingly about the concept with the Manhattan company's principals.

Predictably, however, the *Times* had a different slant on the matter, which the newspaper sourced to the ubiquitous "anonymous director" of the Manhattan Railway:

> We haven't all got nephews who are scientific inventors, but a majority of us are determined to keep the elevated railroad system free of doubtful experiments. There won't be any electric motors on the elevated railroads … you can put that down in black and white.[27]

The foregoing news item was published in 1885, but the month and day are unknown. However, it is indicative of the kind of contradictory statements that issued from Manhattan's officers in regard to electric motive power. At a minimum, it suggests that the left hand did not know what the right hand was doing, when viewed in light of the following news item published by the *Times* on October 2, 1885.

According to the article, several railroad officials [following up on the meetings that took place in November 1884], including Gould, Sage, and Hain of the Manhattan company, took part in a trial run of the nine-ton Daft electric locomotive, the *Benjamin Franklin*, on the double-tracked Ninth Avenue Line between 14th and 53rd streets, a distance of about two linear miles. Dr. Leo Daft (1843–1922) was an Englishman who had conducted previous and promising experiments elsewhere. A third rail was laid between the test terminals, which amounted to about four miles of third rail because of the "up" and "down" tracks. Daft's first test runs were made the night of August 26, 1885, between

10 P.M. and 4 A.M., towing two to four standard elevated railway cars up the long grade. Reporters on hand from *Electrical World* were said to be "enthusiastic."[28]

On November 18, two car loads of Daft's competition, officials of the Manhattan Elevated, and a group from the Society of Civil Engineers participated in another test. Daft ran the train satisfactorily until it came to a sudden halt at just about 30th Street when a jerry-rigged device in the dynamo failed and caused the stoppage. The mechanism was not seriously damaged, but it took some time to make repairs. Those observing the demonstration were said to be impressed, but "the engine was unable to pull more than four empty cars [and] there was some confusion about the normal train size on the elevated lines and the total weight of a typical elevated car."[29]

> "It's well we left [Vice President R. M.] Gallaway behind to run the road tomorrow," said Jay Gould to Col. Hain during the delay [over the minor damage]. Others feared they were stuck for all night. A crowd of boys gathered on 31st Street and shouted to millionaire Gould to "get out and push it."
>
> Eventually, the train got under way again. "The main thing," said Mr. Gould, "was to show that they have the power under control and they seem to have it so here. All that is necessary is refinement of methods to produce success." Russell Sage also expressed himself as believing in the ultimate success of electricity as a motive power.[30]

Daft, however, was not satisfied with the results and was convinced that the *Benjamin Franklin* was too light to pull heavy trains. He withdrew the *Franklin* in December until he could make modifications.[31]

Following closely on the heels of Leo Daft's tests were plans by the Electric Railway Company of the United States, more simply known as the "Edison-Field System." E. H. Johnson, of the company, was quoted in *Electrical World*, April 14, 1885, as saying: "We determined to put our plans in operation on the Second Avenue line, and made a contract with the Manhattan company." The Edison-Field company contracted with the Pullman Palace Car Company of Chicago for a car similar to ones that Pullman supplied to the Manhattan Railway. *Electrical World*, on May 9, reported that the Edison-Field plan would provide each car with its own motor, making it an independent operating unit. But, for whatever reason, car tests that were expected to be held in a few weeks did not materialize. In fact, the Edison-Field car was viewed as a "great disappointment" because no further mention was made of it in the trade journals. Stephen D. Field split from Edison shortly thereafter but continued his work by partnering with Rudolph Eickemeyer of Yonkers, forming the Eickemeyer-Field Company, to design and build electric motors.[32]

Frank Julian Sprague (1857–1934), who became known as the "father of electric traction," was a graduate of the U.S. Naval Academy and one of the most significant inventors to develop a satisfactory solution to electrification of the elevated railroads. After resigning from the navy in 1883, he joined the Edison Company where he worked on electric motor designs. He left Edison in 1884 and established the Sprague Electric Railway and Motor Company.[33]

In December 1885, Sprague presented a paper to the Society of Arts in Boston ("Application of Electricity to Propulsion on Elevated Railroads") that calculated the effects of electricity in place of steam on the Manhattan Railway's Third Avenue Line.

His study was prepared with the assistance of General Manager Hain and others. The Third Avenue Line operated over 8½ miles from South Ferry to the Harlem River, passing through 26 stations, on an undulating line of ascending, descending, and level sections. Steam trains could attain average speeds of ten miles per hour. During peak hours, with 66 trains in operation, the Third Avenue Line was close to full capacity.[34]

In Sprague's view, the capacity of the existing lines could be increased by adding more cars to a train or by increasing the operating speed. However, neither solution was practicable because each would require larger locomotives. "Hence," said Sprague, "we [are] obliged to turn to some other method of locomotion, and that which promises the most satisfactory solution is an electrical system.... I have for a long time been elaborating such a one," he said, "and am now convinced that this is the future method of propulsion for the trains of the elevated road, and it is a near future." Sprague estimated that he could reduce the Third Avenue Line's coal costs by 71 percent with reduced power demand from electrification and much greater efficiency of developing power from a central plant instead of through locomotives."[35] However, he was not able to conduct trials until 1886.

Frank Hain did not control the company's purse strings and was dependent on his board of directors and the executive committee for appropriation of funds. However, his hands were not completely tied, because he could enact immediate changes for the public good that required limited funding.

One of his commitments to public service included changes in ticketing passengers to prevent hardship on the poor. The ticketing procedure in effect required passengers to purchase their tickets at their originating station and surrender them when they left their destination station. However, if they lost or misplaced their ticket en route, passengers were required to purchase a "gateman's check" before they were permitted to leave the destination station. This procedure impacted on all passengers, but especially the poor, because they were required to pay two fares for a one-way trip. Col. Hain's initiative required passengers to relinquish their ticket at the station where they purchased it, as they passed through the door on their way to the platform and the trains. In this way, passengers had tickets in their possession for only a few moments after purchasing them. Col. Hain ordered new ticket machines installed in the stations to implement this plan.[36]

A problem that often had passengers scratching their heads, especially out-of-towners, was the lack of a clear picture of the elevated system's routes and how they could best negotiate the complex system to reach their destinations. As a man ahead of his times, Col. Hain solved the problem ("General Manager Hain's New Idea") by posting large signs in the stations with information that included plain instructions for reaching any destination on Manhattan Island. A map also showed the elevated routes, the names of the stations, their exact locations, as well as directions for transferring from one line to another.[37]

Major improvements on the roads usually were not self–generated but came about as a result of constant pressure from the press. It goes without saying that capital improvements were not at the top of the Manhattan company's agenda because railroad equipment cost money ... big money. However, now and then, public pressure overcame manage-

IV. A Railroad in Flux (1880–1885)

Elevated road at 110th Street, aka "suicide curve," c. 1896 (Library of Congress).

ment's ingrained conservatism, or greed, as the press was fond of saying, and significant improvements were realized, albeit amid petty sniping from the road's detractors.

Long-suffering passengers endured many inconveniences, but none more aggravating than changing trains. A necessary nuisance, the company would say, but a nuisance nonetheless. In some cases, passengers were required to cross a busy thoroughfare to catch their connecting train. At other times, they had to walk a block or two to another station. And, worst of all, the interval between arriving and departing trains was often so short that passengers literally had to run to make their connection, bringing with it the unwanted title of, for example, the "86th Street runners."

"A thrill a minute" was another way to look at travel on the el. The *Times* saw the Second Avenue Line as the ultimate cure for *ennui*. The Second Avenue's passengers will experience a new sensation, "something between a house on fire and a shipwreck. They will find themselves tearing along through the air, just a little above the roofs of four and five story houses, at a speed that will be very likely to make their hair stand on end, provided they are not bald." Between 65th Street and 137th Street, "the track runs down a steep incline, and the cars fly as if they were driven by the wind ... between 30 to 35 mph." A "respectable speed" on a surface road, but on the el, "it is startling." A passenger asked the conductor how fast the train was moving. "Why, we're going a blessed sight faster than we ought to," he said, "that's how fast we're going."[38]

61

Accidents are always regrettable, and often avoidable, but forever a dagger in the shaky reputation of the elevated railroad. With over 200 locomotives hurtling along at 15 mph, and at elevations paralleling the third floor of nearby buildings, accidents were bound to happen. Yet, General Manager Hain made his reputation on concern for the safety of the public. He once "confided to a friend that on foggy nights, when he thought of the trains 'chasing each other up and down the island,' he could not sleep and was often found after midnight on the road assuring himself that everything was in order."[39]

He thoroughly investigated each incident and took decisive action with all the results in hand. Yet, he was defensive at times, even obtuse and testy, showing himself to be a "company man" through and through. For instance, after one collision, Col. Hain persistently denied that he had received a report of the matter. As to whether he proposed to share the information with the public, once he received the report, he bluntly described the collision as "a private matter which did not concern the public." Furthermore, when a reporter suggested that a collision in which one man was killed and another injured was a matter in which the public was highly interested, Col. Hain replied that "the company did not so consider it."[40]

In January 1881, an ice storm wreaked havoc on the elevated roads from the Battery to Harlem. Col. Hain characterized the storm as "by all odds the worst one we've ever had to contend with." Slippery rails, slippery steps and platforms at the stations were dangerous and the general manager anticipated casualties. The greatest danger was from telegraph wires falling across the tracks and impeding the trains, endangering the passengers on board. Fallen trees and telegraph poles also interfered with traffic, and some of the conductors, brakemen, and track walkers had narrow escapes. The wires caused extensive delays and special "wrecking trains" were sent over the roads to clear away debris. However, despite the chaos, Col. Hain anticipated the trains returning to regular service during the evening rush hour but cautioned that "the elevated roads can defy the weather itself, but when it comes to telegraph poles they are obliged to give in."[41]

Collisions were mostly "rear-enders," caused partly because the elevated roads did not deploy mechanical block signals. Safety procedures called for placing a flag man behind the last stopped train to warn approaching trains, but this precaution was sometimes ignored, resulting in collisions "full of murderous possibilities." However, sight rules allowed much closer train spacing, less than a minute apart in rush hours, but caused problems in fog and on curves. With trains running at such short intervals there was little margin for error, such as when a train was forced to halt on a blind curve by reason of a slow train ahead. After one incident, Col. Hain was asked whether he planned to station a flag man or guard full time at a particularly dangerous curve and he replied cryptically: "I can't say because the expense of running the roads is very great in this weather."[42]

The Board of Railroad Commissioners took up the problem of "rear enders" in early 1885. After a series of accidents, the board concluded that "the collisions were the result of the dense fog and the rules of company requiring no definite interval of *space* to be maintained between the trains, although the interval of time was only one minute and a half." Moreover, the board was of the opinion that adoption of a "block system" would "positively forbid one train approaching another nearer than a certain specified distance, say five blocks." Under this plan, a mechanical block system would be put into operation by which a signal would be set at "danger" at the beginning of each block as long as a train is within that block and would not be turned to "safety" until "the train had cleared the other end and got into the next block." The board allowed as how adoption of a mechanical block system would cost roughly $165,000 per year to operate, but urged the Manhattan Railway Company to devise such a system and submit it to the board for approval.

Manhattan's Vice President Gallaway protested the board's recommendation in a letter of February 13, 1885. He took issue with the board's estimate of costs, which the elevated road estimated to be on the order of $226,000 for the first year and $220,000 each year thereafter. Furthermore, he reasoned that the board's block system was intended to prevent collisions primarily in times of fog; whereas, in the company's judgment, very few fog days prevailed in New York City and, then, only for a few hours. While not totally ruling out a mechanical system, Gallaway reminded the commissioners that the company, on January 1, 1885, increased the number of men whose duty it was to signal trains during fog.

Not to be outdone, the board responded by noting that the company's estimate of expenses was "very general and somewhat confused." The board went on to argue its case and asked the company to inquire into "the utility and practicability of providing a system of lighting the entire length of the tracks ... with electric lights to be used in case of foggy weather."

All of this discussion came to naught, however, when the board received a detailed estimate for adopting a mechanical block system. The estimated expense for the first year was $406,744 and $362,920 each year thereafter. In view of the high cost, the board suspended its recommendation "pending the investigation and trial of other devices."[43]

By 1888, the Manhattan Railway had a mechanical block system in place and, in one incident that took place on the Sixth Avenue Line, "the block signal on which Colonel Hain relies to give notice of accidents, sent out the proper notice with all possible rapidity the entire length of the line ... thus preventing anything like an accident ... and scoring one for the 'block system.'"[44]

A major safety issue hounded the company when brakemen did not follow regulations that called for them to close the gates of the cars before giving the signal to start the train. However, the crush of passengers and short intervals between trains sometimes prevented precise adherence to regulations and resulted in unfortunate and horrific incidents. One such case was "little Marie Menzen" who died on the elevated road at Sixth Avenue and 23rd Street on March 25, 1882. A coroner's inquest weighed disclaimers by the trainmen and the claims of Marie Menzen's father who was on the train when she fell between the cars.

The coroner read the company's rules and regulations to the jury and concluded with this admonishment: "Such occurrences as the death of Marie Menzen would continue to happen unless the company provided better means for the safety of passengers. The conduct of the elevated railroad employees was often rude. More trains could not be safely run during [rush] hours, but better precautions should be taken to prevent overcrowding of the cars." The Manhattan Railway's lawyer countered with these insensitive remarks: "Last year the elevated roads carried 85,000,000 passengers and lost only eight. The Hudson River and New Haven Roads lost 41 passengers during the year, but no one heard any great hue and cry over that."

The jury deliberated for about an hour and rendered a verdict that Marie Menzen was killed by falling between the cars of the elevated road. The jury added the following statement:

> We find that this accident was due to the negligence of the middle guard who was stationed on the platforms of said cars, and who gave the starting signal to the conductor while the gates of the platforms were still open and passengers were passing from the platform of the station to the platform of the cars. We further find that even the most careful instructions of the company to its employees will be valueless unless they are enforced with sufficient vigor, and unless the company is careful in the selection of its employees, which, in the present instance, we find has not been the case.[45]

A year later, *The Sun* took Col. Hain to task with an editorial that discussed "The Rules of the Elevated Roads." At issue was "daily violations of rules by the employees of the line," in regard to a regulation specifying that "no train shall start until all the passengers are on board and the gates closed." The brakemen and conductors were said to take "the whole thing" as a "joke" because with the "thousands of people" crowding on the station platforms during rush hours it was difficult to control them without causing delays. Once brakemen decided that the trains were full, they rang the bell without closing the gates, and the trains started up with a "struggling mass of people on the edge of the car platform, from which some are obliged to step back again to the station platform, seeing the uselessness and danger of riding on that train."

Col. Hain was criticized because he was surely aware of the problem but more interested in keeping the trains on schedule than worrying about the safety of the passengers. That said, the newspaper concluded the editorial with this wistful statement:

> The elevated roads are of an incalculable benefit to the citizens of New York and, of course, the managers wish that there might never be an accident of any sort. They have carried hundreds of thousands of passengers under these lax regulations, and fatal accidents have been rare indeed. But there can be no question that this surprising fact is due as much to good fortune as to good management.[46]

Here it should be noted that *The Sun*'s editorial, no matter how well-intentioned and on the mark, was only part of the story. Because, as will be seen five years later,[47] blindly following regulations was not such a good idea either.

After another accident, when it became necessary to amputate a fireman's leg, Col. Hain was more direct about responsibility, saying that the collision was entirely due to the engineer's carelessness, because there was no excuse — the track was straight and he should have been more vigilant. The engineer was arrested and taken to police court but was later released when no complaint was filed. Other culprits received immediate expulsion from service. Most collisions resulted from human error and General Manager Hain could only react after the fact. But his constant vigilance in regard to the public's safety resulted in very few fatal accidents on his high volume roads.[48]

Operating the elevated roads was serious business and required a sense of dedication above and beyond the call. Aggravating side issues came into play, however, and diverted Col. Hain's attention from the bigger picture. Such was the case when a railroad inspector posted a notice in all stations of the Third Avenue Line that prohibited women from the stations, "whether your friends or some other man's friends." This order was met with "excitement and indignation" because it was misconstrued by the female patrons of the road who thought the prohibition applied to them. After considerable backing and filling, the Third Avenue's superintendent pointed out that the order was intended only for female friends of station employees who sometimes visited the stations to gossip and otherwise prevent the male employees from performing their duties. General Manager Hain was "indignant" at the order and recommended dismissal of the inspector from the company. The order was taken down from all stations and the president of the company remarked that the inspector "seemed to have lost his head."[49]

High public visibility as the operating head of a large corporation brought with it social prominence, far beyond what Frank Hain was accustomed to in Keokuk, Iowa. One of his first major social engagements was the annual Martha Washington Ball that attracted many of New York City's great and near-great. The ball was said to be one of the best of the season. The ladies were unusually beautiful and richly attired, and they were adorned with "a notable display of valuable diamonds." General U. S. Grant and his party arrived just before 11:00. The general was accompanied by Mrs. Grant, Ulysses S. Grant, Jr., and wife, General and Mrs. Lloyd Aspinwall. Col. F. K. Hain and his wife were seated in the front row behind two boxes of the city's most distinguished citizens, including the mayor, General Grant's party, bankers, company presidents, congressmen, and Jay Gould.[50]

Not one to look a gift horse in the mouth, Col. Hain saw the elevated railway's lost and found department as a money-maker. All lost articles were put up for sale every two years and Col. Hain invited bids from junk dealers. Among the items on the block in 1884 were 500 pocket books, 800 umbrellas, 100 walking sticks, 200 satchels, 200 books, 50 lunch baskets, two big truck loads of bundles, and a box full of jewelry, spectacles, eyeglasses, tobacco and snuff boxes, and opera glasses. But no money. About 75 percent of the articles were reclaimed on average.[51]

For the fiscal year ending September 30, 1885, the Manhattan, New York, and Metropolitan elevated railway companies reported the following statistics to the Board of Railroad Commissioners:

Manhattan Railway Company
Locomotives, 4 drivers: 240 leased, average cost of each $4,076
Maximum weight of each: 45,680 pounds
First class passenger cars: 696 leased, average cost $2,640
Maximum weight: 26,150 pounds
Average number of cars in passenger trains: 3.71
Average speed of ordinary passenger trains, including stops: 12.5 mph
Average speed of express passenger trains, including stops: 12.5 mph
Average number of passengers per train: 129

Average life of steel rails: circa 15 years
Average life of ties: 10 years
Gauge of track: 4 feet, 8½ inches
Passenger cars are heated with steam, principally Gold's patent; lighted with oil and ventilated by tipping sash in deck roof, and by Creamer's ventilator.
Average number of persons employed (including officials): 3,784
Aggregate amount of salaries and wages paid: $2,412,855

New York Elevated Railroad

Locomotives, 4 drivers: 133 owned, average cost $4,006
Maximum weight of each: 43,200 pounds
First class passenger cars: 327 owned, average cost $2,640
Maximum weight: 26,030 pounds

Metropolitan Elevated Railway

Locomotives, 4 drivers: 107 owned, average cost $4,164
Maximum weight of each: 45,680 pounds
First class passengers cars: 369 owned, average cost $3,395
Maximum weight: 26,150 pounds[52]

Also, for fiscal year 1885, the Manhattan Railway Company carried 103,854,729 passengers, or approximately 285,000 per day, and reported the following earnings[53]:

Gross earnings	$6,796,972
Net income	$1,573,589
Dividends, six percent on $26,000,000 consolidated stock	$1,560,000
Surplus for year	$13,539
Surplus, Sept. 30, 1884	$101,269
Add amount paid Metropolitan Elevated Road in settlement, charged off to cost of Metropolitan lease	$975,000
Add profit on real estate sold	$246,410
Total	$1,322,679
Deduct portion of city structure and personal taxes paid Dec. 6, 1884, chargeable to the period prior to Sept. 30, 1884	$1,387,823
Deficit, Sept. 30, 1884	$65,145
Total deficit, Sept. 30, 1885	$51,605

Clearly, the Manhattan Railway's financial results for FY 1885 were highly impressive in light of the company's ability to make a substantial dividend payout after an extraordinary lump sum payment of back taxes.

V

Facing Down the Challenges (1886–1888)

When asked about reports that a strike by dissatisfied elevated railroad employees was imminent, Col. Hain said the rumors were "baseless." He attributed the rumor of a threatened strike to "one newspaper trying to be sensational" by printing "silly statements" [NYT, June 5, 1886].

The trainmen asked Col. Hain for an increase in wages, but he refused to grant their request, saying that if they do not like the pay they are getting they can [quit] and he can get plenty of Italians who will do the work at half the price [NYT, June 10, 1887].

Almost four years to the day after General Manager Hain put down his first significant challenge from an employees' union, the Brotherhood of Locomotive Engineers took up the engineers' demand for an eight-hour work day. Later on, the trainmen confronted him with demands for a wage increase. But, despite the nagging problems, the company continued to prosper and reported increasingly substantial surpluses brought about by rising passenger volumes.

In May 1886, the Suburban Rapid Transit Company began operation over the Harlem River bridge between the Bronx and a joint station built by the Manhattan company at the head of Second Avenue. Essentially, "the Suburban Line made connections with the Second and Third Avenue lines at 129th Street and Second Avenue in Manhattan. After through trains ran to lower Manhattan from the Bronx, the Suburban Line became an extension of the Third Avenue Line."[1]

As Colonel Hain's reputation spread in railroad circles, he was offered the position of superintendent of the Philadelphia and Reading Railroad. While he declined the offer, it was a tribute to his firm hand in labor negotiations and positive results on the balance sheet. However, his signature achievement occurred during the Great Blizzard of 1888 when he kept the trains running despite the worst storm on record.

In keeping with his increasing prominence Frank K. Hain and his wife gathered social steam, so to speak, and appeared with NYC's elite at upper crust social events. And they lived the part by being among the first residents of the upscale Navarro Apartments, aka the "Spanish flats," at 165 West 58th Street.

Built in 1885, Spanish flats was NYC's first cooperative apartment house and consisted of eight eight-story buildings with 128 units facing Central Park South. It was "proclaimed the most elegant apartment house in New York, the largest apartment house in the world, and the most important building project ever undertaken, in terms of its novelty, magnitude, and cost."

Each house had a separate name and address, named after a city in Spain; Frank and Annie Hain resided in the "Barcelona." The complex was constructed by Jose de Navarro, a Spanish-born financier and a director of the Metropolitan Elevated Railway Company, and designed by architects Hubert and Pirsson. The living units each held 12 apartments of "extraordinary dimensions." The largest had a 23 × 29-foot drawing room, a 14 × 29 reception room, 20 × 23 dining room, an 18 × 20 kitchen with several large pantries, six bedrooms from 22 × 24 to 14 × 18, three baths with tubs, and three rooms for servants. The flats sold for $15,000 to $20,000, with annual maintenance charges running $1,000 to $2,000.[2]

General Manager Hain greeted the year 1886 with another challenge from a trainmen's union. This time, however, the stakes were raised because the elevated railroad engineers brought in P. M. Arthur, chief of the Brotherhood of Locomotive Engineers, from his office in Cleveland, to promote their cause. The issue was that the men were sometimes compelled to work more than ten hours a day for eight hours' pay. The grievance stemmed from 1880 when the engineers received $3.50 for eight hours work and were asked by the then general manager to assist the company by working ten hours a day without an increase in pay. The engineers agreed, but only until the following spring. However, the men complained that their hours increased little by little until sometimes they now worked more than ten hours for eight hours pay.

After discussing the problem with his engineers, P. M. Arthur asserted that their demands were "just," and "they ask for nothing that is not reasonable." As a practical locomotive engineer, Arthur felt that a man should not be required to run an engine on an elevated road for more than eight hours because it is much harder than driving on a surface road. He has no breaks from the moment he enters his cab and is worth every penny of $3.50 for eight hours' work.[3]

Master Mechanic Peeples (Thomas Whitson Peeples) of the elevated road had a different perspective. The company was prepared to make concessions, but was unlikely to comply with the men's demands. "The men are fickle," he said, "if they are scheduled to work only eight hours, they will report for duty later than they now do and quit earlier and, thereby take compensation in another way." He reasoned that "an engineer on the elevated road has a hundred dollar job … the best job in America. After all, an engineer can make $108 in a month."[4]

The battle lines were drawn. P. M. Arthur sent a letter to General Manager Hain and asked for a meeting. He received an immediate response from Col. Hain's secretary who wrote that the general manager was prepared to meet with Arthur and a committee of engineers on Wednesday at 11:00.

However, on Tuesday, the day before the meeting, Col. Hain issued a directive that circulated among all employees of the elevated roads:

V. Facing Down the Challenges (1886–1888)

The Navarro Apartments, aka "Spanish Flats," 165 West 58th Street; Frank K. Hain's residence, 1886–1896 (Office for Metropolitan History).

> Inasmuch as a number of engineers and firemen employed by this company have expressed dissatisfaction with the prescribed hours of labor, the time has come when the interests of the company demand that it should know at once who are for or against it, and to that end *engineers and firemen must immediately sign their names to this paper, thereby asserting their fealty to the corporation from which they derive the means to support themselves and their families* [author emphasis].

The engineers greeted the highlighted portion of Col. Hain's directive with "derisive laughter." However, before the engineers had time to "agitate" further, another directive from Col. Hain came to their attention:

> ... [the] company has decided to close its Second and Ninth Avenue lines, withdrawing all trains, commencing this day, and until further notice, and operate the Third and Sixth Avenue lines with loyal employees. Meanwhile, the company asks the kind indulgence of the traveling public, with the assurance that safety will be the first consideration.

P. M. Arthur was sitting down when he read the directive, but stood up before finishing it. His face was flushed, and he spoke with a tremor in his voice: "If there is a strike of the engineers on the elevated roads, the responsibility for it will rest on the company."

The surprise and indignation among Arthur and the men resulted in considerable posturing about the possibility of a strike. However, apparently realizing that Col. Hain had called his bluff, Arthur took a face-saving stance: "The Brotherhood of Locomotive Engineers does not issue orders for a strike; it merely sanctions a strike when it is based on just and reasonable grounds. If the Second and Ninth Avenue lines stop in the morning, the Sixth and Third Avenue lines will work until the results of our meeting with Col. Hain are known. If he refuses to meet us or to redress the grievances laid before him, the men on those lines will go out [on strike]."[5]

Later in the day, Arthur told a reporter: "All things considered, General Manager Hain's treatment of the men on the roads was most shabby. Nothing has been done either by myself or men to warrant such a procedure and it was wholly uncalled for."[6]

Meanwhile, a committee of ten engineers met with Col. Hain in his office to reiterate their grievances and request him to withdraw his directive. Col. Hain promised to examine their grievances carefully and render his decision at the scheduled Wednesday meeting. The committee was satisfied with his response, but their chairman sought assurance. "Col. Hain, will you treat this matter as we do between man and man and be ready with your answer on Wednesday?" Col. Hain answered affirmatively and added: "Give me time; don't push me to the wall, and you will be surprised when you see the schedule I will make out."

A reporter visited Col. Hain at his residence that night and asked why the company had taken the initiative to cancel the Second and Ninth Avenue trains. He replied that "the advertisement which will appear in the papers contains all the company has to say at the moment." But what about the public? "There is nothing more to be said. [The public] will have to wait patiently until tomorrow to see. We took off the Second and Ninth Avenue trains to be prepared." "Suppose, Col. Hain, that the fight should last for a month. What then?" The elevated road manager contemplatively scratched his head, and then, after a moment's silence, replied ambiguously: "My bump of combativeness is not very large."

The reporter also saw Vice President Gallaway who was "somewhat more communicative than his General Manager." After a brief discussion of the possibility of a strike, which Gallaway thought not likely to happen, he had this to say:

> The whole trouble is due to the younger men in the employ of the company who have never run a surface engine. Three-quarters of the present engineers were formerly barbers, tailors, or shoemakers, whom we took when the road opened and taught them the business.... The old fellows, who have run upon the surface roads, know that they have a "pudding," whatever that may be, and would not go into this, but, belonging to the brotherhood, they are forced to. The elevated engineers are better paid than the surface railroaders. The average speed is not over 15 miles an hour.... Then, too, ... every one of the day men can go home and stay there every night, while the engineer on the surface lines cannot be with his family more than two or three times a week.[7]

Settlement of the difficulties between the engineers and the company was achieved at the Wednesday meeting between Arthur, the engineers' ten-man grievance committee, Col. Hain, and Vice President Gallaway. The meeting lasted two and one-half hours and resulted in an "amicable understanding." The engineers agreed to work for the company at the old schedule of wages, but on a new time schedule. That is, they would receive $3.50 per day for nine hours' work or less. For any extra work over the nine hours, the engineers were to be paid at the scheduled rate per hour.

Manhattan Directors Sidney Dillon and Cyrus W. Field "flitted about the room in which the consultation was held." Director Dillon was the first to give reporters an inkling as to how the discussions were progressing: "There won't be no fighting," he said. Cyrus W. Field, "oily, chilly, and stately, carried his gray hair and whiskers, his new overcoat and rusty hat as he appeared at the prisonlike gate which shut reporters out of the sacred precincts. With a face wreathed in smiles such as few but Dukes and Princes and Kings are usually permitted to see, he looked over the plebeian reporters and said: 'Gentlemen, it's all been settled on a nine hour basis.'"

Afterward, Arthur briefed the men. "No man," he explained, "should grumble at giving nine hours work for $3.50." Furthermore, "I know how men sometimes feel when they have won a victory. I hope, when you go to your duties, you will not assume an air of braggadocio or brag to your fellows of what you have accomplished.... I know some of you are liable to say when you get into your roundhouses: 'We fetched 'em to time.' This is wrong."

Arthur continued. "Let me say, too, that notwithstanding the unfavorable reports I have heard of Col. Hain, I must admit, for him and Mr. Gallaway, I have never been received more courteously or been treated more kindly than by those two officials. I am satisfied that if you do your part, they will do theirs."[8]

Chief Engineer Arthur returned to Cleveland the following day. The *Times* summarized the results of his visit in this way: "On the roads everything worked smoothly. The victorious engineers and firemen remembered their chief's advice and did not brag, but attended to their duties. Master Mechanic Peeples [of the company] was as suave as usual, and his manner did not show that the company for which he works so faithfully had been worsted or that he entertained the shadow of a grudge against the victors."[9]

General Manager Hain was probably baffled by the *Times*' and Chief Engineer Arthur's rosy assessment of the negotiations. Especially since it was Col. Hain who called the trainmen's bluff, and allowed them no more than a face-saving, cosmetic victory, much as he had done four years before.

The Suburban Rapid Transit Company

Up to 1886, New York City's elevated railroads all operated within Manhattan Island, beginning at South Ferry and City Hall, and extending northward to their respective terminals on the east and west sides at the Harlem River. In addition, the 34th Street and 42nd Street spurs operated east and west. After the city annexed the 23rd and 24th wards (Bronx County from 1914), there was a call for extension of the elevated lines across the Harlem River into the "annexed district" (hereafter referred to as the Bronx). In 1880, the Suburban Rapid Transit Company (SRTC) was formed under Chapter 606, Laws of 1875, to provide rapid transit for the Bronx, and four main routes were approved and established: Central Route, East Side Route, Fordham Avenue Route, and the Eighth Avenue Route. "Under its charter, the SRTC was obliged to connect with existing trunk line railroads terminating in the Bronx, and to make a physical connection with existing east side elevated railroads in the Borough of Manhattan. These were the Third Avenue Line and Second Avenue Line, both then controlled by the Manhattan Railway Company."[10]

After the SRTC was organized, the Rapid Transit Commissioners approved, on March 15, 1882, construction of a bridge over the Harlem River. Work began on October 24, 1883, and it was completed on November 29, 1886. While the bridge was under construction, elevated railroad structures were built in the Bronx and a joint station was built by the Manhattan company at the head of Second Avenue. The SRTC's lines were ready for operation on May 17, 1886. The Suburban trains came to the joint station at Second Avenue from the north, using the westerly side, and the Manhattan's trains came from the south on the easterly side.[11]

On March 27, 1886, the SRTC leased the New York, Fordham and Bronx Railway Company and merged with it on April 9, 1886. Under a lease dated April 1, 1891, the Manhattan Railway Company, on June 4, 1891, took control of "all the railway lines, equipment, property and franchises of the SRTC, in return for a yearly rental of $240,000." From that day forward, the SRTC became the Suburban Division of the Manhattan Railway Company. On May 26, 1893, the Manhattan company adopted a five-cent fare for a continuous ride in Manhattan, across the Harlem River, and into the Bronx. So, a passenger could ride, without paying an extra five cents, between any points served by the SRTC line in the Bronx and the Second and Third Avenue elevated trains on Manhattan Island.[12]

The first through service of the Second and Third Avenue trains from South Ferry to Bronx Park, and from City Hall to 177th Street (Tremont) was in September 1896. Through trains were then operated only during rush hours. All trains, except locals, were made through trains two years later.[13]

By FY 1895, the Suburban road operated over 8.885 miles of single and double track. The line carried 5.5 million passengers, a reduction of 3.3 million passengers from the previous fiscal year, but consistent with the reduction of passenger volume on the other Manhattan lines. From the time the Manhattan Railway Company assumed control over the Suburban, the Suburban averaged over 6.6 million passengers per year between FY 1892 and 1895.[14]

Wrangling with the Brotherhood of Engineers was only the first of General Manager Hain's labor challenges in the period between 1886 and 1888. Several more thorny issues popped up, and he dealt with them in his forthright manner.

In June 1886, when asked about reports that a strike by dissatisfied elevated railroad employees was imminent, Col. Hain said the rumors were "baseless." He knew of no grievances against the company and had received no complaints. He attributed the rumor of a threatened strike to "one newspaper trying to be sensational" by printing "silly statements." Indeed, some of the trainmen who were shown the story "declared it absolutely untrue." The men said they were "perfectly satisfied under the new rule; that they have short hours and good pay, and want nothing more."[15]

However, rumors of a possible strike persisted. Col. Hain was quoted as saying that he was "not going to lose sleep in worrying over mythical dangers." He believed that the men would come to him directly if they had grievances, because "they were not led by foolish men."[16]

A month later, trainmen were said to be "uneasy" because several of them were discharged for being members of the Knights of Labor and because a "large number" of new men were hired to replace them. Col. Hain assured the trainmen that he did not intend to discriminate against the Knights of Labor and that he did not care whether they belonged to any organization or not.[17]

Later in the year, Col. Hain had the fortuitous opportunity to ingratiate himself with his principal antagonists. It came about when 300 delegates of the International Brotherhood of Locomotive Engineers held their annual convention at the Metropolitan Opera House. Opening ceremonies were attended by the Grand Chief Engineer and his associates, as well as several political figures including New York City's Mayor Grace, Governor Leon Abbott of New Jersey, and the Honorable Chauncey M. Depew, a state politician and president of the New York Central and Hudson River Railroad. President Cleveland sent regrets.

The welcome was extended by New Jersey Governor Abbott (the Governor of New York was invited, but did not respond) who described the delegates as a "conservative, law-abiding organization of intelligent, hard-working men." The Honorable Chauncey Depew delivered a "stirring address" that conveyed the following inspirational message:

> The great Republic owed all its greatness and glory to the railroads.... No better men worked in the world than locomotive engineers. They led sober, regular, and industrious lives.... Thanks to the Brotherhood the engineer of today [is] a very different man from what he was 23 years ago. Blasphemy was his conversation and whisky [sic] was his nerve tonic in those days, but this [has] all been changed.... The leader of the Brotherhood should be a man of sense, courage, and virtue — of sense, to know the Brotherhood's demands; of a courage to help him resist urgent pressure from either side, and of a virtue that would prevent him from ... plunging his fellow men into penury.[18]

The following day General Manager Hain invited the delegates and their wives for a ride on the elevated railroad. In the evening they would visit the Young Men's Christian Association for a program of entertainment.

Two special trains bedecked with flags took the visitors on an excursion over the entire elevated system. They set a record of 25 miles in two hours and ten minutes without special effort to make time. Behind the lead train trailed five new cars "shiny as a newly coined seventy-cent dollar [sic]." The seats were filled "in a twinkling" and the train moved off, leaving about 200 of Superintendent Hain's guests to ride with excursion train #2. Along the way, the guests passed the hat to collect business cards of the delegates for Col. Hain, as well as to collect a tip for the trainmen. The excursion was pronounced a "great success."[19]

Col. Hain announced that the directors of the company, "without being asked," decided to increase the pay of guards and conductors who had been in service to the company for three years from $1.75 to $1.85 a day and $2.20 to $2.30 a day respectively. Formerly, a brakeman got $1.50 a day for the first year of service, $1.65 for the second year, and $1.75 after that; conductors got $2.00 the first year and $2.20 after that. The decision affected about 400 trainmen or more than one-half of the company's work force. Col. Hain said that the rates paid by the Manhattan company were the highest paid for similar service on any railroad in the United States.

However, the raises were by no means satisfactory to the men and a committee was sent to notify Col. Hain. The committee expected "big things" from Col. Hain, but instead he made an order that left the workers worse off than before. Under the new agreement a conductor would get $2.00 the first year and $2.30 after that if his record was clear. A brakeman would get $1.75 for the second year and $1.85 afterward if his record was clear. In the trainmen's view, Col. Hain's plan sounded like a raise until it was understood that probably no more than four men on the four roads had a clear record. For instance, a "faithful" brakeman applied for a job in the office, but his superintendent refused to give him a certificate of "clear record." Among the worst of the charges against him were that he reported late twice, had failed to wear his uniform trousers, and once spoke to a man when the train was going around a curve. "You can see by that what a clear record means."

Unless the trainmen reached a more satisfactory agreement with Col. Hain at their next meeting, "there is a strong possibility that a strike will occur, and that the engineers and firemen will support the trainhands."[20] The outcome of the discussions was not reported.

Other employees of the Manhattan Elevated were seeking advantage in their own way. For example, an elevated road employee remarked to a *Times* reporter: "You newspaper men are always ready to find fault with us fellows, but you wouldn't give us a bit of a lift, would you?" The reporter assured him that he could indeed provide a "lift" if it were in a "proper direction." Whereupon the elevated employee elaborated on the hardships of a monthly pay day. The men had asked Col. Hain to be paid twice a month, but Col. Hain told them the company could not afford it because it would "overwork the cashier and his assistant, and the men would get drunk oftener, neglect their duty, and endanger the lives of the public."

The employee asserted that this was "both absurd and unjust" because there are "thousands of sober and reliable men" willing to work for the company if there were assurances that they would be paid weekly or bi-weekly. The present system, he claimed, had a "tendency to keep on the road men not of the best class. If we are short of money," he said, "we must go to money-lenders for an advance in order to buy bread. They charge us ten percent a month even if the loan is made for less than a month."[21]

Complaints about wages took many forms, about as many as there were employees of the roads. In another case, several of them assembled to complain about the company's new rule to pay them by the hour instead of by the day. This change was adopted because of bills in the state legislature that made ten consecutive hours a day's work on the surface and elevated roads.

Under the old system, the elevated employees were paid as follows: telegraph operators, $2.25 per day; ticket agents, $2.00; platform men, $1.65; gatemen with over a year's service, $1.50; under a year, $1.25; and porters, $1.20. Under the new pay-by-the-hour rule, the wages were: telegraph operators, $1.85; ticket agents, $1.68; gatemen, $1.25 and $1.05; platform men, $1.37; and porters, $1.00.

The men first got wind of the new system when some of them were summoned to the office of the general ticket agent and "ordered" to sign the new agreement. When one of the men wanted to know more about it, he was told: "You can read, cannot you?" The man still wanted more time to read the agreement, but the chief clerk went out of the office for a moment, returned with a company detective, and pointed out the recalcitrant trainman to him. The detective said menacingly: "All right, we'll look out for him."

The men claimed that the company was rolling in money since reduction of the fares to five cents, while their work had been doubled. They had sent a petition to Col. Hain about a year ago asking for an increase in wages, but he refused to grant their request, saying bluntly that if "they did not like the pay they were getting they could [quit] and he could get plenty of Italians who would do the work at half the price."[22]

The trainmen's claim that the company was "rolling in money" was not without justification. Until 1886, the rate of fare on the elevated roads was ten cents for all distances at all hours except between the "rush" hours of 5:30 A.M. to 8:30 A.M. and 4:30 P.M. to 7:30 P.M. when the fare was five cents. However, after experimenting with reduced fares on the Second Avenue and Ninth Avenue lines, the company reduced the fare for all lines, over all distances, at all hours of the day and night to five cents, effective November 1, 1886. The results were an immediate increase in the number of passengers carried and an increase in net earnings. A comparison of data between November and December 1885 and the same months of 1886 showed that the reduction of fares on all roads amounted to an increase of 8,877,960 passengers carried and an increase of $26,758 in net earnings.[23]

While the reduction in fares was welcome relief to the traveling public, and boosted the Manhattan Railway's profits, an article in *The Sun* brought an unexpected safety issue to the public's attention. The newspaper questioned whether, with increased travel (because of the reduced fares), would the elevated structures be "subject to a strain which they had not before been called on to bear?" Col. Hain's reaction was that "the growth had been foreseen and carefully provided for; that on the Sixth Avenue line the structure has been strengthened systematically during the last four years, and that a like work is now going on with the Third Avenue line." Evidently satisfied with Col. Hain's reassurance, the article went on to say that the Manhattan company has "not only served the public with admirable punctuality, but they have done it with a proportion of accidents which falls below that on the best managed surface railroads of any country. That the people may travel over the elevated roads without fear is made pretty clear by Mr. Hain's figures and explanations." However, the article concluded with the following admonishment:

> But the conclusion we have expressed before we must now express again, and it is that New York cannot afford to put its sole reliance for rapid transit on the elevated roads alone. However well managed, they are unequal to the wants of the public, and already are overcrowded to a very uncomfortable degree, at both night and morning. We need imperatively and at once an underground railroad, such as the Arcade Company proposes.[24]

The elevated roads' telegraph operators had their own unique grievances. Some of them became dissatisfied and considered a strike because they were paid $2.25 a day and had to work 12 hours a day, 7 days a week. In addition, they were required to sell tickets.

In comparison, Western Union telegraphers received $65 a month and worked nine hours a day, with Sundays off. Also, Superintendent Hain, it was said, opened a compulsory night school where telegraphers must teach telegraphy to gatemen. The telegraph operators believed that the elevated road wanted to reduce their wages still farther. If a strike was called, "which is not improbable," the commercial telegraph operators would not replace them.[25]

Later on, Col. Hain again came under fire on the same issue because of his School of Telegraphy at the Chatham Square station. The operators claimed that the school would train men who would be recruited from the extra gatemen and trainmen because they would work at a much cheaper rate than the current operators. The newly trained telegraphers were expected to receive $55 a month instead of the $70 to $75 a month received by the current telegraphers. The person in charge of the school did not see why the school should be opposed so violently. "We are simply teaching these men telegraphy with the idea of benefiting them," he said.[26]

In November 1886, Stephen D. Field, now associated with electrical engineer, Rudolph Eickemeyer, announced a new design for an elevated railway electric locomotive. "This was a short 'steeple cab' locomotive, with a center control cab and sloping compartments at each end. The locomotive was mounted on two four-wheeled trucks, one of which was unpowered while the other was powered by an electric motor designed and built by Eickemeyer." The locomotive was put to test in September 1887 on the north track of the 34th Street branch of the elevated road. However, the locomotive could pull only one car at eight miles per hour and the design elicited no interest from the Manhattan company.[27]

Between late 1885 and 1886, Frank J. Sprague conducted experiments on a short section of elevated track at the Durant Sugar Refinery on East 24th Street. "A key feature of Sprague's design for the test car was the adoption of a 'nose-suspended or wheelbarrow' method for mounting the motors so that they were directly geared to the axle," which solved "what had been a source of endless problems for early electric railway designers." "Sprague's application ... became an almost universal method for mounting electric motors."[28]

Over the next several months, Sprague conducted a series of tests that were attended by Jay Gould, Cyrus W. Field, and General Manager Hain. One such visit did not go so well as Sprague later recalled:

> Desiring to make an impressive demonstration of how readily the car could be controlled and braked in the short distance available for movement, I handled the controller rather abruptly, whereupon the fuse blew with a violent flash and Mr. Gould attempted to jump off the car. My explanation that this young volcano was only a safety device was not convincing and he did not return.[29]

Some observers feel that the above incident left such an unfavorable impression on Jay Gould that he turned away from the concept of electric motive power because of it.

In May 1886, the experiments shifted to the Manhattan Railway's 34th Street branch and were attended by Cyrus W. Field, General Manager Hain and other Manhattan officials. The elevated road supplied a standard elevated car for the tests, and it was equipped with a variety of equipment required for electric operation and "two traction motors were mounted in 'wheelbarrow' fashion on one of the car's two trucks." After some trying moments, when the motors failed to respond to electrical current, the test was a success. "For two hours every feat which could be tried with the machines was attempted without a failure."[30]

Encouraged by the May results, the tests continued through December 28, 1886, when they were brought to a close. But, as Sprague later remarked: "In all those months, so far as I can remember, not a director or stockholder of the Manhattan road ever took the slightest interest in what was being done."[31] In short, "[the company was] not interested in spending money to replace an existing, money-making operation."[32]

Sprague devoted the next couple of years to electrification of street railways, which, in 1887 and 1888, "led to his great success at Richmond [the first practical electric-powered street railway] and a boom in electric railways."[33]

Inventor Leo Daft returned to the elevated tracks with his *Benjamin Franklin* for more trials during late 1886. However, the tests showed that Daft was working with inadequate details from the el's representatives. "The *Franklin* was constructed in the belief that 55 to 60 horsepower was required for pulling trains. It was not equal to the 22-ton steam locomotives, which had over twice the horsepower, and it could not pull more than two loaded cars up the steep grade at 13th Street. Since a normal train was four cars in length, the *Franklin* was a disappointment and removed from the line."[34]

However, two years later, in October and November 1888, Daft returned to the Ninth Avenue Line with an improved *Benjamin Franklin*. Trial runs "showed the *Franklin* capable of pulling eight empty cars (the maximum train length and a load in excess of 54 tons) up the 13th Street grade at 7½ miles per hour. With the standard four-car trains, the *Franklin* made 25 miles per hour and on two occasions was reported to have pulled three cars at 30 miles per hour." Nevertheless, "even though Daft's 'new' *Benjamin Franklin* was a marked success, doing more than asked of it, the elevated railroad's owners decided to continue with their steam locomotives."[35]

Col. Hain was said to be in "high feather" after General U. S. Grant's funeral because his elevated roads had surpassed previous passenger records. On an average business day his trains carried about 320,000 passengers, but on the day of the funeral, the passenger count increased to 400,000. For the 24 hours from Sunday at midnight to Monday at midnight, the trains carried 535,932 passengers. "Our men stood by us bravely," remarked Col. Hain, "and did such valiant service that we did not have to employ an extra man." He issued the following official notice:

To all Officers and Employees:
The unprecedented traffic on Monday, 19th inst., when 535,932 passengers were carried without accident or material delay, is cause for warmest congratulation for your patience, devotion to duty, and extraordinary care under most trying circumstances. The traffic was distributed as follows: Second Avenue, 88,310; Third Avenue, 248,599; Sixth Avenue, 161,436; Ninth Avenue, 42,587–535,932.
/s/ F. K. Hain, General Manager[36]

On another matter, related to a heavy increase in elevated traffic because of tie-ups in the surface lines, Col. Hain claimed: "We can carry 800,000 passengers today without overstraining our facilities, and we can carry that big number, too, with far greater ease than we could have taken 500,000 a year ago."[37]

A *Times* reporter asked General Manager Hain what he knew about a rumored plan in Albany to build another elevated road in Broadway, extending from the Battery and connecting at 34th Street with the Sixth Avenue road. Col. Hain knew nothing about the supposed project and drolly suggested that "a hunt be made for the individual who is said to have in his pocket the bill to permit a company to build the road."

The reporter then called on Director Russell Sage's office to inquire whether the undertaking was part of a scheme to connect the elevated system and the New England road at the Brooklyn Bridge with the Long Island Railroad Company. The "cerberus of the outer office" refused to allow the reporter to meet with Director Sage but agreed to take a note to him. He returned in a few minutes with a verbal message from Sage who had not heard anything about the scheme. However, the cerberus volunteered: "That's what he says, you know, but he laughed when he said it, and maybe he knows all about it."[38]

A report surfaced that Colonel Hain was offered the position of general superintendent of the Philadelphia and Reading Railroad at a large salary. The press reported at least two versions of a conversation that took place between Col. Hain and Jay Gould regarding the above position and the General Manager's salary. The following version appeared in the *New York Tribune* of May 24, 1886, and was sourced to *The Philadelphia Press*:

> Colonel Hain's great ability was recognized some years ago by railway managers so that he received many tempting offers. All of them he declined to consider until at last one came through Mr. Austin Corbin [owner of the New York and Manhattan Beach Railroad, later President of the Long Island Railroad, and a Director of the Brooklyn Elevated Railroad], which, if accepted, would have made Colonel Hain the executive manager of the Reading system. With that was a salary offer so tempting that in justice to his family, Colonel Hain felt compelled to consider it. Jay Gould heard of this offer, and he sent for Colonel Hain.
>
> He said to him, "Colonel, I hear that the Reading Railroad people have made propositions to you to go into their service; is it true?"
>
> "Yes, Mr. Gould, that is so," Hain replied.
>
> "Well, you should have informed us," said Mr. Gould.
>
> "I did not do it, because, in the first place, I have never informed you of other offers, and, in the second place, I do not think it right to use an offer as a club with which to get an increase in salary. I should either have accepted that offer in the belief that you were paying me all that you thought I was worth, or I should have declined it."
>
> Here Mr. Gould began to tear up paper, as was his habit, when he was deeply interested. At last, he said: "Colonel, how much are we paying you?" and Colonel Hain replied: "Six thousand dollars."
>
> Mr Gould looked up in astonishment, and he afterward confessed that he had forgotten that Colonel Hain's salary had never been raised. He said to the Colonel: "Do you mind telling me what the Reading people have offered you?" The Colonel named a sum nearly three times the amount he was receiving from the elevated company.
>
> "Is it the salary alone that tempts you?" Gould asked, and to this Colonel Hain replied: "I felt compelled in justice to my family to consider this proposition solely on account of the salary."
>
> Then Mr. Gould said: "Then dismiss this subject from your mind. You are as valuable to

V. Facing Down the Challenges (1886–1888)

the elevated company as you can be to any other corporation and your salary will be taken care of at once. Hereafter, if you feel convinced that you are earning a better salary than you receive, let us know, and I do not think there will be any disagreement between us." At the next Director's meeting Colonel Hain's salary was increased to the sum offered him by the Reading Company.

Five months later, the press followed up the above account with another news item, sourced to an anonymous director of the company, who acknowledged that Col. Hain had received an offer from the Philadelphia and Reading, but was "not likely to accept it." He was said to be proud of the honor because he began his career as a machinist's apprentice with the Reading. While Col. Hain did not accept the offer, an interesting side issue developed when the anonymous director asserted that working for the Reading would be "much heavier" than at the Manhattan Railway and therefore "Col. Hain has not the strength required for duties of the position." This discussion prompts a flash back to 1861 when Col. Hain suffered from adynamia and malaria during service aboard the *Iroquois*. The effects of those debilitating illnesses apparently carried over into the future and impacted on his decision to accept the Reading's offer.[39]

Another account, *Times*, December 4, 1892, reported that the Reading offered $12,000 and that Col. Hain was earning $6,500, whereupon Gould increased his salary to $15,000.

No year was complete unless the *Times* got in its two cents worth on the evil "robber barons." In this example, the newspaper took delight in briefly describing the "Manhattan squeeze" that was put on Cyrus W. Field by his partners because he lowered the price of a ride on the elevated from ten cents to five against their wishes several years before.

> Jay Gould and Russell Sage are triumphant; Cyrus W. Field's scalp has been taken.... Mr. Field made a brave fight, but he did not realize until the end came that he was to be struck down in the very house of his friends. He knows a good many things now that he didn't even dream of a week ago; he learned the value of professing friendship and declared partnership; he has seen what dollars and cents have to do with loyalty; he discovers how cheap is duplicity and double-dealing and downright betrayal.[40]

It was known as the "white hurricane," and it would go down in history as one of the worst natural disasters ever to befall a major city. The "Great Blizzard" of 1888 began on Sunday, March 11, as a light rain when temperatures were fairly mild for the time of year. The temperature fell, the winds grew in ferocity and the rain turned to sleet and then snow. When New Yorkers woke up for their work day on Monday they were looking at two to five feet of snow and drifts up to thirty feet in some areas.[41]

> Before the day had well advanced, every horse-car and elevated railroad train in the city had stopped running; the streets were almost impassable to men or horses by reason of the huge masses of drifting snow; the electric wires — telegraph and telephone ... were nearly all broken; hardly a train was out from the city or came into it during the entire day; the mails were stopped, and every variety of business dependent on motion or locomotion was stopped.[42]

As the day progressed, the storm lost none of its intensity. The streets were littered with debris and the horse-cars were lying on their sides, entrenched in deep snow. The city scene resembled a battleground. Dusk fell and the ferocious blizzard continued.

The elevated roads were in chaos. The rails were slippery, making it dangerous to round curves, almost impossible to climb steep grades, or to come to a stop at the stations. The deep drifts impeded trainmen who first needed to clear the snow before they could address running the trains. However, the wind had other ideas, because as soon as a drift was cleared, the howling wind blew another in its place. The switches and movable rails were frozen and laborers brushed them with salt water, but the salt water froze in the pails. "At the headquarters of the elevated roads there was the usual ignorance of what was going on."[43]

By Wednesday, the 14th, the elevated trains were running again. But it was not without a lot of determined work:

> Colonel Hain reached his office this morning at eleven o'clock. He had been taking since midnight his first rest for some forty hours.
> "I'm too tired to talk this morning," said the General Manager, with weary good nature, "but the tracks are clear. The gangs of shovellers and ice pickers worked all yesterday and last night, and every inspector and inside man was on hand. The first care was to get the ice out of the switches and lubricate them. Afterwards, there was a general clearing up and straightening out. Luckily our telegraph and telephone wires were not injured and we were able to tell exactly where everything was throughout the whole system. We're all right now."
> [Colonel Hain] has been the right man in the right place, and the town ought to put up a statue to him.[44]

The paralyzing blizzard was not only an event that brought acclaim to General Manager Frank Hain for keeping the trains running, but it was an exclamation point to the need for a more efficient transportation system than the elevated roads were capable of delivering. To Mayor Abram S. Hewitt, "the snowstorm was nothing less than a vote of confidence from God for underground rapid transit."[45]

The *Reading Press* inaugurated a weekly feature in its Sunday edition that included biographic sketches, including photographs, of "men whose names are known to everyone, [but] whose faces are unrecognized when seen on the streets." These individuals included "men of national reputation who have never given a photograph to a newspaper." The first such prominent person was Frank K. Hain in a portrait entitled: "A Bright Berks County Boy." After outlining his professional career, the *Press* had this to say about him as a person:

> He is a very quiet man, whose alphabet has only twenty-five letters. The letter it lacks is "I." He has a retiring manner, which is nevertheless not at all unnoticeable. There is a dry humor about it which reminds one not a little of that of ex-Senator Platt. [Thomas C. Platt, Republican Party leader in New York State who served briefly in the U.S. Senate in 1881 and again from 1897–1909].
> Perhaps there is a phlegmatic Pennsylvania Dutch strain in him which has stood his nervous system in good stead. Think of the strain on the man who knows that his alleged "blocks" [train delays] are made the scapegoat for the sins of every belated husband, every recreant lover, every tardy clerk or salesgirl of the 500,000 people his trains carry daily. Now that the *Press* makes known his face to wives, sweethearts and employers the excuse will no longer go.[46]

Accidents continued to be an unavoidable problem and the fatal accidents naturally received considerably more attention from the press than the minor "rear-enders." Pinning blame was a constant exercise and the elevated road usually took the (dis)honors.

However, an article in the *Railroad Gazette*, sourced to the *New York Herald*, favorably portrayed the Manhattan company's medical department and its ability to handle injuries to the company's trainmen. Dr. Field, one of two physicians attending the roads, went to great length in explaining the mechanics of reporting injuries and the department's state of readiness for every emergency. He also noted that of the 4,000 employees it was the repairmen, couplers of cars, trackmen, and flagmen on duty who suffered the most injuries.

> But the most fruitful source of accidents is the thoughtlessness and ire of passengers attacking our trainmen — "guards" they are called. The gates must be shut when ordered. Now [but] a day or two ago we had one of our guards here who may probably lose his eye. His condition was very serious. An irate passenger, because the gate was shut, struck him across the eye with a heavy cane, and the poor fellow may lose his sight forever.... These assaults occur almost daily, and they are quite numerous on the midnight trains.[47]

Despite the Manhattan company's record of fairly rapid and informative responses to the causes of accidents on the elevated lines, the *Tribune* was convinced that Col. Hain had ordered his trainmen to suppress information about matters that put the company in an unfavorable light. The feeling was that, in order to keep their job, the only safe course for the trainmen was to "keep their mouths shut." "Almost without exception whenever inquiry is made concerning a collision or breakdown, ticket sellers, gate keepers, and guards alike refuse to give any facts, and try in every way to keep passengers and reporters in the dark." Moreover, before Col. Hain came to the elevated system, it was "not especially hard to get at the truth concerning accidents," but once he became general manager, "although he says he has issued no order imposing secrecy, the lips of all subordinates have been as tightly sealed on such matters as if they were closed with Portland cement."[48]

One of the most high profile accident victims was the "little widow in black," a Catharine (Kate) Sheehan, who was crushed under a train at the 93rd Street station of the Ninth Avenue Line as she tried to get on the rear platform of a passenger car. The *Times* reported that the body was "found to be horribly mangled and crushed out of all semblance of shape below the waist," and the gruesome story went on from there. "Railroad people" advised the police that Sheehan made a "frantic effort" to board the train after the conductor closed the gate and missed her footing, causing her to fall between the cars. However, a rumor circulated that Sheehan's "death had not been accidental" because the guard slammed the gate in her face when she attempted to board the train, and the force of the blow threw her onto the track between two cars. The *Times* found witnesses who put the blame entirely on the elevated road; while "railroad people" were equally adamant about placing the blame on the victim.[49]

Col. Hain conducted his "thorough personal investigation of the facts," and felt that Mrs. Sheehan's actions spoke for themselves:

> The facts are that the gates had been closed and the engine had started when Mrs. Sheehan rushed out of the waiting room. A strange and sudden aberration of mind must have come upon her, for she ran across the platform and placed her hand upon the forward gate of the second car. She was dragged along a few steps, when in a twinkling the momentum of the

train whirled her between the car and the platform and she was crushed to death upon the track before the gateman, who realized her peril and sprang forward to save her, could reach the spot where she had stood. It is a sad case and has given me a feeling of melancholy today which I have been unable to shake off, yet I know that no one in the service of the road can be blamed in the slightest degree, or could have prevented the unfortunate occurrence.[50]

Another gruesome and fatal accident took place later in the same year that closely resembled the Sheehan incident. According to the *Times*, "in this city there has not been a casualty so revolting in detail and as exasperating because of the utter lack of common sense and humane feeling which caused it as that which resulted in the death of Philip Baer." Baer attempted to board a Second Avenue train just as the conductor was closing the gate and "the actions of this conductor [were] so brutal and so extraordinarily devoid of even decent discretion that [the Police Court] issued a warrant for his arrest on the charge of homicide."

According to witnesses interviewed by the newspaper, Baer tried to board the train, but the conductor slammed the gate shut and left Baer clinging to a narrow edge on the car's platform. The train began to move and Baer shouted: "Let me on, for God's sake, I can't get off now." However, the conductor, instead of letting Baer pass through the gate, shoved him back on to the ledge and caused him to go down between the cars and the station platform. An "intelligent Italian barber" reported that "the opening was only wide enough to admit his body to the hips [and] the moving train kept twisting him around like a corkscrew and I could hear his bones crack." Etcetera.

Col. Hain was quoted after the incident: "I have very little to say. The affair was sad, very sad, but the conductor was only obeying the orders of the Company that the gates shall not be opened. This order is backed by an act of the Legislature of 1881." When asked if the conductor should have shown some common sense when he saw that life was in danger, Col. Hain replied: "Undoubtedly, if I or one of my lieutenants had been there we should have ordered the conductor to open the gate, but we cannot afford to allow our thousand employees to use discretion."[51] Col. Hain elaborated on the incident in another quote attributed to him: "The poor fellow [the conductor] probably has a family to support on his dollar and a half a day; he couldn't afford to risk his job. He was between the devil and the deep sea."[52]

Col. Hain's insensitive public remarks resulted in a heavy backlash:

> [For the general manager of the elevated roads] to intimate as a rule governing the conduct of the system ... that any employee who ventures to depart at all from his ordinary instructions for the purpose of saving a human life will be dismissed from his position, is an affront to the instincts of humanity that ought to be resented by this community. If [Col. Hain] thinks so little of human life ... then it is the plain duty of the directors to get a new manager as soon as possible.[53]

In a bizarre incident, a fireman was struck by a signal post when he was lighting the headlight of his engine and received severe injuries. A recent similar accident caused Col. Hain to seek a solution to the problem. His initial reaction was to change the location of several signals to remove the causes of danger, but because of technical considerations, it would be easier to change the current configurations. In the meantime, he concluded that the accidents owed to the "negligence of the employees and could have been avoided had they used ordinary care."[54]

The "most destructive collision in the history of the elevated railroads" took place just south of 104th Street on the Ninth Avenue Line. General Manager Hain blamed an engineer, but others blamed the accident on a "frog" that "jumped." It was a switching accident that took place on a three-track section at midmorning and involved a five-car train driven by locomotive engineer W. G. Gilchrist. No passengers were involved because the locomotive was detached from the passenger cars.

The company had a rule against making switches at high speeds, but apparently engineer Gilchrist disobeyed orders and his engine jumped the track at a "frog," and instead of rolling toward a west track, "shot to the right" over the east switch. Gilchrist reversed his engine, but seeing that a collision with empty passenger cars was unavoidable, he shouted to the fireman and both jumped from the cab. The engine went one way and the passenger cars the other, crashing into guard rails, before coming to a halt in a cloud of smoke. It was a miracle, according to onlookers, that the engine did not fall to the street below. Terrible as it was, no fatalities or injuries occurred.

General Manager Hain sent for Engineer Gilchrist at once, but he did not respond to the summons. Col. Hain was conducting a thorough investigation and if Gilchrist was found at fault he would be discharged.[55]

An accident waiting to happen was the way the *New York Times* looked at another collision that took place on the elevated road in the vicinity of Chatham Square. A Second Avenue train bound southward crashed into a Third Avenue bound northward and blocked traffic for about an hour. Col. Hain responded to the matter by placing the blame on the carelessness of the engineer on the Second Avenue train and declared that he was suspended from service. However, the *Times* was not satisfied with Col. Hain's explanation because the newspaper saw the incident as part of a larger problem at Chatham Square. While the engineer may have been careless, opined the *Times*, the recklessness of his employers (i.e., Col. Hain) was more apparent.[56]

After the collision at Chatham Square, the Railroad Commission communicated with Col. Hain with a view to making changes that would ensure greater safety for passengers and prevent grade crossings.

General Manager Hain responded with a letter in which he went into great detail about the reasons for the collision and reflected on the irony of the press now suggesting that the road "return to the method in vogue before the existing plan was adopted, and against which the newspapers and the 8,000 passengers who made the daily transfer uttered vigorous and long-continued protests."[57] "[In any case], I beg to say the present method of operation is the more satisfactory to the public, for the reason that all necessary transfers are made on a level, and without a fatiguing climb over a high bridge. As to the safety and efficiency of the interlocking system in use at the point in question, I have to say that it is manufactured by the Union Switch and Signal Company of Pittsburgh, and is the best device known for the purpose."

The Railroad Commission responded with a suggestion that a red gate or bar across the Second Avenue track might eliminate the danger. However, Col. Hain thought an

Elevated station, Chatham Square, c. 1880 (Library of Congress).

additional "torpedo signal" and an additional flagman on the platform would be better and he ordered these additional precautions to be taken at once.[58]

In May 1887, during an early morning rush hour, the trains at 14th Street and Third Avenue were blocked because of a fire. The fire occurred in a tailor shop on the Bowery and blocked the north-bound track between Grand and Houston streets. At this time, the trains were filled with working men anxious to reach their places of employment. So anxious, in fact, that many of them left the cars and walked along the three-foot wide track-walk. About this time the track was cleared and a train just north of the station started toward the platform, whereupon one of the passengers on the track-walk tried to climb onto the train. This action resulted in a portion of his body protruding beyond the side of the car sufficiently to strike other passengers. Eleven of them fell to the street and four died. The passenger who caused the disaster escaped injury and all efforts to locate him were fruitless. Col. Hain's investigation continued.[59]

A cylinder head blew out on a locomotive that was drawing lightly loaded cars on the Ninth Avenue Line during the morning rush hour as the train neared the 23rd Street station. The equipment failure brought the locomotive to a halt and backed up the trains behind it. Col. Hain said that equipment failures can occur at any time to any locomotive and that it happens as frequently on the surface railroads as on the elevated ones. "We can't and nobody else can tell just where a piece of iron is defective. The engines are fully equal to the work they are put to."[60]

V. Facing Down the Challenges (1886–1888)

The Bowery, March 5, 1900 (Library of Congress).

An accident occurred on the Third Avenue elevated road at 85th Street because of the "too ardent zeal of a switchman." The accident prompted speculation that the tracks were perhaps carrying more trains than they were built to handle and that the switchman overreacted in his haste to accomplish his job.

Col. Hain was asked whether the roads were capable of handling the increased traffic. He had no conception, he said, nor did anyone else, when the roads were first operated that the traffic over them would reach its current high volume. "Do you think [the roads] are safe?" he was asked. He answered:

> They are completely, perfectly, and absolutely safe, in my opinion and in the opinion of some of the most competent engineering experts in the country. The management of the roads has taken every precaution to make them safe by strengthening them beyond the required standard. Even before the increased traffic demanded it, the strengthening process was inaugurated, and there has not been much cessation to it. The road beds are heavier, and in every way calculated to withstand a far greater strain than at the outset was calculated to be necessary. The material, too, is in the best of condition, as longitudinal and transverse sections of iron have been given to [the Stevens Institute] for test purposes, and [they] have pronounced them of the best quality and in a better condition to bear strain than when first put into position.[61]

A collision occurred at 76th Street and Third Avenue that resulted in injuries to six passengers and one employee, and the death of one employee. The accident took place during the Great Blizzard when a train stalled in the snow and was being assisted by another engine, forming a so-called double-header. As they approached the 76th Street station, a preceding train was stalled in the snow. Unfortunately, the hand brakes of the double-header were filled with ice and snow that rendered them useless. Thus, it was impossible to stop the double-header from crashing into the train ahead. The engineer of the colliding train was pinned against the boiler and died of internal injuries shortly after being extricated from the wreckage. Col. Hain did not find fault with the engineers, but attributed the accident to the weather conditions.[62]

Blown cylinder heads on the elevated locomotives grew more frequent, but with no results more serious than alarm and delay. Col. Hain said such accidents happened every day on the surface roads and scarcely anybody noticed them, but when they happened on the elevated roads, the incidents were greatly magnified. When asked about safeguards to protect people on the streets below, Col. Hain replied: "How can there? The people must stand from under." He added that the engines underwent daily inspection.[63]

> The care accorded the red devils [the Forneys] was surely above average. Inspections were unusually vigilant. Operating crews were expected to report, in writing, even the slightest defect. At the same time a terminal inspector made his own examination. At the end of the day both a hostler and a yard supervisor were required to make yet another pilot-to-draft-gear inspection. Once a month each engine was given overall light repairs and a boiler wash. Every twenty months it would receive an overhaul at the main shops. Some parts were replaced on a mileage-renewal schedule. Axles were replaced every 250,000 miles no matter what their condition might be. Crankpins went into the scrap-bin after 125,000 miles. While in service crankpins were tested every thirty days with four blows from a twelve-pound sledge hammer.[64]

A rear-ender took place at 64th Street and Ninth Avenue when an engineer "ran" a warning signal and plowed into the rear of the train in front. The collision resulted in partial derailments and two "trucks" falling to the street. The passenger cars were prevented from falling by the safety chains and transverse girders of the structure. The engineer who ran the signal was dismissed from the service by Col. Hain.[65]

The public often had their own unique requirements, many times without having all the facts in hand. For instance, residents of Harlem petitioned the road for a new station at 130th Street to accommodate passengers who were currently obliged to use either the 125th Street or the 135th Street stations. The petition argued that owing to the large increase in West Harlem's population and the "concentration of traffic lines at Eighth Avenue and 125th Street, passengers are crowded in an uncomfortable if not dangerous manner on the station and approaches thereto." The inconvenience largely applied to the residents of 128th and 129th streets.

Col. Hain replied that the improvements were being considered by the board of directors. However, he explained, "a new station is a matter of $30,000 to us, and therefore, worth careful consideration. When citizens demand a new station they forget the cost and the effect another stoppage point will have on the schedule."[66]

Personnel issues beyond wages and compensation also required General Manager Hain's attention. For instance, a complaint was filed with Col. Hain that jeopardized the position of conductor no. 892 of the elevated road. According to the complaint, four "rough-looking colored men" boarded a Third Avenue train, and on their way to their seats, one of them stumbled over a woman's foot. He made some insulting remarks about the woman in a "filthy language." A passenger took umbrage to his language, "whereupon the colored man and his friends pounced upon him and pounded him severely." The women in the cars became frightened by the incident and appealed to the conductor to intervene, but he refused on the grounds that it was not his business to stop the disturbance. When the train stopped at 34th Street, a passenger asked the conductor to have the offenders arrested. Again he refused. Col. Hain, when apprised of the incident, remarked that if any part of the offense could be established, the conductor would be dismissed. Moreover, the "colored men's" language was sufficient for the conductor to eject them or cause their arrest.[67]

Passengers on the elevated roads during the winter of 1886 complained about the heat. Some of the cars, they claimed, were perfectly heated, while others were cold, although all cars had the same kind of (Gold's) heating system.

The problem was not with the apparatus, explained Col. Hain, but with the attendants who neglected to uncouple the steam pipes when the cars side-lined at night. Water accumulated in the pipes during the freezing nights, plugging the pipes and preventing steam from flowing through the pipes to the radiators. This problem necessitated the installation of "traps" that automatically drain the condensed water from the pipes and radiator. According to Col. Hain, obstructions in the heating systems have not occurred once in the trains equipped with the steam traps. He was equipping all trains as rapidly as possible.[68]

In 1888, notices in the press solicited investors in the Julien Electric Traction Company of which Col. F. K. Hain was one of six directors. This "choice investment" was capitalized with $3 million, par value $100 per share. The Julien Company was equipping cars on the Fourth Avenue surface line with its battery-powered system and was "strongly endorsed by Col. F. K. Hain, the New York and Harlem Railroad, and by horse railroad men generally."[69]

By order of Col. F. K. Hain, the Manhattan Elevated Railway auctioned off unclaimed items that had been accumulating in their property room for the past year. The auctioneer, "in a high treble voice knocked down the most incredible articles at the most incredible prices." Among the items sold were a brand new pair of pantaloons for 55 cents; one "Marie Antoinette" was "knocked down" for a quarter; 19 pairs of "lost and homeless" spectacles brought $2.75. The buyers had a lot of fun and gave fictitious names to the auctioneer. For instance, "Mrs. Rootbeer" bought 10 pairs of unmentionables for $2.45. "In short, everything that man or woman has been known to wear since the beginning of the century went at most ridiculously low figures."[70]

On the summer social circuit of 1888, Newport, RI was reported to be having a "great season." Among the prominent visitors were Col. Frank K. Hain and his wife who were staying at the Ocean House. Newport was a wealthy society resort that one trendy magazine described as "the fashionable queen of all watering resorts, for summer pleasure." The Ocean House was built about 1841 and was one of Newport's first large hotels.[71]

For fiscal years 1886 to 1888, The Manhattan Railway Company reported earnings as follows (*NYT*, December 24, 1887, December 22, 1888):

	1886	*1887*	*1888*
Gross earnings	$7,352,982	$8,016,887	$8,587,489
Net income	1,659,631	1,578,132	1,918,742
Dividends	1,560,000	1,560,000	1,300,000
Surplus for year	99,631	18,132	618,742

The figures indicate that the road's profits were rising dramatically under General Manager Hain's leadership. Gross earnings increased by $1,234,507, net income by $259,111 and the total surplus skyrocketed to almost $620,000, albeit assisted by a reduction of $260,000 in dividend payments. The annual increase in passenger volume was unreported, but in November 1886, the company reported over 13 million passengers as against about 9 million in the same month a year earlier, a daily increase of over 140,000 passengers.

Colonel Hain could rightly bask in his success. But he had a lot on his plate and the responsibility seemed to weigh on him, because he came through as testy at times, blunt, curt, and cryptic. He didn't show a whole lot of empathy, either, given his reputation for concern about the traveling public. By today's standards, $12,000, or even $15.000 a year, seems like inadequate compensation for his level of responsibility and the pressure he was under.

The responsibility of operating a major railroad did not always embrace the big picture. Unforeseen side issues often took center stage regardless of Col. Hain's wealth of experience, management ability, and best intentions. For instance, the *Times* of January 31, 1886, took great delight in highlighting the following incident, which has been liberally edited, but quoted at length in order to retain the flavor:

It Was the Goat's Night Out

A short reign of terror on a Sixth Avenue elevated train

At the 125th Street station of the Sixth Avenue road, the down train received a passenger of a belligerent turn of mind in the shape of a billy goat. The goat's fare was duly paid by his escort, and he stepped aboard with peace and dignity and commended himself to the kind attention of his fellow passengers by a mildness of demeanor, which was as beautiful as it was unnatural. However, no sooner had the train started than the goat began to exhibit symptoms of war. He first rose up on his hind legs and issued a general challenge to everybody in the car, and on being remonstrated with by the mild old lady who owned him, promptly butted her into a state of helplessness and hysterics.

Then he considered it his duty to climb over one timid old man and begin a vigorous assault and battery on another who was desperately trying to throw himself out of the window. Having knocked out these two, he amused himself by slugging four terrified citizens and then bethought that it would be funny to make an onslaught on a fat woman who cowered at the other end of the car.

Having reduced her to a state of insensibility he began a two-legged war dance before his own reflection in the windows, and entertained himself by pulverizing the imaginary goats he saw therein until the train came to a stop. Brakemen and passengers entered both ends of the car and were neatly fired out again in tumultuous heaps. The train resumed its journey and the goat continued to butt brakemen, smash glass, and terrify the ladies until the train reached 53rd Street when the engineer providentially brought the train to a permanent halt.

A council of war was held and a strong force of ticket takers, station agents, and police, armed to the teeth and desperate, made a concerted rush into the car and succeeded, after a terrific struggle, in getting the goat down and ending the reign of terror.

The superintendent of the Sixth Avenue road considered that the best way of compensating for the damage done to the car was to fire the man who sold the goat's ticket, the man who took the ticket, and the brakeman who let the goat on. This was rapidly done, and peace once more swayed travel on the Sixth Avenue Line.

It goes without saying that Colonel Hain was not immediately available for comment about the incident.

VI

Leadership Changes (1889–1892)

Opponents of the third track and other "grabs" by the elevated road are very hopeful that Col. Hain's admissions now reflect a determination on the part of the elevated road officials to begin the New Year by telling the truth [NYT, January 10, 1892].

The citizens of New York are slow and slothful, stupid, cowardly, unready, inert, blind, narrow, and mean-spirited for their inability or unwillingness to provide other and sufficient means for transporting passengers within the city's limits. The inadequacy of the elevated roads ought to give a powerful and much-needed impulse to the lagging project of a rapid transit route underground [NYT, October 12, 1892].

Frank K. Hain achieved a professional milestone when he was promoted to second vice president and membership on the Board of Directors of the Manhattan Railway Company.

In 1892 the deaths of Jay Gould and Cyrus W. Field changed the leadership equation at the Manhattan company. George J. Gould assumed the presidency of the firm after his father's death, but he was not the same dominating figure.

General Manager Hain's heightened profile resulted in his appointment to prestigious civic positions. And rumors began to surface that he was in line to assume a managerial role in other major railroads. For instance, a Philadelphia newspaper reported that a syndicate planned to construct an elevated railroad in the City of Brotherly Love and that F. K. Hain had accepted the position of general manager. However, the following day, Colonel Hain announced that he would not go to Philadelphia's elevated roads nor would he in anyway be involved with their management.[1]

Enhanced prominence, however, did not free him from attacks by the press. If anything, he took more "heat" than heretofore because of the elevated roads' perceived sins, chiefly the company's failure to lead the charge for an improved, integrated rapid transit system. If the press is to be believed, the elevated roads were a disgraceful public conveyance and Colonel Hain was as responsible as anyone for their dismal conditions. However, by now a half-million people a day traveled the elevated roads, and the company prospered, as earnings swelled in direct proportion to increased volumes of passengers. And the roads showed flexibility by handling significant spikes in passenger traffic during holidays and special events.

Integrated rapid transit. A buzz word that the elevated railway's critics rolled out at every opportunity. What did it mean? The press saw it as a system of elevated, surface, and subsurface public conveyances that alleviated congestion on the streets of New York City. But the emphasis was on construction of a subway. After all, an underground railway had been in existence in London since 1863. And an electric line — the City and South London — opened in 1890. Not that the London "tube" was perfect by any means, because its route was shorter and the trains smaller than the elevated system, but it was a step in the right direction. Some argued that the subsoil in London was more conducive to sustaining underground tunnels than geological conditions in New York City. But the real reason for the equivocation by the 18 New York companies was the prospect of a squeeze on their short term profits. Capital expenditures of the sort envisioned were enormous. And while bond issuances and funding from city and state could have eased potential short falls, senior officials of the relevant companies were not philanthropists. They were in business to make money, and the money was flowing in. "Don't fix it if it ain't broke" was stamped indelibly on their pocketbooks.

Franklin K. Hain (*Biographical Directory of Railway Officials of America*, 1889).

Did the public care? Yes and no. The public traveled in quick-time from A to Z on the elevated roads, and they grumbled a bit, but at five cents a ride, they did not complain very loud. Moreover, the public was not a cohesive entity and their complaints gained little traction except when one or another issue was highlighted in the press — only to be forgotten shortly thereafter — when the elevated roads reacted with cosmetic adjustments. So, when the press put on its white hat and unleashed its arrows on behalf of the "public interest," the attacks largely wallowed in a sea of public apathy.

The Manhattan Railway Company reported the following data to the Board of Railroad Commissioners for the fiscal year ending June 30, 1890:

> Number of passengers carried: 185,833,632 (509,133 per day)
> Average number of persons employed (including officials): 4,673
> Aggregate amount of salaries and wages paid to them: $3,053,510
> The company receives $5,000 per annum from the U.S. government for carrying mail over all lines.

Equipment
> Locomotives, 4 drivers: 158 owned, 133 leased; average cost of each: $4,099
> Maximum weight of each: 45,680 pounds

VI. Leadership Changes (1889–1892)

First class passenger cars: 452 owned, 469 leased; average cost of each: $2,671
Maximum weight of each: 26,150 pounds
Passenger cars are heated by steam, lighted by oil and ventilated by sash in deck and Creamer ventilators.
Eames' vacuum brake and standard draw bar and link and pin used on all cars.
There are 20 towers at junctions and terminal points equipped with the Lorenz safety switch and in almost constant use.[2]

Manhattan Railway Company, General Order No. 6, dated November 11, 1891, was issued by President Jay Gould. R. M. Gallaway, vice president of the company resigned to accept the vice presidency of the Merchant's National Bank. George J. Gould was elected first vice president of the company, and Col. Frank K. Hain, second vice president and general manager. Reports heretofore sent to Mr. Gallaway were hereafter to be sent to Mr. George J. Gould. Col. Frank K. Hain, was named to the board of directors in place of John H. Hall, deceased. Col. Hain continued to be in charge of the operating department as heretofore.

Cyrus W. Field died at age 72 on July 12, 1892, at his summer home at Ardsley Park, near Dobbs Ferry, after an illness of several months. According to his obituary, "it was learned that in 1881 Mr. Field was worth about $6 million. In 1887 he was squeezed out of $1 million by Jay Gould in the elevated railroad deal of that year. His fortune still further shrank in succeeding years, and when the Field, Lindley, & Wiechers crash came he raised $500,000 by mortgaging all his real estate and by putting up all the securities he possessed. This money was turned over to Edward M. Field, but it was only a drop in the bucket in meeting his son's debts. After his death, one of his friends declared, he was not worth $100. The funeral was attended by family, friends, and five passenger coaches filled with prominent citizens, including Frank K. Hain, who came from Grand Central Station on a special train. Jay Gould and Russell Sage did not attend the funeral.[3]

Four months later, on December 2, 1892, Jay Gould died at his NYC home, 579 Fifth Avenue. He had suffered from pulmonary consumption for several months and his death was attributed to hemorrhage of the lungs. Several business associates and the press speculated about his worth and a consensus of the financial community put it between $65 million and $100 million, with some estimates as high as $150 million. Among the early callers to the home after Gould's death was Frank K. Hain who was "much affected, and said that he had lost a good friend." He remained there "most of the day, receiving those who entered to offer sympathy, and looking after matters generally."[4]

George Jay Gould (1864–1923), inherited the management of his father's properties and assumed the presidency of the Manhattan company. Like the other Gould children, George inherited a one-sixth share of his father's estate. He also received a special bequest of $5 million for "having developed a remarkable business ability and having for twelve years devoted himself to my business, and during the past five years taken entire charge of all my different interests." He was already first vice president of the Manhattan Railway Company; president of the Pacific Mail Steamship Company; vice president of the Texas Pacific; second vice president of the Missouri Pacific and the St. Louis and Iron Mountain Road; vice president of the Western Union Telegraph Company and a member of the

George Jay Gould and wife, Edith Kingdon, c. 1908 (Library of Congress).

Executive Committee and its Board of Directors; a Director of the Wabash and International and Great Northern; and a member of the New York Stock Exchange.[5]

However, the "Crown Prince" was not a "chip off the old block." For a while he got by on his father's reputation, but he did not have the same shrewd intelligence and work ethic. He did not focus on details and was more of a socialite, preferring lavish parties at his New Jersey mansion and vacations in Europe to running his father's business empire full time. He had married an actress, Edith Kingdon, much to the family's disdain, and later took up with a show girl, Guinevere Sinclair, by whom he had three children, known in the family as "George's bastards." He later married Guinevere after Edith died in 1921, but she, too, died a few months later. (Edith Kingdon died November 13, 1921, while playing golf with her husband on their private nine-hole course at their estate in Lakewood, New Jersey. She was thought to be about 56 years old.) George J. Gould died in France on May 16, 1923, at age 59.[6] He was a well-known figure in railroad and social circles, but his accomplishments did not come close to matching his father's.

When he was heir-apparent as president of the Manhattan Railway Company, the *Times* reported the following anecdote about George Gould under "Phases of City Life," an intermittent feature that enabled the newspaper to take wry or humorous "pot shots" or "sound off" on issues without committing to a formal editorial.

> A story is going the rounds of the brokers' offices that [it wasn't long ago that] Mr. George J. Gould took his wife and one or two of her friends into the Sub-Treasury Building. He was known to the chief officers in the building, but not to the custodians of the vaults. When the little apartment wherein are stored the gold certificates was reached, one of the attendants handed a package containing $10,000,000 in gold certificates to George Gould with the remark, "There, just take that in your hands, and you can hereafter say that at one time in your life you were a millionaire ten times over." George took the package, and, saying very soberly, "That is a great deal of money," handed it back. When the attendant was subsequently informed as to the young millionaire's identity, he exclaimed, "Well, that's all right. He may have held that amount in checks or bonds before, but I'll bet he never held it in currency until today."[7]

An old Irishman had this to say:

> George Gould was making one of his last trips as president of the Missouri Pacific. His private car was laid out on a siding for some reason or other, and he got out to stretch his legs. An old Irishman was tapping the wheels. Gould went up to him and said:
> "Morning. How do you like the wheels?"
> "Not worth a durn," was the reply.
> "Well, how do you like the car?"
> "It's good 'nough for de wheels."
> "What do you think of the road?"
> "It matches de car."
> George Gould looked at the old chap for a minute and said:
> "Maybe you don't know who I am?"
> "Shure I do," retorted the wheel-tapper.
> "You're Jarge Gould, and I knew your fadder whin he was President of de road, and by gab, he's going to be President of it again."
> "Why, my father is dead," said Mr. Gould.
> "I know dat, and de road is going to hell," was the reply.[8]

Summarizing the street *and* elevated railroad corporations' results for 1889, the *Times* observed that the year "appears to have been a prosperous one." Gross earnings increased by about $1 million over 1888 while operating expenses decreased. Even after paying out a larger amount in dividends, the surplus for 1889 increased to $1.8 million. All roads, street and elevated, carried a total of 389 million passengers, almost half of whom were carried by the Manhattan company. The Manhattan's gross receipts were nearly as great as the 17 surface roads and its net receipts were considerably greater.

As for accidents in 1889, the elevated roads reported 9 persons killed and 32 injured while carrying half the passengers; whereas the surface roads had 16 killed and 102 injured. The *Times* concluded by claiming that the passenger business was out-distancing the facilities, and "if the need for rapid transit were to be fully met, it would expand as it cannot under the present cramped conditions."[9]

By 1891, New York City's Board of Rapid Transit Commissioners was becoming increasingly interested in extending the existing elevated roads or developing a subway system. On March 15, electrical engineer Frank J. Sprague addressed William Steinway, chairman of the Rapid Transit Commission, and advocated an electric-powered subway for the city. However, the commissioners were "finding the building of rapid transit to be an exceedingly difficult topic," evidently due to problems with financing the huge costs and opposition from the elevated railroads. Jay Gould, perhaps still smarting from his misadventure with the earlier Sprague test, ventured to say that "there is no electric motor in existence or likely soon to be invented, capable of drawing heavy trains rapidly and economically over the required distances." As a result, Frank Sprague's proposals in 1891 went for naught. Sprague resurfaced in 1893 with a new proposal, but a number of powerful critics, ones Sprague politely referred to as "existing corporate interests," were against electric power and, "once again, nothing happened."[10]

On Columbus Day weekend of 1892 the crowds of additional people in the city for the holiday taxed the capabilities of the elevated railroads, according to the *Times*. The newspaper discussed the problem in an editorial and took to task the citizens of New York for their "slow and slothful, stupid, cowardly, unready, inert, blind, narrow, and mean-spirited" inability or unwillingness to provide "other and sufficient means for transporting passengers within the city's limits" since 1885, when they became aware that the city had outgrown the elevated railroad system. Furthermore, the crush of passengers during the Columbus Day holiday provided "new evidence of the inadequacy of the elevated roads [and] ought to give a powerful and much-needed impulse to the lagging project of a rapid transit route underground."[11]

However, General Manager Hain was more up beat. He announced that during the Columbus Day holiday the elevated roads carried 945,000 passengers on Monday, 901,000 on Tuesday, and a record 1,075,537 on Wednesday, for a total of 2,921,537 — nearly as many people as lived in New York City and its suburbs. The fares received for the three days amounted to $146,076.85.[12]

Integrated rapid transit was like a nagging virus and difficult for the elevated roads to get rid of. In late 1892, NYC's Rapid Transit Commissioners met with representatives of the Manhattan company to consider various plans in regard to the establishment of a viable rapid transit system. The *Times* characterized the meeting as "strongly suggestive of a love feast." Both sides pledged to work together, but little was accomplished. Among the issues was how the Manhattan Elevated would tie into a comprehensive rapid transit system, including underground transit if, indeed, it was decided that the elevated roads would connect up at all. Predictably, the Manhattan committee tabled no proposals, preferring that initiatives come from the Rapid Transit Commissioners.

An interesting sidelight developed when Commissioner Spencer engaged in a verbal sparring match with his business partner, J. Pierpont Morgan, chairman of the Manhattan company's rapid transit committee. Spencer made the point that the commission had "spent much time and labor" considering the development of a comprehensive rapid transit system without inclusion of the elevated roads because they were unlikely to provide a solution to the problem. The Commission's plan was to devise a separate and distinct system that would "ensure much better service than seemed probable with the elevated road." "Mr. Morgan received with a grave face the official utterances of his partner."[13]

The *Times* never had to look very far afield to find fault. Take, for example, property damage. The newspaper asserted that the Manhattan Railway, since its inception, had tried to "evade by every manner and means" payment of property damages to owners of real estate abutting its elevated roads. The company tried various devices with mixed success but now had a new scheme. They were trying to use the October Grand Jury of the Court of General Sessions to "aid them in their little enterprise." In short, the company planned to frighten 25 lawyers by having them indicted for "champetry and maintenance" because the lawyers illegally incited people to litigation against the company.

When the company's plan was readied, Col. Hain visited the district attorney's office and laid out the evidence. Affidavits from Col. Hain and others detailed the "grievous way in which the lawyers had been offending against the peace of the county — and incidentally, of course, against the peace of the Manhattan Railway Company." These papers were submitted to the grand jury and related how the "lawyers had been going about looking up people who had no idea of suing the company and getting them to place the cases in their hands."

The lawyers, however, felt assured that the company's case could not succeed, because many of the lawyers were among the most reputable members of the profession. The grand jury was in session throughout the afternoon and the results of their deliberations were not reported.[14]

In another property issue, General Manager Hain thought he "got square" with the people living in the vicinity of Second Avenue and 116th Street who permitted their neighbors to sue the company for $12,000 in property damages because of their proximity to the elevated station. If the station is a nuisance, he said the company would take it away. However, the people had second thoughts when they came to realize that more than 3,000 persons per day were using the station and a considerable inconvenience would be felt if it were removed. The neighborhood held a "mass meeting," and a committee of 20 was appointed to work with their neighbors to retain the station.[15]

In December 1890, Harlem residents complained that extension of the Ninth Avenue Line to 135th Street caused long delays between 5 P.M. and 8 P.M. An "indignant Harlemite"

Elevated road and street scene near 116th Street, 1898 (Library of Congress).

said that unless something was done to improve the schedule, "the Harlem supper and the Harlem breakfast will have to be soldered into one meal."

Col. F. K. Hain "smiled earnestly" when his attention was called to the problem. "[The delays] no longer exist," he said. "They were done away with about two weeks ago by the new time table, under which the Ninth Avenue train service was extended to 135th Street." "I deny absolutely," added Col. Hain, "that such delays exist. Whatever delays there are are largely due to the failure of passengers to get off quick enough at the stations. Of course, on a railroad where 3,500 trains are run daily, it is impossible to avoid delays, but the new time table has reduced them as much as can be done."[16]

In mid–1891, the *Times* aired out a particularly heinous example, in the newspaper's view, of the Manhattan company's devious operations. Under the heading "Tools or Fools," the *Times* took Jay Gould to task, and other officials of the company, for laying a third track on the Ninth Avenue Line before obtaining the approvals to do so. Specifically, at issue was Gould "making his elevated railroad a solid three-track structure from 59th Street to 155th Street, instead of the two-track structure, one track on either side of the street, with an open space between for light and air to the street below, such as the law allows."

The *Times* saw it as "farcical" that Jay Gould "recently" went before the Rapid Transit Commission and appealed for the right to lay a third track on the Ninth Avenue Line from 59th Street to 155th Street despite the fact that the track from 59th Street to 65th Street was already complete. Furthermore, several more sections of the third track, including a construction house, iron girders, and ties were in various stages of completion up to 155th Street.

"It will from this be seen that Gould has practically built his third track from 59th to 155th Street before asking if he could build it. With his girders all in and whole sections of the track tied and railed, his work is almost done." Gould's "Lieutenants" had been "sneaking it in" for several years while referring to their work as "putting in switches."

"He evidently had that thought in mind when recently before the Rapid Transit Commissioners he became so enthusiastic in telling the Commissioners what a public benefactor he was, he forgot that he had been building nothing but 'switches' on Ninth Avenue, and candidly confessed that his company was laying a third track there, and that as soon as it was completed express trains would be run."

A reporter asked Police Captain Killilea, in whose precinct part of the third track was laid, why he did not send out his men to arrest the gangs working on the tracks because they were in violation of the law. "Col. Hain came to me night before last," he replied, "and assured me on his word of honor that the railroad was making no effort to lay a third track. He told me that the company had no intention of antagonizing the authorities. They would wait for the third track until the Rapid Transit Commission gave them the right to build it. The work they are doing now, he assured me, was merely putting in switches."[17]

However, the *Times* did not let the issue die there. For, several months later, the newspaper reminded its readers of the "illegal third track" that had been under construction on the Ninth Avenue road "in defiance of law." This track, the *Times* asserted, was masqueraded as a "switch" in previous explanations by the elevated railroad. However, now the truth was out. "It is boldly declared to be a continuous middle track for express trains." And Col. Hain "admitted it" when he said that men have been engaged in laying the track "for some time" and that it will be finished in "about two weeks." "The spirit of confession" has led the Colonel also to "admit" that his road is "wholly inadequate" to handle the glut of passengers expeditiously after the theatres are over. However, he is working up a schedule to accommodate everybody who is trying to get home after the theatre as one element in his plan to improve the general schedule.

Col. Hain claimed several reasons for the irregularity of his train services. The road was running at full capacity and was overtaxed to handle the immense increase in passengers during the rush hours. Trains rapidly followed one another and it was unsafe to run them any closer. He laid the fault for this inadequate service to his engineers and firemen who did not always seem equal to their duty of running their trains on time.

However, the *Times* did not accept that explanation, declaring that the success of the "grabbers" in getting all they want on Ninth Avenue had led Col. Hain into these admissions about the inadequacy of the elevated road service. Furthermore, "it will not be forgotten, however exuberant he may be, or to whatever extent he may now inculpate himself and his superiors, that the things which he now admits are those against which citizens have been complaining for a long time, and about which Col. Hain has been at some pains to make a complete and emphatic denial."

Finally, the *Times* indulged in a bit of wishful thinking. Opponents of the third track and other "grabs" by the elevated road were "very hopeful that Col. Hain's admissions now reflect a determination on the part of the elevated road officials to begin the New Year by telling the truth."[18]

However, it must be pointed out in connection with both of the above examples that the complaints surfaced as the company was making a determined effort to enlarge its capacity and improve service in response to public demand. That management, including Col. Hain, went about constructing the third track on Ninth Avenue in a deceptive way was not excusable but, perhaps, was rationalized as the only sure way to get the job done expediently. Whatever the case, the *Times* hardly qualified as an unbiased reporter when it chose to focus on the negative aspects of the company's performance without mentioning the positive results. Hypocrisy it is called.

Also, in Harlem, the rapidly expanding population in the vicinity of 116th Street and Eighth Avenue necessitated the construction of high-rise apartment buildings to house residents on the four sides of a single block. As a result, the crush of passengers trying to reach the elevated trains by stairs during rush hours became a major inconvenience. To alleviate the problem, the public pulled together funds and caused a four-elevator tower to be erected from the street to the elevated railway station. The Manhattan Railway, under an agreement with the public, agreed to run and maintain the elevators.

However, it was not a perfect world, and soon it became evident that the company was running only two of the elevators and the inconvenience to passengers continued. A sign on top of the elevators limited the cars to 15 people, but during rush hours as many as 19 people came together. "Those who use the elevators can attest that when 15 persons get into a car they are brought into a closer relation with each other than is consistent with a natural fear of pickpockets."

The company's elevator operators took their share of the heat "because their every movement suggested the movement of an automaton to dirge music." And, with only two elevators in operation, the "automatons" did not please everyone with the manner in which they handled their cars. In nine out of ten cases, it took longer to make the elevator trip than it did to climb the long stairs. Why? "Ask Col. Hain."[19]

In two other "Phases of City Life," the *Times* reported the following anecdotes about the Manhattan's managers:

> There are at least three New Yorkers who would find it impossible to travel incognito on the elevated roads. They are Jay Gould, George Gould, and Col. F. K. Hain. There is not a guard, conductor, or ticket "chopper" on the entire system who doesn't know each and all of them by sight. Let one of them enter an elevated train and the guards at either end of the car in which the magnate happens to sit instantly drops his habit of mumbling inarticulate gibberish and announces the names of the stations in faultless elocutionary style. When either of the Goulds or Col. Hain leaves the train the guard on the platform always makes a pull at his cap, by way of salute. Both the arch-millionaire and his son invariably acknowledge the salute by raising their hats. Sometimes Col. Hain does so, too, and sometimes he doesn't.[20]

Also,

> In each car on the elevated railroads are two or more framed placards headed: "Notice to Passengers." For lo these many years passengers have gleaned from these placards the information that the rules of the company prohibited the admission of "disorderly or intoxicated persons" to the cars; also that "passengers will not be allowed to stand on the platforms while the train is in motion." [However, no] attempt has ever been made to enforce the two rules during "rush" hours. Col. Hain, the General Manager of the elevated roads, has the reputation among his subordinates of being somewhat of a martinet. It is a pity that he is not sufficiently a martinet to be able to enforce his own rules.[21]

The press had unlimited ways to make "points." For instance, in a long article, the *Tribune* asserted that the Manhattan company "retains in its service the employees who have been most conspicuous in acts of brutality to passengers." Moreover, these brutes were unlikely to be dismissed from service. Col. Hain's secretary acknowledged retention of the "brutes" and it was "not denied by Col. Hain, whose indignation at the newspapers will not permit him to utter a word for publication." Col. Hain's secretary defended his chief by saying that "he has so often been misquoted ... that he no longer chooses [the newspapers] as a vehicle to reach the public, whom, however, he will enlighten in due time and in his own way."

The article allowed as how "Col. Hain, as an individual [is not] generally detested, though it is hard to think of him apart from the corporation with which he is identified." The *Tribune* opined that Col. Hain may "at heart abhor the system" that he operates and "only lacks the courage to resign his place." Continuing in the same vein, "the elevated railroads are managed in a way most offensive and injurious to the community, and their frequent condemnation is natural and proper." While it is hardly possible to man the elevated roads with "perfect gentlemen," the "servants of the Manhattan company owe at least as much consideration and self-restraint to its patrons as it patrons owe to them."

Finally, the crux of the matter. The company's claim that its trainmen have been mal-treated by passengers is a "bogus defense" because the newspaper had never heard of trainmen being "punched and jumped on and dragged off the cars" in the manner that passengers have suffered at the hands of the trainmen. Col. Hain's appeal for police protection for his men from the "violence of passengers has been universally received as an audacious and … rather irritating jest." All of that said, the newspaper made "no appeal for a neglect of reasonable discipline on the trains and platforms of the Manhattan company." But "it's an outrage that so much profanity and obscenity should be tolerated, that cigar stumps and puddles of tobacco juice should be allowed to offend decent people and that so many drunken blackguards should be admitted to the cars." The community "will not cheerfully acquiesce in the theory … that the regulations are to be kept or broken according to [the trainmen's] momentary inclination, that they are free to maim and disfigure the disobedient and that the passenger who remonstrates deserves to have his head broken."[22]

Two days later the press reported that Col. Hain had applied to the police commissioner for deployment of six policemen to be detailed at night at the terminal stations of the elevated roads "to protect the defenseless trainmen from the assaults of ferocious passengers." His application was denied.[23]

"Phases of City Life" took a wry look at the qualifications of the el's trainmen:

Col. F. K. Hain, General Manager of the elevated railroad system in this city, was riding uptown on the Sixth Avenue road not long ago with a friend. At one of the stations a guard stuck his head through the doorway and shouted: "B-a-c-h-kittycat street!"

Nobody in the car manifested any surprise, but in a few seconds Col. Hain turned to his friend and said: "You would find it difficult to believe that that guard was at one time a teacher of elocution, wouldn't you?" "Well, yes," replied the friend, looking at the Colonel as though he expected that a joke was forthcoming. "I don't believe it either," grimly responded Col. Hain, "but that is what he claimed to have been when he applied for this job."[24]

No matter how often the detractors of the elevated system sought to nail the perceived evil-doers to the wall, very little could be said against General Manager Hain's reputation as a motive expert. His opinions on the safety of the tracks and terminal facilities on the New York–Brooklyn Bridge were solicited by the bridge trustees during their hearings in 1889.

"Heaven be praised, we are through" was the "fervent ejaculation" of counsel for the bridge trustees after 33 hearings that dragged on for 100 hours. The last witness was Col. F. K. Hain who was called on behalf of the bridge to show that the proposed plan to run trains on the bridge at 45-seconds headway was entirely practical. He testified that he operated about 32½ miles of double track road in New York and ran trains for nearly a year on the Third Avenue road, a distance of eight miles, on 45-seconds headway. He was not doing so at the time, however, because of lack of terminal facilities. The shortest headway on which trains on that road were run was one minute and ten seconds. After examining the plan of the bridge trustees, Exhibit 4, Col. Hain said, as an expert: "I will say that this is a feasible and positively safe plan for doubling the carrying capacity of the bridge. It is far superior to the Wellington circular plan."[25]

A statistical increase in deaths on the elevated roads in 1891, in comparison with the previous year, prompted the *Times* to seek the reason from Col. Hain. However, he was not in the office on the day of the reporter's inquiry, and Col. Hain's secretary, W. J. Fransioli, answered for him.

Fransioli said that in all of 1890 six people were killed on the elevated: three passengers and three employees. Three employees were killed — their own fault. Two passengers committed suicide and another fell down the stairs of a station. "And," said the secretary with some pride, "we carried last year 189 million passengers."

Already in early February 1891, four of the road's employees had been killed, and Fransioli described them as follows: One employee had stepped into a train he did not see; another was drunk on duty; another committed suicide; and the fourth suffered from his own carelessness. None of these deaths were the company's fault. The company could not force men to be careful, and Col. Hain had spoken to the division heads and cautioned the men to be more careful. And the company posted notices warning them to be careful.[26]

A fireman was one of the fatalities during a collision at 148th Street and Eighth Avenue. Col. Hain's initial impression was that the accident occurred because of dense fog — "one of the severest we have had to contend with." However, if his investigation found that the engineers of either train were not sufficiently alert on the occasion, they would be "properly taken in hand."[27]

A company car cleaner died one night on a section of tracks near 69th Street and Third Avenue. His body was discovered in a tool house. How he came to his death was not immediately clear, but blood marks along a nearby guard rail suggested that he was struck by a train. A blood trail led from the tracks to the tool house, but it was not determined whether he crawled to the tool house or was carried there by an unknown individual. The car cleaner had reported to work earlier in the evening and was dismissed because he was intoxicated. He was later seen in a local saloon, but it was not known how and why he returned to the tracks. Col. Hain's investigation continued.[28]

Fortunately, few accidents were fatal, but all accidents counted against the company's reputation. Later, in December 1891, "an old gardener" was barely alive after "brutal treatment" that he suffered at the hands of a guard on the Second Avenue Line. As the train arrived at 14th Street, a crowd got off and the gardener was the last to step off. However, as he was about to put his foot on the station platform, the guard "slammed the gate shut and gave him a vicious push in the back." He turned to the guard, but before he realized what happened, the train began moving and he was rapidly nearing the end of the platform. He held on to the top of the gate and the guard refused to open it, which resulted in the gardener dangling from the side of the train, hanging from the gate by his finger tips. He was finally able to get his feet up on the narrow platform and stand there, but the guard still refused to open the gate, effectively leaving the gardener outside the train in a precarious position until the train arrived at the next station. The gardener planned to engage a lawyer and sue the company for damages.

The incident prompted the *Times* to recall a similar incident several years ago.[29] On that occasion, Col. Hain declared that the guard was not at fault. "Our rules," said he, "forbid a guard to open a gate after the train has started under any circumstances. A guard who violated that rule would be dismissed from our service. If a man through his own carelessness gets killed the railroad company should not be held responsible."[30]

The foregoing incident, and similar ones in the past, portray General Manager Hain as arbitrary and insensitive. Certainly, the el required procedures to handle the glut of last-minute passengers, because the trains could not be delayed endlessly without public backlash. While there is some logic to Col. Hain's position, if accurately reported, his rigidity created a public relations nightmare that might have been avoided if more thoughtful procedures were in place. Slamming the gate in passengers' faces, with the potential horrible consequences, was a black mark against Col. Hain and the Manhattan Railway when they were in need of all the friends they could get.

In the same vein, the *Times* took Col. Hain to task for his unresponsiveness after a rear ender that occurred on the Sixth Avenue Line. *Heedless of Any Danger ... Elevated Roads Indifferent To The Safety of Passengers ... Too Busy Taking In Nickels To Bother About Precautions to Save Lives — No Explanation of Sunday's Accident Given.*

A "gentleman" who was on one of the trains told a reporter that "so far as he could observe," the cause of the derailment was a break in the iron that fastens the "truck" to its tender. He said that the truck had been loosened and made it possible for it to bound over the heavy timber of the guard rail. Furthermore, the flanges of the truck were so weak that a slight force would drive them off the track.

A reporter called on the offices of the company to learn "if officials had investigated the matter or made any effort to find out who or what was responsible for the accident." Meanwhile, "the people" asked: "Is there any guarantee that this will not occur again? Will trains be stopped before they topple over and cause death and destruction to [the people] on board or in the streets below?"

"Whatever the company may have found out, if it took the trouble to make any investigation, it kept to itself and made every effort to hush up the affair." Inquiries were referred to Col. F. K. Hain, but he sent out word from his private office that he would not see a *Times* reporter. He would not be asked any questions about the accident and he would answer none. He would make no statement. "He had no time to devote to such matters as answering questions about accidents."

But the *Times* was persistent and their reporter learned that the engineer of the second train was color blind and did not recognize the red danger signal on the rear of the train ahead. Furthermore, the company did not know how many of its engineers were capable of distinguishing red signals because not all of them had been examined for color blindness.

Company officials refused to release any information as to the engineer's color blindness. The company, the *Times* asserted, has been "too busy gathering in the public's nickels to insist on some troublesome details which might sometimes save the lives of some of the people the road is carrying. It would interfere with the company's business, and human beings only account for a nickel each, anyway, so far as the company is concerned."

VI. Leadership Changes (1889–1892)

However, the *Times* "induced" the engineer, a 14-year veteran of the road, to tell his side of the accident. "It happened in just this way," he explained. "The sun was very bright and right in my eyes and the rear car of the train that was stopped was in the shade of a big building. I could not see it. I shaded my eyes with my hand and looked out of the fireman's window. I then saw it just ahead of me. I jumped to the throttle and reversed, but it was too late. I was on the train and we struck the rear car."

A surgeon of the road explained that tests for color blindness had been given to all employees who worked on the trains for the past six or seven years, but employees who were on duty before then were not tested and the company did not know whether some of these employees were color blind or not. On March 19, 1886, almost six years earlier, *Railroad Gazette*, reported that the elevated road's physicians examined all employees for color blindness, sight, and hearing deficiencies. Employees who were not in "sound condition" were transferred to other positions where their physical limitations would not be of consequence.

As to why these men had not been tested, the surgeon replied: "It would make trouble. There is no law in the state which requires companies to make examinations for color blindness, and if we were to find some men who could not distinguish the signals and discharge them, the probabilities are that a strike would follow. If there was not a strike, there would be serious trouble, for it would be thought a hard thing to discharge an old employee for such a cause."

When asked if the records would not show whether the engineer of the second train had been examined for color blindness, the surgeon said they would. However, General Manager Hain was in charge of the records, and therefore, they were "secrets" of the company.[31]

Again, these incidents illustrate that Col. Hain did not do himself or the Manhattan company any favors with his adversarial attitude. After all, his concern for the safety of the traveling public was a cornerstone of his reputation. But empathy and safety are two different values, and Col. Hain's record, by the above examples, is uneven at best.

Another noteworthy rear ender occurred when a switch engine plunged into the street from the Third Avenue Line between 118th and 119th streets and was "smashed into small pieces." The accident was caused by a southbound train crashing into the rear of the switch engine. Despite the heavy guard rails, the weight of the engine and its tender plowed through and fell 35 feet below. No one was killed, but one man was slightly injured.

General Manager Hain carried out an immediate investigation. Meanwhile, the *Times* developed its own spin and pronounced the accident "avoidable." Moreover, the nature of the accident and causes were such that a "great fatality" was waiting to happen if nothing was done to rectify the situation. So far, asserted the *Times*, "great good luck" had kept the elevated line immune from fatality and clearly pointed out the need for "an improved system of safe and adequate rapid transit."[32]

A somewhat lesser accident, but still an accident of concern, took place at 158th Street and Six Avenue at mid-morning on a Sunday. A train with a blown cylinder head was stopped on the tracks, and while the engineer was disconnecting the engine, another train ran into the rear of it, causing moderate damage to both trains and delaying traffic for about 30 minutes. After an investigation of the incident, Col. Hain charged the engineer of the stopped train with carelessness and dismissed him from the service.[33]

The New York–New Jersey Bridge Act empowered Mayor Grant to appoint one commissioner to the NY–NJ Bridge Commission, and he selected Isidor Straus, brother of Oscar S. Straus, former Minister to Turkey. Isidor Straus was an officer of R. H. Macy & Company and a Democrat. Governor Hill also had one selection, and he chose Evan Thomas of New York. The state legislature had already appointed Andrew H. Green, Charles M. Vail, and Col. F. K. Hain to the commission. The proposed bridge was to be located "somewhere between 10th and 181st Streets."[34]

Shortly after their appointments, the commissioners met to elect officers and carry out such business as came before them. Andrew H. Green was elected president, Charles M. Vail, treasurer, and Charles H. Swan, secretary. Andrew H. Green was a lawyer, city planner, and civic leader who played an important role in several projects including Riverside Drive and Central Park, and he was once president of the NYC Board of Education.[35]

Almost before the Bridge Commission got its sea legs, the *Times* saw evil. It all began at 214 Broadway where a sign informed tenants and visitors that the New York and New Jersey Bridge Commission was located within. The sign was of interest to beholders because the names of several individuals on the commission were well known. However, it was not at all easy for a reporter to obtain more information than the sign conveyed. An office was located up one flight, and contained a plain desk, a chair or two, a typewriter, and the "benevolent visage" of Secretary Charles H. Swan who "beamed" upon callers. However, in the *Times'* view, Secretary Swan was "clearly more interested in learning to play with his typewriter than in giving away the business or doings of the commission."

However, under the law passed by the state legislature, the commissioners were appointed to invite subscriptions to a preliminary stock fund of $300,000, ten percent in cash. The subscribers would form a company to assume the management responsibilities, while the commissioners controlled the location of the bridge and all important details of construction.

At issue for the *Times* was the manner and means by which the company would obtain the necessary land and reimburse the property owners, because the language of the law clearly enabled the company, if negotiations failed with property owners, to claim the land by what amounted to "eminent domain." Judge Greene, who fathered the bridge bill in Albany, declared: "The bridge is to be only a link in a great system. Our engineers are at work to provide suitable connections between the bridge and all the railroad stations on both sides of the river."

Commissioner F. K. Hain described Judge Greene's statement as "Greek to him and seemed to think that [such plans] were easier to talk about than to accomplish." He felt certain that the Manhattan company "wanted no extensions or connections unless guaranteed against damage suits by owners of property."[36]

Later on, the Commissioners of the New York–New Jersey Bridge project met in Jersey City to receive the report of the committee appointed to open the books and receive subscriptions to the company's stock. The meeting, "of course," was held behind closed doors, but the "bland" Mr. Charles Swan greeted a *Times* reporter with the "cheering announcement that the stock — $1 million — had all been taken, and nothing was left to do but to go ahead and organize the company" so the work on the bridge could go forward. However, a reporter who was "somewhat inquisitive as to the ways and means of the prospective company" was "overwhelmed" by Mr. Swan with the gentle reproof that: "Mr. Andrew H. Green and Col. F. K. Hain would not allow their names to be connected with any enterprise that is not all right."[37]

Col. Hain increased the scope of his business activities when he became a director of the Pine Forest Land and Improvement Company, a real estate development firm that built the luxury Lakewood Hotel at Saratoga, New York. The hotel was said to be the finest on the Atlantic coast and able to accommodate 1,000 guests. Nathan Straus of R. H. Macy & Company was president of the Pine Forest Company. The Lakewood opened in January 1891 and among the invited list of distinguished guests were the governors of New York and New Jersey, the mayor of New York City, prominent businessmen, and the directors of Pine Forest, including F. K. Hain. The company also planned to break ground later in the year for the construction of a large hotel on Lower Saranac Lake.[38]

Later in 1891, Frank Hain was one of several well-known investors in a real estate syndicate that had purchased Chauncey, "a superb tract of riverside land" north of Yonkers, in the village of Dobbs Ferry, that catered to potential buyers of permanent homes or vacation properties. The tract was laid out "similar to Central Park" and adjoined properties of some of the "wealthiest and shrewdest New Yorkers," including Jay Gould. Chauncey could be reached by the New York and Northern Railroad after passing through the gates of the Sixth Avenue and Ninth Avenue elevated lines at 155th Street. New express trains were added on the el to shorten travel times "very materially."[39] (The inventory and appraisement of Col. Hain's estate revealed that he owned two commercial certificates on the Chauncey property totaling $9,000 but of nominal value at the time of his death.)

Perhaps because his previous international experience in Russia, F. K. Hain was among the attendees at a dinner meeting at Delmonico's to form an organization to promote trade between the United States and Mexico, Central and South America, the West India Island, and other Spanish-American countries.[40]

In their role as socially responsible individuals, Col. Hain, Cyrus W. Field, and Cornelius Vanderbilt were among the notables seated on the podium during the fifteenth anniversary of the Railroad Branch of the Young Men's Christian Association at the Railroad Men's Building on Madison Avenue. Cornelius Vanderbilt delivered a short speech declaring that "our efforts here are but a part of an important work for railroad men extending over a large section of our country."[41]

Evacuation Day was a patriotic celebration to commemorate November 25, 1783, the date when the last of the British, "who had stayed in New York to harass the citizens," sailed away forever and allowed George Washington to ride down Broadway as head of the American Army in a free city. Many Americans arose early on Evacuation Day to raise flags in celebration of the event. Col. Frank K. Hain was among "the many well known people present."[42]

In keeping with his enhanced prominence, General Manager Hain and his wife were seen more frequently on the upper crust social circuit.

In July 1889, Col. and Mrs. F. K. Hain vacationed at the Scarboro Hotel, Long Branch, New Jersey. An "unusually busy season" was highlighted by a "full dress hop" for 200 guests. Mrs. Hain wore a white brocaded silk, and her niece, Miss Wallace, of Philadelphia, was in white lace with pearl ornaments. Later in the week, the actors summering at Long Branch put on a benefit performance at the Ocean Theater for the Monmouth Memorial Hospital. Col. and Mrs. Hain attended the performance. Many of the ladies were in evening dress.[43]

Just after Christmas 1891, Jay Gould introduced his daughter, Miss Helen Gould, into New York society with a reception at his home. The late Mrs. Jay Gould, although very popular in the upper circles of New York, did not seek social prominence. Miss Gould was described as a "tall, slender young lady of great personal attraction." A list of prominent and distinguished guests were invited and among the attendees were Mrs. Ulysses S. Grant, Mr. and Mrs. John Rockefeller, Mr. and Mrs. Andrew Carnegie, Mr. and Mrs. J. Pierpont Morgan, Col. and Mrs. F. K. Hain, and others. President and Mrs. Harrison and other senior U.S. government officials sent regrets.[44]

Evelyn Louise Demorest, daughter of Mr. and Mrs. William Jennings Demorest, was married to Alexander Garretson Rea of Philadelphia at Collegiate Reformed Church. Among the distinguished guests who attended the reception were Mr. and Mrs. William Rockefeller, former Governor and Mrs. James Bedle of New Jersey, and Col. and Mrs. Frank Hain. The father of the bride was a magazine publisher and Prohibition leader who ran for mayor of New York City on the temperance ticket. His wife, Ellen Curtis, was well known for building a fashion empire.[45]

In July 1892, "celebrities" Col. and Mrs. F. K. Hain vacationed at the Oriental Hotel on Coney Island, one of three large hotels that were the "epitome of a gracious and leisurely age." The Oriental was the "most snobbish" of the three and served "rich customers" who often stayed the entire summer. The hotel took pride in its cuisine which was served in "immense" dining rooms where the evening dress was formal. Pinkerton detectives patrolled the grounds and beach to provide security.[46]

For the three years (1890–1892), the Manhattan Railway Company's gross and net earnings increased by over $1.4 million and almost $700,000 respectively. After dividend payout of $1.8 million, the company reported a surplus of $1,179,946 for FY 1892. Passenger traffic (including the Suburban branch) increased by almost 27 million to a total of 215,122,575 in three years.[47]

The Manhattan Railway was a highly successful financial enterprise. However, at a salary of $12,000 or $15,000 a year, Frank Hain did not share in the wealth, and in fact, he was not a stockholder in the company. But he was not in the business for the money. He had a higher calling ... to manage a major railroad in the world's most important city, just about any way he saw fit, as long as the railroad generated significant profits for its owners. And he did not waste his opportunity.

VII

The Depression Takes Its Toll (1893–1896)

Amid horrible noises and Diphtheria-inducing stenches, weak women, men young and old, and helpless children are packed in together until contact becomes indecent—All because the Company "cannot afford" to keep a full force at work and run the necessary number of trains [Comments by a "keen-eyed French journalist," *NYT*, September 25, 1893].

I do not anticipate any trouble with the switchmen. They are sensible men, and have worked their way up until they receive the maximum pay of $75 a month, and have one day off a month, with full pay. I do not think that is so bad in these hard times. Wages have been reduced in almost every branch of work, and these men ought to be willing to work two extra hours a day rather than have their wages reduced [Col. Hain, *NYT*, April 26, 1894].

The end of the 19th century saw America free-fall into a deflationary tailspin. The financial collapse of the Philadelphia & Reading railroad on February 23, followed by the National Cordage Company on May 5, touched off the Panic of 1893—a depression that took down as many as 15,000 businesses, 600 banks, and 74 railroads and occupied the nation's attention for the next four years. Farm foreclosures dotted the landscape, and 20 percent of the workforce was unemployed. European investors withdrew their funds from U.S. banks and soon American depositors pulled out their savings. The stock market plunged dramatically and investors lost their life savings. It was the worst economic depression up to that point in U.S. history.[1]

During this time, Frank K. Hain was promoted from second vice president to vice president of the Manhattan Railway Company, placing him second in command behind President George J. Gould. He was also beset with personal health concerns that required him to cut back on his work schedule and assign more responsibility to his assistant, W. J. Fransioli.

General Manager Hain's final three years at the helm were marked by a decline in the elevated roads' passenger traffic and gross earnings, reflecting the severe economic climate, the public's growing dissatisfaction with elevated transportation, or a combination of both. For the period 1893–1895 gross earnings fell by almost $1.7 million, while passenger traffic declined by more than 31.5 million. Nevertheless, while the numbers were clearly on a downward trend, in Frank Hain's final year, the road's deficit was offset by a surplus of over $5 million carried over from prior years, while passengers still numbered well over a half million per day.[2]

	1893	1894	1895
Gross earnings	$11,137,051	$10,138,143	$9,397,572
Net earnings	4,926,891	4,042,586	3,983,608
Dividends	1,800,000	1,800,000	1,800,000
Surplus	1,111,816	240,180	(277,952)
Surplus up to June 30, 1894		$5,623,197	
Total surplus June 30, 1895			$5,345,245
Passengers carried	219,621,017		188,072,615
	(601,427 per day)		(515,259 per day)

Nonetheless, despite the clearly declining numbers and depressed economic conditions of the times, critics saw only "exorbitant profits of the elevated railroads" that "probably" would result in an effort to pass a bill at Albany to reduce the fare from five cents to three cents a ride. "One of the men" said to be supporting this initiative took issue with the Manhattan Railway's annual report for 1893 and asserted to the *Times* that "management is somewhat extravagant, notwithstanding the magnificent profits of the corporation" and "moreover, these inordinate profits are constantly increasing." This article revealed its true colors, however, after several paragraphs devoted to questioning the company's report. According to the above one of the men, "the obvious conclusion is that the city should build, own, and operate its own system of rapid transit lines." "A prominent financier of this city" endorsed this viewpoint and "declares it to be the most practical of any method yet devised for the immediate construction of the much-needed lines of rapid transit."[3]

However, a year later, the *Times* declared that the decline in earnings for 1894, while "unexpected, [was] not incomprehensible," but demanded an explanation. The newspaper consulted Vice President Hain and Director Sage and determined that operating costs were increased because the Second, Sixth, and Ninth Avenue lines had been completely equipped with 90-pound rails. More than 9,000 tons of rails were used, costing about $200,000, and new cross ties to support the heavier rails came to another $54,000. In addition, the company purchased 20 new locomotives for about $5,500 each. These costs, amounting to more than $360,000, were charged to operating expenses.

The *Times* educated its readers by pointing out that the "old fashioned custom of railroad bookkeeping would have required such expenditures to be charged to a construction or equipment account," whereas lately such charges in regard to "betterment and offsets to wear and tear" are often charged to operating expenses. According to Col. Hain, if the charges had been applied to the construction or equipment account, then the percentage of operating expenses charged to gross earnings would have been about the same as the previous year (1893).

The *Times* graciously concluded its analysis by allowing as how "there is evidently no desire on the part of the Manhattan management to give outsiders an exaggerated idea of the value of the stock of that company. Certainly increasing the apparent percentage of operating expenses would not have the effect of 'bulling' the stock."[4]

A severe cold wave in January 1893 was particularly hard on Harlemites "thanks largely to the poor train service on the elevated roads," according to the *Times*. On January 17, when the temperatures ranged between 5 and 22 degrees, "the elevated trains, never very prompt or reliable," fell far behind schedule on the Ninth Avenue and Sixth Avenue roads "where blocks are by no means uncommon." Predictably, the delays came during rush hours, which resulted in over 40,000 people living above 59th Street who didn't make it home for dinner that evening.

The trip from Warren or Barclay Street to 59th Street on the Ninth Avenue Line, which ordinarily takes about twenty minutes, took over two hours. The trouble on the Sixth Avenue Line began from about 23rd Street and for nearly two hours the trains were "bumped and pushed along twenty or thirty feet at a time until they got above 65th Street."

On the Ninth Avenue Line, "hundreds of people" got out of the stalled trains, which at one time extended from 59th Street, "as far as the eye could see," and walked along the tracks to the nearest station."

A reporter contacted Col. Hain at his office and he "calmly confessed" that the delay was due to the cold.

Col. Hain went on to explain that

> The engine attached to the No. 9 express on the Ninth Avenue Line, which was due at 59th Street, began to lose steam on account of the intense cold after the 50th Street station had been passed. When she got on the grade from 53rd to 59th Street, which is very severe, she got stalled, and her engineer could not get steam enough to move her. After some delay, the engine from the train behind was detached, and by shoving the stalled express it was moved into the 59th Street station and over the grade. In the meantime, trains on both the Ninth and Sixth Avenue lines had been coming up behind and they were all held, as a matter of course, by the crippled express. Some of the trains were held over an hour and a half, and by the time they could be moved, the water in their boilers intended only for a through trip to Harlem, was exhausted and they had to stop at 61st Street to get a new supply. This, of course, caused another delay.

As to whether the delay to the express could have been prevented "if the proper kind of an engine had been drawing it":

"No, Sir; it couldn't have been prevented. Such a thing is liable to happen at any time when a severe cold snap comes on."

"Would it have happened on an underground road?"

"I am not running an underground road," replied the Colonel sharply. "I am running an elevated road. If people want to ride in sub-cellars, they can perhaps keep warmer than they can in the fresh, open air."

"You can't promise, then, that the people living in Harlem will not find themselves suspended in midair again for a couple of hours or so?"

"I can promise nothing. It depends on the weather. All the railroads are late these days. A train to Philadelphia frequently loses two hours, but the people think nothing of it. If they get delayed on the elevated, however, from exactly the same causes, they make a great fuss over the matter."[5]

Frank K. Hain attained a new level of prominence when he was selected to join in honoring Princess Isabel of Spain — the "Infanta" — and her entourage of royal visitors to the city. An evening celebration at Madison Square Garden kicked off the occasion. Many of New York City's prominent and distinguished citizens attended the affair and sat in some 42 boxes with their peers. Col. and Mrs. F. K. Hain were guests of Mrs. Theodore Sutro, vice president of the Kindergarten and Potted Plant Association; Miss Helen Gould, President.[6]

The following day, the city feted the Infanta and her party in ceremonies that lasted from late morning until late afternoon. The day began at the Hotel Savoy as the Infanta entered a carriage with her party and proceeded to visit the Stock Exchange. She "wore a driving costume of soft ashes of roses, and a fashionable chip hat trimmed with flowers [and] carried a pink parasol."

The party spent a quarter of an hour at the Stock Exchange where "pandemonium raged on the floor" when the Infanta appeared and the welcoming committee presented her with a basket of Jacqueminot roses. From there the Infanta was driven to the Equitable Building where she was greeted by the president of the Equitable Life Insurance Association. Following a late breakfast, the Infanta and her entourage proceeded to tour the U.S. Weather Bureau in the upper floors. She was delighted with the panoramic view of lower Manhattan and the Bay from the main tower which led her to exclaim: "This is one of the most glorious sights it has ever been my fortune to behold. Great, indeed, is America and its people."

The Infanta's party next traveled by carriage to the Brooklyn Bridge where, all along the way, they were greeted by a "mass of cheering people" and were received by the mayor of Brooklyn. The return trip was made in a private cable car with the Infanta, Prince Antoine, and Marchioness d'Arco Hermosa.

Arriving at City Hall, Colonel Frank Hain greeted the royal party and Mrs. Hain presented the Infanta with a basket of roses. After the welcoming ceremony, the royals boarded a special elevated train of two cars that was decorated with the Spanish and American flags. The first car carried newsmen, while the second was reserved for the Infanta and her party, two members of the celebratory committee, D. W. McWilliams, secretary and treasurer of the Manhattan Elevated Company, and Col. and Mrs. F. K. Hain. The train made a run to Chatham Square and the Battery, and then along Sixth Avenue to 58th Street where carriages were waiting to take the royal party to the Savoy Hotel.[7]

Annie Hain played a role in welcoming the Infanta, because she was the wife of one of New York City's most visible and successful businessmen. She was also known, in her own right, to be a patroness of the New York Musical Society and the Students' Club of New York University. But her prominence took on greater significance when she joined with many of New York City's high profile "society women" to petition the state legislature for the right to vote. Although women's suffrage did not come about in the state of New York until 1917, she continued active in the cause by enrolling in New York University Women's Law Class to enable her and her associates to "better protect their rights." In so doing, she was a member of the Portia Club, a professional society for women lawyers and women interested in the law, that advocated, among other things, appointment of a female judge. This was at a time when women lawyers were uncommon and looked upon with disdain by their male counterparts. A commentary in 1890 put the situation in perspective:

> ... The woman lawyer in the abstract has not yet attained her majority — the novelty of her very existence has scarcely begun to wear off, and the newspapers publish and republish little floating items about women lawyers along with those of the latest sea-serpent, the popular idea seeming to be that the one is about as real as the other.[8]

I've been working on the railroad ... for sure, a job to be sought after ... especially when times are tough. Good pay ... and the days aren't so long ... well, maybe a little longer than necessary ... but who could argue with bread on the table? ... *all the live long day*. That is, until the *Times* embarked on one of its crusades. Such as in September 1893, when the newspaper asked Monsieur Raymond de l'Epee, a visitor from France, to ride the city's elevated trains and provide the public with his evaluation of the "accommodations." M. de l'Epee was more than eager to accept this assignment. "I realize both the compliment and the gravity of the task intrusted [*sic*] to me by a great American newspaper," he declared. "I am to thrust myself into intimate acquaintance with a great American institution, and then I am to tell Americans candidly, but politely how it appears to me. Very well, I accept the compliment and the task together."

M. de l'Epee's evaluation of the elevated roads filled more than five full length columns in the *Times*. No doubt M. de l'Epee had plenty of ammunition, but pomposity and verbosity were his long suit. Over-indulgence in his conclusions, real or imagined, would not be a fair telling of the elevated roads. However, the *Times*' subheads tell the story in a nut shell from the newspaper's perspective:

> Picture by a keen but dispassionate observer of hardships in a single trip: Amid horrible noises and Diphtheria-inducing stenches, weak women, men young and old, and helpless children are packed in together until contact becomes indecent — Bodies wrenched and tortured as in the days of the Inquisition — Platforms jammed by passengers forced to violate the rules of the Company, risk physical disablement without legal redress, and suffer all the discomforts of inclement weather if they wish to breathe — All because the Company "cannot afford" to keep a full force at work and run the necessary number of trains.[9]

De l'Epee's "revelations" took on a life of their own. As to be expected, the *Times* received numerous letters of approval in response to the criticisms by "the keen-eyed French journalist." To be "fair," however, the newspaper presented excerpts from "a long letter in defense and eulogy of the elevated system, and — wonderful to relate — it was signed by a lady." Excerpts:

> Your correspondent, M. de l'Epee must have a very vivid imagination. I have traveled the elevated for a dozen years, and although I have stood up several times for short distances I

cannot see why the press constantly agitates popular opinion against the elevated. Possibly because I am a lady I find the employees more courteous than does M. de l'Epee and have less trouble in finding a seat.

With all fairness to a corporation that has always given me my nickel's worth, I would say that his account is a beautiful picture from the imagination of one who evidently expected a dollar's worth for five cents.

The elevated is giving us better service than any other line of conveyance. If not, why do 500,000 ride on it daily, M. de l'Epee?

Now the hammer fell. The writer of the above letter identified herself only as "Mrs. M.," but the *Times* determined that she was a Mrs. A. Merritt of 157 West 104th Street, and the newspaper sent a reporter to interview her at her "pretty, vine-embowered cottage, standing back from the road." The reporter found her to be a "pleasant-faced little woman" who responded frankly to questions. "Oh, I didn't write that letter," said she, "but my husband did and signed my name to it." And, it turned out, that her husband was Abram L. Merritt, an employee of the Manhattan Elevated Company since 1881. Furthermore, he was a telegraph operator, worked in the train dispatcher's office, and "subject to call for any kind of confidential or special work from Col. Hain."

The *Times* concluded that "Mr. Merritt's zeal may be commendable, but the protest to which he appends the signature of 'Mrs. M.' will not win many persons from the judgment of M. Raymond de l'Epee."[10]

The *Times* did not let go and printed two more letters in support of M. de l'Epee's critique:

From "Mrs. H:" ... M. Raymond de l'Epee has simply written plain facts and time and time again all he has mentioned has been my actual experience.... Your valuable paper has done much to right the wrongs of the people. Can you not take up this matter and eventually provide us clean, wholesome-smelling elevated cars? ... "Mrs. M." must be very blind, and the glasses she wears very rosy-tinted, indeed, to write as she has done.... Thanks for your delightful newspaper.

From "A Harlem Reader:" ... What your correspondent experienced in his trip is what we who use the road twice a day can vouch to be true in every particular, especially in regard to the odor from the lamps. It has been decided by the best medical authority that this is a menace to health.... The Health Department should take some steps to stop this practice of lighting the lamps some two hours before dark and then turning them very low to economize, until the air is filled with the nasty smoke and odor.[11]

Still more. "Apparently stung and shamed by the pungent comments of M. Raymond de l'Epee, the Manhattan Elevated Railroad Company has nerved itself to provide something in the shape of approved accommodations for the traveling public. Seven additional trains have been put on the Sixth Avenue Line and seven additional on the Third Avenue." The *Times* also learned that Col. Hain ordered 75 new cars to replace old passenger cars on the Sixth Avenue road. Several of them had already been put into service and three trains of them were in operation. The new cars were considerably improved over the old cars because they were neater and better ventilated and lighted with new lamps similar to ones in use on all first-class surface roads. And, the *Times* snidely remarked, "one does not expect to have oil drop on one's clothing from them."[12]

VII. The Depression Takes Its Toll (1893–1896)

But no matter what improvements were made, the *Times* saw the need for increased train service on all roads. In the newspaper's view, more trains and passenger cars meant less trains "packed to suffocation," and an increase in the number of trainmen to run them. However, according to one trainman: "The fact is, the company is in no hurry to send out more trains. The company is in business to make money. When the additional trains are run they will cost at least $200 more per day to maintain. The company saves this every day the cars are kept off the road." And, even with the extra trains, "it seems as though the crowd is just as great. All the people on the platform crowd into the first train that comes along. The number of persons to be accommodated grows larger every year, while the elevated road is still just as it has been for several years, and apparently is not going to increase its facilities. Perhaps the officials want to goad the public on to granting them more privileges in the line of rapid transit."

All of that said, it was beyond belief that trainmen, or any employee of the Manhattan company, ventured talking to reporters in light of Col. Hain's regulations against doing so. "The trouble with us," said one of them, "is that we never can tell whom we should or should not talk to." That was because Col. Hain forbade employees from talking to reporters, and he went so far as to check on the men by sending an employee posing as a newsman to interview some of them. Afterwards, the "undercover operative" reported back to Col. Hain what he had learned and retribution followed depending on the circumstances.[13]

This issue goes back at least as early as 1887[14] when Col. Hain denied giving orders to suppress information about accidents or breakdowns on the elevated lines.

In 1894, the entire elevated system consumed 200,000 tons of anthracite at $4.20 per long ton. Late model locomotives carried 2,500 pounds of coal and consumed an average of 54.6 pounds per mile. The Forney locomotives also consumed a total of 400,000 gallons of water a day from Westchester County via the Croton Aqueduct. Cost: $1.00 per 1,000 cubic feet. In 1898, each Forney consumed 26 gallons per mile. And business was brisk, to say the least. During rush hours, passenger cars that normally seated 48, were packed with 100. Trains operated on a 40-second headway and each stop was limited to between 10 and 15 seconds. There were 192 stations, but a typical train stopped at only 25 of them during a 9-mile, 35-minute trip. "The red engines never seemed fatigued. Like frisky terriers, they scampered along the tracks ... average speed around 15 mph ... and when compared to the pace of the street traffic below, it was positively a full gallop."[15]

A veteran newspaperman, identified as "Howard," wrote a regular column from New York City for the Sunday edition of the *Boston Globe*; this one dated March 11, 1894, and headlined:

HOWARD'S LETTER— One of the Great Charms of Newspaper Work — Opportunity of Meeting Men of Extraordinary Mold — Picture of Three Masters of their Profession: Dan Lamont [Secretary of War under the second Cleveland administration], Henry Irving [English stage actor of the Victorian era], and Hain of New York.

"Howard" lauded Lamont and Irving and then went on to glorify NYC's elevated system for being instrumental in the development of the "uptown" from 23rd Street to

110th Street and beyond. In so doing, he calls readers' attention to the "nerviest man in New York," Col. F. K. Hain, under the subhead:

A Trip on the L

Stockholders come and directors may go, but Hain retains his grip forever. He makes the purchases, he maps out the schedules, he hires and discharges the men, he is the disciplinary power, he is the absolute master and manipulator of this great general convenience, on the successful management of which depend the comfort, the safety, aye, the very existence in peace and quiet of 800,000 [sic] people every day.

The Colonel is a small, wiry, full-bearded man, quiet in manner, simple in taste, honest in dealing, straight forward in every line of action. He is known of course to men of affairs, but the great army who chip in their 10 cents daily, five up and five down, never saw him and know nothing about him save in a general way that there is an individual of that name.

At the Manhattan Railway Company's annual meeting in November 1894, the stockholders elected Frank K. Hain to the position of vice president (promoted from second vice president) and general manager, thereby becoming second in command to George J. Gould, president.

An officer of the company, whose initials are illegible, sent an undated, handwritten congratulatory note to Col. Hain. The note apparently refers to his promotion to vice president of the company. It reads as follows:

Colonel! General Order No. 7 [No. 6 was dated November 11, 1891] is just to hand. I congratulate you heartily,—and hope today may be the first day of a long, honorable and prosperous career. The way to start on that career is, not to perk yourself on superior genius or attainments,—but to count yourself a little child led along to it by a divine hand reached out of the heavens and you holding by it,—and the right feeling in you should be to grip that hand with gratitude for the bounty of Providence and the good will of your brethren, and to resolve to hold fast by it in future, whatever betides. That is the right spirit of man,—as we know both by the record and by our secret consciences. By that spirit only can we be free & happy, and strong.

Colonel! The Construction Committee has given me a holiday for 10 days or 2 weeks from Tuesday next,—the first I have asked for since coming here,—to give my young ones a little play. Mr. Sloan will attend to the needful formalities during my absence. That is the plan, but if you think of anything that may make a postponement desirable I will postpone.

If this note looks rather boldish & freeish to you on a first look please be persuaded that you have not caught its meaning which is simply frank & sincere congratulations and good wishes.

Yours ...[16]

The depressed economy, and resultant drop off in passenger traffic, required General Manager Hain to, well, economize. In one measure, he ordered switchmen of the elevated roads to work ten hours per day instead of eight without an increase in pay. Col. Hain refused to give any reason for this order, but had this to say:

I do not anticipate any trouble with the switchmen. They are sensible men, and have worked their way up until they receive the maximum pay of $75 a month, and have one day off a month, with full pay. I do not think that is so bad in these hard times. They receive higher pay and work shorter hours than men in similar capacity on the steam surface roads and other elevated roads. Wages have been reduced in almost every branch of work, and

Cartoon, *The World*, June 27, 1893. "Who is this man, papa?" "Col. F. K. Hain, my son." "Is this his little playtoy?" "No, that is his little model of an improved elevated station and car."

these men ought to be willing to work two extra hours a day rather than have their wages reduced.

The switchmen were "not inclined" to say what they intended to do about the situation.[17]

Col. Hain also reorganized the work schedule of the engineers and firemen to their great displeasure. The new schedule transferred 13 engine crews to the "extra list" where they had little chance of working more than once a week. The new schedule also required the men to take an hour or so break during the day rather than allowing them to work continuously until their work was completed. The result was that the men's work day was extended to 12 to 14 hours. Not ones to take the order lying down, however, the

Brotherhood of Locomotive Engineers and Firemen held a secret meeting to consider their response. After deliberating the issue, the engineers and firemen were reported to be "greatly exercised" over the new work schedule that, they claimed, was in direct violation of their agreement with the company. However, a chief engineer of the road thought everything could be settled amicably once a committee had an opportunity to discuss the matter with Col. Hain.[18] The outcome of the issue was not reported.

Accidents continued to plague the elevated roads, but they were mostly run-of-the-mill rear-enders.

However, a serious collision took place on the Second Avenue Line at 46th Street when the lead train was required to stop because of a warning flag on the track ahead. A second train, running one minute behind and traveling at 15 mph, failed to notice the stalled car in front of it and plowed into it at full speed. The rear car of the forward train was knocked off the tracks and one end was thrown sideways on an iron beam supporting the tracks and almost fell into the street. The rear platform of the car was "smashed to pieces." The water tank on the second locomotive was torn open causing water to deluge passengers in a surface car on Second Avenue. Most of the elevated passengers got out through the windows. Two women fainted. The engineer of the second train claimed that his air brakes failed. However, after his investigation, Col. Hain declared that the accident was caused by the engineer's "inexcusable carelessness." The engineer admitted his fault.[19]

A politically sensitive accident occurred at the City Hall terminus of the Third Avenue Line when a train of four cars ran into the bumpers at the station. Several passengers were knocked to the floor, and panic ensued, but no serious injuries were reported. The engineer claimed that he could not control the engine because the "ejector" was mysteriously out of order and prevented him from working the brakes properly. Damage to the train was slight, but the bumpers were badly smashed. Repairs amounted to "a few hundred dollars."

Col. F. K. Hain was asked if the accident was caused by circumstances beyond the engineer's control:

> Certainly not. The accident was absolutely inexcusable. One of our strictest rules is that an engineer approaching a terminal must have his train under control, and particularly so in the case of the City Hall station, which we regard as our most important terminus. It is an up grade from Chatham Square to City Hall, and that fact of itself should retard the progress of the train and aid the engineer in keeping his train under control.
>
> If the ejector or any part of the air brake apparatus was out of order, it is singular that the engineer did not discover it until he reached City Hall. The engineer has been suspended, and company is making a rigid investigation of the circumstances attending the accident. Our present view of the matter is that it was inexcusable.[20]

While Frank Hain was consumed with railroading, he was not one dimensional, for he displayed a commitment to social issues. For instance, he and Russell Sage were re-elected to the Board of Trustees of the West Presbyterian Church, located at 165 W. 105th Street and Amsterdam Avenue on Manhattan's upper west side. The West Presbyterian was a prominent place of worship in New York City, and its origins dated back to a Sunday school founded in 1887.[21]

VII. The Depression Takes Its Toll (1893–1896)

A Committee of Twenty, appointed by Mayor Gilroy, raised and distributed from their own funds $80,000 for relief of the unemployed of the city. Among the contributors and committee members were Cornelius Vanderbilt, William C. Whitney, John Jacob Astor, Andrew Carnegie, John D. Rockefeller, and Frank K. Hain.[22]

The Seventh Annual Conference of the Railroad Department of the Young Men's Christian Association closed a two-day session of railroad officials and employees from all parts of the country, and as far west as Denver. More than 250 delegates, representing 98 railroad associations, with a membership of over 20,000, were present. In one of the closing messages to the conference, Frank Hain remarked: "The noble work in which your association is engaged among railroad men has done the greatest amount of good, in making men better morally and physically."[23]

In April 1894, opponents and proponents of women's suffrage mustered their resolve in preparation for submitting their respective petitions to the State Constitutional Convention. "Society women," such as Mrs. John D. Rockefeller and Mrs. Russell Sage, as well as Annie R. Hain, held several parlor meetings in support of women's suffrage, but the turnouts became so large that it was necessary to transfer the gatherings to a large ballroom.

Among the themes abounding within the anti-suffrage movement were such controversial notions as: "They say that women demoralize politics, and politics demoralize women." And the suffragists were not tame about launching lofty pronouncements of their own: "These women [the antis] are enjoying the rights for which we have been working for half a century. It seems the highest of ingratitude that after our labors, and now that we are getting the key to the whole situation, so that we can keep what we have and get what we want, they should try to keep us out of it."

The petition died in the legislature, but surprisingly, the majority of the signees in favor of women's suffrage were men, including Col. F. K. Hain.[24]

Ever the patriot, Col. Hain frequently visited public schools and presented the students with American flags, because he believed "the pupils should be taught an intense patriotism."[25]

The *Brooklyn Eagle* of July 14, 1894, reported on the "Hain Club," membership in which included a number of Brooklyn people and aides of Col. F. K. Hain. The club had "beautifully situated quarters" at Lake Mount Basha in the Catskills where the 15 members could enjoy one of the "coolest summer resorts in the state." The "large and comfortably appointed club house" was situated on a hill about 60 feet from the lake and commanded a "very beautiful view of the surrounding country." Moreover, the Hain Club was a "hospitable entertainer and its steward a man of merit in his position. The members and their wives and daughters make the visitors feel at home with that freedom which accompanies only refinement and good sense." The members included the Manhattan company's chief engineer, a senior superintendent of the road, and Col. Hain's assistant, W. J. Fransioli.

From its inception until September 30, 1895, the Manhattan Railway carried 2,410,845,487 passengers. Between 1885 and 1895, the company consolidated its position as the kingpin of New York City's rapid transit system. Capital stock was increased to $30 million, and 1,487 shareholders, more than double the number of shareholders 10 years earlier, received a 6 percent dividend totaling $1.8 million ($1.56 million previously). Leading the way were gross earnings for the fiscal year ending June 30, 1895, which increased three-fold from FY 85, while profits soared from a deficit position to a surplus of over $5 million. Passenger train mileage increased at the same rate as gross earnings, and the trains carried an average of 515,000 passengers per day (up from 283,000). The number of locomotives in service increased from 240 to 334, and first-class passenger cars in service almost doubled to 1,122. Miles of track, sidings and turnouts in service increased from 81.44 to 102.26. And by 1895, the 5,363 wage and salary employees (including officials) of the elevated roads earned a total of $3,608,548.[26] The Manhattan Railway Company amounted to a wonderfully successful financial enterprise if there ever was one.

But the critics claimed that while the board of directors got rich, the public got short-changed at best. The road took citizens' properties by what amounted to eminent domain and paid them a pittance for the privilege of placing once-successful businesses in the shadows of trestles, track, and stations, thereby diminishing property values. What's more, ashes, cinders, and oil spewed from the trains down to the unfortunate pedestrians below. Climbing the long, steep steps to the stations was always a chore. And once the passengers got there, the cars were poorly lit with smelly oil lamps, and heat in the winter was marginal. The development of a convenient, viable underground rapid transit system stalled while the Manhattan's directors equivocated.

VIII

Steam Versus Electric Heats Up

Electricity is the power of the future in our business, and we must keep up with the times. The contract for the work has been given to the Westinghouse Electric Company, which will give us what we want [Col. Hain, *NYT*, June 14, 1895].

When Col. Hain was asked if he thought the transportation question of the near future would be solved by the use of electricity, he said: "I don't believe it will be to any greater degree than at present; in fact, I don't think that during a life time it is likely to come" [*WSJ*, October 13, 1895].

Electrification of the Manhattan Elevated Railway received extended warm up time. The subject was talked about and analyzed to death, and the company sponsored several tests of alternative motive power. But little to no progress was made toward replacing steam with electricity. This, despite the fact that elevated railroads added to New York City's increasing congestion, accidents were an ever present hazard, and air pollution had become a major public issue. Moreover, in a large city where real estate values were skyrocketing, local government wanted to free up the elevated's real estate by placing the tracks underground.[1]

Electric locomotive development had been underway since 1835 when a Vermont inventor built a model electric locomotive that ran around a circular track. After several other early inventors experimented with small battery operated engines, German industrialist Werner Siemens, in 1879, built a small-scale electric railway using a third rail to feed power to an electric locomotive. His car carried up to 30 passengers at a time, at about four miles per hour, over a distance of 600 yards.

In 1883 Thomas Edison and Stephen Field incorporated the Electric Railway Company for debut at the Chicago Railway Exhibition. Their three-ton, fifteen-horsepower prototype locomotive ran at about nine miles per hour on a three-foot gauge track traversing over one-third of a mile. By the end of the exhibition, Edison and Field's electric locomotive had pulled 26,805 passengers.[2]

The handwriting was clearly on the wall. Champions of the public interest demanded electric trains and electric lighting in the cars. The elevated railroad system was seen as antiquated and destined for replacement or integration into a true city-wide rapid transit

The Siemens electric motor on a trial run at the Berlin Industrial Exhibition, 1879. The car hauled up to 30 passengers at 4 mph over a distance of 600 yards (Siemens Corporate Archives, Munich).

system that included a subway. Yet, the Manhattan company's management equivocated. "Yes, we agree" ... "No, we don't" ... and "We're working on it" were their responses for a decade and a half. Pressure from the *New York Times* was intense, but the company held fast. And Frank Hain was no better than his superiors because he failed to stand up and be counted. As a man who knew everything there was to know about motive power, he must have had plenty of opinions. But what were they? Or was it simply a matter of doing whatever necessary to maintain the status quo on orders from his superiors? Or was it because he and his closest associates were captives to steam?

Evidence that the problem was deeply rooted was apparent after General Manager Hain visited the Chicago World's Fair in the summer of 1893 and had a first-hand opportunity to observe operation of the so-called Columbian Intramural Railway. Upon his return he wrote an article for the *New York World* about his impressions. It is telling that he reminisced eloquently about the old time steam locomotives, without mention of electric. Had he been clairvoyant, he would have seen that the world's first permanent elevated electric railway, the Metropolitan West Side Elevated Railway, would open in Chicago a mere two years later. Moreover, in rapid succession, Chicago's electric road connected to the city's steam-powered elevated lines in 1897, and the latter were converted to electric motive power by the end of the century.

The fair was held on 630 acres at Jackson Park on Chicago's South Shore, opening on May 1 and continuing to the end of October. The transportation building that par-

VIII. Steam Versus Electric Heats Up

ticularly impressed Col. Hain was a modern polychrome structure in contrast to the classic white stucco architecture that housed the other exhibits. Following are excerpts from his lengthy article in the *World*:

> My object in going [to Chicago] was only to see the World's Fair, and I must confess that it surpassed all my expectations. I was especially interested in the Transportation Building and its contents. What a wonderful part of this most wonderful of exhibitions. It is gratifying to see that ... the United States is far ahead of the rest of the world in everything that contributes to comfort and speed in travel.
>
> The most striking object lesson in the phenomenal advance that has been made in railroading was the exhibit of the New York Central's glorious engine 999, with Sawyer, that splendid fellow and prince of engineers, in charge of it, side by side with the old De Witt Clinton engine.
>
> The queer little train of open coaches behind the De Witt Clinton engine made a contrast with the palatial Wagner cars that was perfectly startling.... Sawyer can look back on a good deal of advancement in the way of railroading. He is the oldest engineer on the Central road, and is the faithful chap who said at the time of the big strike: "As long as this right arm of mine can pull a throttle it shall pull it for the New York Central."

In May 1893, President George J. Gould of the Manhattan Railway Company declined the proposal of the Rapid Transit Commission to extend the elevated railroad system because of compensation issues. The *Times* saw it this way. "No corporation is going to provide rapid transit facilities for this city as a philanthropic undertaking, and anybody who expects the Manhattan company to act from a desire to benefit the public must be unfamiliar with the history of that concern and the character of its management. If there is no profit in sight, the soulless corporation will not consent to pay the city for the privilege of incurring expense just to benefit the public." The public wanted increased and better means to travel between upper and lower Manhattan. However, if the public's expectations were to be met, the company must go to work immediately on extending and increasing its facilities in order to carry more passengers, more rapidly, and more comfortably. "It is not expected that it will do this merely to be obliging." Furthermore, Mr. Gould's rejection of the Commission's proposal could not be regarded as terminating the negotiations because "nothing is final in the way the matter is now left."[3]

In December 1894, Director Russell Sage, being in "a talkative mood," spoke out on rapid transit and the Manhattan's plans for improvement of the elevated service.

> The Manhattan Railway Company intends to build crosstown branches, so that the public will have the benefit of quick rapid transit to all parts of the city. The company will do all it can to accommodate the public, and it has some new improvements in view which will make traveling on the elevated railroads a pleasure. The criticism ... that the elevated roads have reached the height of their popularity is absurd on the face of it. The only rapid transit in New York City for years to come will be the elevated railroad and the underground trolley system. Under the present system the elevated roads have nothing to impede their travel, and, with the improved service that we intend to furnish, I think rapid transit in its true sense will be realized.[4]

The *Times* learned in April 1895 that Col. Hain would leave shortly for Chicago to inspect the electric trains running on the Metropolitan West Side Elevated Railroad. He was said to be making the visit "under instructions," and if his report was satisfactory, it could lead to contracts for equipping the Manhattan roads with electric cars.⁵

While the steam versus electric cauldron was boiling, the press frequently sought out Frank Hain for his opinion. For the most part he equivocated on trial balloons sent aloft by the rival Westinghouse and General Electric companies and their supporters. And, if one is to believe statements attributed to him by the press, Col. Hain could be accused of speaking deceptively. The following are but a few of the contradictory press reports.

The *Times* learned in June 1895 that the Manhattan Railway Company was "preparing" to replace steam motive power with electric on several of its lines in accordance with a plan submitted by the General Electric Company. The conversion to electric would require erecting and equipping large power plants and installation of an electricity-conducting third rail over the entire length of the system. The cost was put somewhere between $2 million and $3 million.

Rumors of a change had been circulating for more than a year while railroad men had been watching the performance and operation of an electric system in Liverpool, England. The Columbian Intramural Railroad at the 1893 Chicago World's Fair also had been "watched" with similar interest, but apparently not very seriously by Col. Hain who attended the fair. Now that Chicago's Metropolitan Elevated Railway had just begun operation, managers of the Manhattan Railway Company were said to be determined to install a similar electric railway in New York City. However, when Col. F. K. Hain was asked about the proposed change, he incredulously replied: "This is the first I have heard of it. I know nothing about it."⁶

Two weeks later, the *Times* reported from Pittsburgh that the contract for an electric motive power system for the Manhattan Elevated was awarded to the Westinghouse Electric Company. The official announcement reportedly was made by F. K. Hain when he and "one of the Goulds" (Frank Gould) arrived in Pittsburgh to visit the Westinghouse Works and examine their system. Col. Hain was quoted as saying:

> Electricity is the power of the future in our business, and we must keep up with the time. It is not true, as has been reported, that the Edison (i.e., General) Electric Company is to furnish the Manhattan Elevated Road with electrical equipment.
>
> The contract for that work has been given to the Westinghouse Electric Company, which will give us what we want. The contract will involve $6 million to $8 million of electrical apparatus and is based on fair business terms, which, I believe, will be profitable to the Westinghouse Company. It will not mean a change in our roadway, but will give a much cheaper system of operation than that in use at present.⁷

Then, the following day, and without so much as a question or explanation, the *Times* reported a contradictory statement by Col. Hain:

> It is a splendid story, but it is, unfortunately not true. We have not contracted with the Westinghouse Company for an equipment of the elevated railway. [Nor have we] formed any alliance with the Westinghouse Electric Company "forever shutting out the General Electric Company from our patronage." The statement that the Westinghouse Company had accepted the contract at a price which General Electric would not take is also untrue.

We have not even definitely decided on abandoning steam for electric motive power [author emphasis].

We have thought electricity might be cheaper and more convenient. On this trip I will make it a point to convince myself of the adaptability of electricity to run trains on our elevated system. If I am satisfied on that point, the probabilities are that we will finally give up steam and substitute electricity as a driving power. Of course, I cannot yet say who will get the contract for the equipment.[8]

On June 25, Col. Hain was quoted as saying that "nothing definite in regard to the introduction of electricity on the elevated roads had been decided upon."[9]

In August 1895, George J. Gould and his family, "browned by the sun and in excellent health," accompanied by five servants, and one hundred pieces of baggage, returned from Europe aboard the steamship *Paris*. Gould and his family had been to Norway, Denmark, and then on to Germany where they were present at the grand opening of the Kiel Canal. Afterwards, they visited The Netherlands, England, and Scotland, pausing only for dinner with the Lord Mayor of London.

A *Times* reporter caught Gould's attention long enough to ask his opinion about plans for substituting steam motive power with electric on the elevated roads:

I must first talk with Col. Hain about that. He has inspected the system in use in Chicago. We must carry 600,000 people a day, and the question is, can we do that with electricity without a hitch? I hardly think we can at the present time. It is possible, perhaps, but we must look into the matter carefully before we put the public's convenience at stake. When we can see our way clear to put in electricity without putting the public in the street, we will do so. It is a good thing.[10]

However, seven weeks later Col. Hain offered a different perspective when he spoke to the matter in an interview with the *Electrical Review*, which was later carried by the *Wall Street Journal*:

[General Manager Hain of the Manhattan system] states that the management has no definite plans in reference to the adoption of electricity as motive power. He sees no reason for believing that it is likely to be used during the next year, or in fact two or three years. When asked if he thought the transportation question of the near future would be solved by the use of electricity, he said: "I don't believe it will be to any greater degree than at present; *in fact, I don't think that during a life time it is likely to come*" [author emphasis].[11]

Ten days later, the *Wall Street Journal* reported on a conversation with a "gentleman closely identified with the Manhattan":

There is less said about rapid transit (these days). The reason is that the Manhattan is giving the best rapid transit service New York City has ever had and fully as good as it can get in any underground system. The management has seen the necessity of increasing the speed of its trains and to that end has brought about the shortest time on record between the Battery and Harlem. If the train service is continued, there will be less demand for an underground rapid transit and steadily increasing difficulty to get the city to spend money for a new system.[12]

In December 1895, George J. Gould was called to testify before the Assembly Special Committee about the New York street railway system. His testimony went like this:

Q: (Mr. Gould), what do you think of building an underground railway?
A: I think it is possible to build an underground railway, but that it would not pay financially.
Q: Is that your opinion?
A: Yes Sir. I don't think that an underground railway can ever be a paying investment in this city. It is not paying in London, where the circumstances are better than they are here.
Q: What do you regard, Mr. Gould, as the best and most feasible system of transit in New York?
A: I think an elevated road equipped with electricity would be best. We are at present experimenting with electricity.

Gould said that he was aware of complaints about the lighting of the elevated cars. The company had planned to adopt a gas system about a year ago, but as electricity was coming into prominence, it was decided to hold off on the gas system until the company shifted to electric motive power. He indicated that expense was a factor and that surface cars had an advantage over the elevated roads because they did not have to pay for right-of-way.[13]

Then, in early February 1896, the *Times* learned that the Manhattan company was about to put an electric motor into operation on the elevated roads. General Manager Hain was said to have been testing motors manufactured by the Electric Storage Company of Philadelphia for several months and the tests were so satisfactory that the manufacturer was asked to submit specifications for the New York elevated system.

However, President Gould and General Manager Hain, while "admitting" that negotiations for using electric motive power had progressed satisfactorily, were "non-committal regarding the details." It was estimated that equipping the entire system with electricity would cost $5 million to $8 million and that the money would be raised by a bond issue.

An officer of the Manhattan Railway, speaking on condition of anonymity, said that with electric motive power the elevated roads could be operated at six to seven percent less than with steam. The Ninth Avenue Line was likely to be the first equipped with electricity; because most of the experiments had been conducted on that line and because it had three tracks, the change from steam to electricity will be greatly facilitated. The Ninth Avenue Line would be followed in order by the Second Avenue, Sixth Avenue, and Third Avenue lines.[14]

Three days later, on February 5, 1896, the *Times* reported that "after a protracted and careful investigation, the management of the Manhattan Railway Company came to the conclusion that a combined system of third rail and storage battery is best adapted to meet the requirements of the elevated roads" and it was decided to equip the 34th Street shuttle lines (Ninth Avenue Line) with the system. Moreover, the officers of the company were said to "feel sanguine that the test will demonstrate the practicability of equipping all of their lines the same way." The installation work was to be conducted by the Electric Storage Company of Philadelphia, assisted by the General Electric Company. The total cost of implementing the system would amount to about $6 million.

Col. Hain's involvement with electrification of the elevated roads came to an end shortly after the foregoing episode when he entered a sanitarium for a rest and recuperation. His responsibilities were taken over by his assistant, W. J. Fransioli, whose work load had been increasing for over a year because of Col. Hain's illness.

VIII. Steam Versus Electric Heats Up

Frank K. Hain had come a long way from a farm in Berks County, Pennsylvania, through the engine rooms of federal gunboats, and stop-overs in out-of-the-way places with catchy names, like Renovo, Susquehanna Depot, and Keokuk. He was "the guy in the boiler room" who worked his way up to rub shoulders with New York City's rich and famous. Mostly known as financiers and entrepreneurs, this elite and sometimes unscrupulous group included the Manhattan company's owners and, true to their wealth, they lived like emperors. Although Frank Hain's place in New York City's society required him to "keep up with the Joneses," he could not compete with the truly wealthy without sacrificing his values. But a lot was expected of Frank and Annie Hain socially despite their position in the second tier of the city's stratosphere. Thus, they frequently were seen at places and events where only the financiers and entrepreneurs were accustomed to promenade.

Frank K. Hain's first job as an apprentice machinist was about all that could be expected of a 17 year old with a public school education. And it was probably a good job where he could look forward to rising in the ranks to become a master mechanic. Coming from a family of farmers, small businessmen, and blue collar railroaders, he hardly could expect much more. The railroad industry was coming on strong in America then, so Frank Hain had a promising future. However, somewhere in his life's progression he developed a strong sense of patriotic duty. Perhaps he was strongly influenced by the fact that his grandfather and other ancestors fought against the British in the Revolutionary War. Otherwise, there was little reason why he would volunteer for two tours of duty with the navy and join the militia when Lee's forces invaded Pennsylvania. If it were not for illness suffered during his naval service, Frank Hain might well have by-passed the railroad and pursued a long and satisfying career as a naval engineer.

Ironically, his career in railroading came about almost by chance because, after four years with the Philadelphia and Reading and a year aboard the USS *Colorado*, he turned up as an unlikely manufacturer of leather goods in Danville, Pennsylvania. However, lady luck shined on him because two good things happened in Danville. First of all, he made the acquaintance of Jay Gould and must have left a lasting impression. In an age when free-wheeling financiers developed many enemies, aggressive promoters like Gould necessarily watched their backs. Thus, it was highly important for Gould to win over a straight-arrow like Frank Hain, because loyalty and trust sometimes were worth far more than gold and silver.

Frank Hain met and married Anna Rebecca McWilliams at about the same time. She was a driven woman for her era—a woman's liberationist ahead of her times and a patriot as well—and she apparently had a strong influence on her husband, coming as she did from a well-to-do family of achievers. Thus, Frank Hain had a lot going for him when he took over the operational helm of the Manhattan Railway ... a powerful superior who trusted him and a wife who was at ease in the upper levels of New York society. And he helped his cause considerably by shunning politics, not seeking great status for himself, and avoiding the kiss of death by not criticizing his superiors when he had ample opportunity to do so.

Although he was on the ascent, it is a wonder that Frank Hain maintained his equilibrium in view of the turmoil embracing the elevated railroads. Little more than a year after his arrival in New York City, the railroad entered into receivership. Management was under relentless attack by the champions of the public interest and the offensive did not abate during Frank Hain's 16 years at the operational helm. All the while, by most accounts, it was the public be damned while the owners lined their pockets without regard for comfort and convenience on the elevated trains. In short, Frank Hain's introduction to New York City was in the midst of a highly conflicted atmosphere. But he rolled with the punches and pursued management's objectives with a single-minded purpose. Often tarred with their brush, rightly or wrongly, he made a name for himself as a highly competent railroad manager whose chief concern was the safety of the traveling public.

By any stretch of the imagination, Frank Hain produced extraordinary results. He managed the daily operations of 334 locomotives that hauled 1,122 passenger cars over 102 miles of track. About 2.5 billion passengers traveled the elevated roads during his tenure, and in his final full year, the company enjoyed a cumulative surplus of over $5 million and the elevated trains conveyed 515,267 passengers per day. What's more, most important to him and a remarkable achievement, no passengers were killed while riding his trains.

Yet, Frank Hain came up short on his ability to interact cooperatively with the public and press. He was compassionate but an austere individual who grew up in a strict and unemotional family. Some might say he was a poster boy for the stereotypical "Pennsylvania Dutchman." He was prone to committing public relations gaffes when a more measured approach to confronting contentious issues would have reduced pressure on himself and the company's owners. Some of his irritability may have been because of deteriorating health, overwork, personal financial concerns, or any combination of the above. But the public record reveals a consistent pattern of uneven behavior that one would not expect from a senior manager with his level of experience.

Thus, while Frank K. Hain had a significant record of achievement in a city that was not easy to please, he probably would have received far greater accolades, and positioned himself to reap greater financial rewards, if he had paid more than lip service to public diplomacy.

IX

A Martyrdom to Duty

The final two years of Frank K. Hain's career were marked by failing health. The consensus was that he was suffering a "nervous breakdown" brought on by overwork. According to one report, "no man in New York was more widely known than Col. Hain" and, in one year, he was said to have discussed railroad matters with 15,000 to 18,000 citizens, besides railroad officials. Perhaps sensing uncertainty about the direction of his health, Frank Hain wrote his last will and testament on December 22, 1895, appointing his wife as executor. The Will was witnessed by George A. Post and his wife, Minnie Post, of 140 W. 103rd Street.[1]

As will be seen from the following reports, in the 16 months from August 1894 to December 1895, Frank Hain's social schedule picked up, which may have been a purposeful diversion to help him minimize stress. Of course, these occasions were only the ones reported in the press, so he could have had many other social engagements or "breaks in the action" that were unreported.

- Mr. and Mrs. Frank K. Hain spent the 1894 summer season at Long Branch, New Jersey, and stayed at the West End. Among the events of the season were the Annual Proprietor's Ball and the Open Air Horse Show. Prize fighter "Gentleman" Jim Corbett visited Long Branch, and Ethel Barrymore made her first appearance on stage at the West End Amusement Hall as Lucy in "The Rivals."[2]
- "Without display or ostentation" the Gould Memorial Church at Roxbury, Delaware County, New York, was dedicated in October 1894 to the memory of Jay Gould and

F. K. Hain, c. 1895 (author's collection).

his wife by their children. The newly constructed church was "cruciform in shape" and built of St. Lawrence marble. With fixtures, interior decorations, memorial windows, and organ, the cost exceeded $100,000. Miss Helen Gould was responsible for the invitations to members of the church, the Gould family, close friends, and business associates. Among the invitees were Col. and Mrs. Frank Hain and senior executives of the Gould railroad empire.[3]

- A large pre–Christmas reception was given by Mrs. D. A. De Lima to introduce Miss De Lima to society. Among the callers were Col. and Mrs. F. K. Hain, Count von Bismarck, and Baron Uechtritz.[4]

- About 10,000 persons visited the Bicycle Show at Madison Square Garden, including Col. F. K. Hain. This was about the time that the "bicycle craze" hit New York, and General Manager Hain may have been thinking about how the el could accommodate passengers and their bikes. (In the summer of 1897, special bicycle cars were introduced on Sundays on the Ninth Avenue Line from 155th Street to Rector Street to carry passengers and their bikes. Cyclists toted their bikes up to the stations and into the cars where a row of side seats had been removed and bicycle racks installed. Riders with bikes paid 15 cents or 25 cents for a couple. The bicycle cars were very popular, but the service was discontinued by the end of 1897 and not resumed).[5]

- The wedding of Jay Gould's daughter, Miss Anna Gould, to French Count de Castellane took place on March 4, 1895, and 80 of her "intimate friends" were guests at a breakfast celebrating the event. Among them were Col. and Mrs. F. K. Hain.[6]

- The summer season at Fire Island, the most popular resort on the East Coast, opened with music and song. Among those who rented cottages in June 1895 were Col. F. K. Hain and family.[7]

- A "distinguished party" arrived in Greely, Colorado, in July 1895 via a Missouri Pacific train and consisted of Frank Jay Gould, Miss Helen Gould, Col. and Mrs. Frank K. Hain, Miss Ida J. Casto, Miss Alice Northrup and William Northrup, both of Tarrytown, New York. (Misses Casto and Northrup were nieces of Jay Gould, while Frank and Helen were his children.) The group arrived from St. Louis on a pleasure trip and were expected to visit Denver and probably continue on to the West Coast.[8]

- The summer season in the Catskills saw many prominent arrivals, including Col. and Mrs. F. K. Hain in August 1895.[9]

- Col. and Mrs. Hain were among the arrivals at the Laurel House in Lakewood, New Jersey.[10]

- Mayor Strong hosted a reception at his home in December 1895 for many city officials as well as the president of the Board of Education, Col. F. K. Hain, the police commissioner, superintendent of buildings, four justices, and the president of the Board of Aldermen.[11]

However, Colonel Hain's diversions were too few and too late. His friend, George Westinghouse, warned the directors of the Manhattan company that unless they gave Col. Hain a vacation, they would be in danger of losing his services altogether. But Col. Hain refused to rest, saying that his office required his personal attention and no substitute could conduct it to his satisfaction. His physician urged him to leave his work and go where he would be beyond reach of the telephone, telegraph, and newspapers. But Col. Hain steadfastly refused to follow his doctor's advice until about January, when his condition became so alarming, he convinced himself to take a vacation. Some of his associates thought he went to Florida, but actually he spent a few weeks in Washington and Virginia, where he seemed to improve. But his physician was not satisfied, and his wife and confidant, George A. Post, persuaded him to enter the Clifton Springs, New York, sanitarium where he could get a complete rest.[12]

William A. Ewing, M.D., 134 W. 58th Street, his personal physician, stated:

> Col. Hain always had his mind on his work. He was not content with working daytime. He took his cares home with him, and at all hours of the night he had messengers at his home, and would receive reports and send out orders if there was any trouble on the elevated lines. He was ever ready to get out of bed and go to any place on the lines where his presence seemed to be required.[13]

Director Russell Sage had this to say:

> [After discussing the situation with George Gould] I went to him and told him to go away and drop his work altogether until he was thoroughly rested. We didn't care how long he remained away, so long as he got well.[14]

Colonel Hain was admitted to the Clifton Springs Sanitarium in March 1896. The institution was founded in 1850 by Dr. Henry Foster, a graduate of the medical college of Western Reserve University. The sanitarium was situated around sulfur springs in the Finger Lakes section of the state of New York. The area was served by the New York Central & Hudson River Railroad, which provided convenient access for the patients who visited the facility for rest and recuperation by the springs. In addition to the sulfur waters, Dr. Foster developed several types of baths for his patients and stressed the need for proper diet and the benefits of walking and other forms of exercise. Over the years, the sanitarium grew from wooden buildings into a massive 244-feet-long, five-story brick structure with a solarium on the roof and a chapel attached. By the time of Frank Hain's brief stay at the sanitarium in 1896, it was a brand new, mostly state of the art facility for its time.[15]

Annie Hain, who accompanied her husband to the sanitarium, sent several messages from Clifton Springs informing their friends and associates that Col. Hain was greatly improved and hoped to be getting back to work soon. However, it was wishful thinking.

> Clifton Springs, NY, May 9, 1896—Col. Hain's Horrible Death. Colonel F. K. Hain of New York committed suicide at 3 o'clock this afternoon by crawling under west bound freight train No. 289 on the New York Central Railroad. The freight had uncoupled two cars to make an opening at Crane Street and was backing up to couple up again when the body was discovered by one of the trainmen who immediately stopped the train. The body was found to be cut in two parts and the right arm was severed from the trunk.[16]

This shocking incident brought forth eloquent tributes from the rank and file to the most senior officials of the New York railroad world, as well as complimentary editorials from respected newspapers.

New York Times, editorial, May 12, 1896:

> Col. Hain. Whether or not the late Superintendent of the Manhattan Railway was driven to temporary aberration of mind to take his own life, there can be no question that his death was really due to his disease. Nor can there be any question that his disease itself was the consequence of the seriousness with which he took his responsibilities as the manager of the elevated railroad system, so that it may really be said of his death that it was a martyrdom to duty.
>
> The success of his [work] is to be found in the wonderful immunity of the roads from extensively fatal accidents [and] has been remarkable considering the [volume] of the traffic. [However], it is necessary to make a distinction between the management of the system as a business enterprise and the management of it as a practical problem in transportation. On the financial side it is a record of unscrupulous greed, chicanery, and want of respect for the rights of others which has made the corporation to be regarded, with justice, as a public enemy. Upon the practical side, as a problem in railroading, it has been admirably handled, and its General Superintendent, who was a stranger to the stock jobbing and the litigation of its owners, is entitled to the chief credit for its success in this respect.

George J. Gould, on behalf of the executive committee:

> He possessed rare judgment in the selection of the men who assisted him. His practical knowledge enabled him to judge unerringly of their qualifications and to reject incompetency.... He was courteous in manner, just, and anxious that no wrong should be done to any man.... He deeply felt the responsibility that rested upon him of care for the enormous number of passengers that daily fill the cars of the elevated roads. Night and day, his vigilance was exerted to guard their safety.[17]

One of the station men at 58th Street, where Colonel Hain was frequently seen because of the proximity of his home:

> I doubt whether any man will ever be able to gain the same general esteem of the railway men as did Colonel Hain. There are many causes why our dead chief was so cordially liked, but it was due perhaps more than anything else to the fact that all of us knew that we could always go to him with either requests or grievances without the least fear of any unfavorable consequences.... There was no detail too small for the Colonel to give his attention to.... I have known him to be called from his bed several times in the course of a week to superintend something that happened to go wrong somewhere on the line.[18]

Brooklyn Eagle, editorial, May 11, 1896:

> ... The human and intellectual side of the Manhattan elevated system was reflected in him, for he did not regard the property as a commodity or speculation, but as a public agency to be conducted along lines of fair dealing with the public, and proper respect for its rights.

Railway Gazette, May 15, 1896:

> ... Those who saw Colonel Hain often in the last year or two must have observed a certain loss of elasticity, although his mind was still clear and vigorous.... He was a man of extraordinary qualities as a disciplinarian and as an executive officer ... a man of great resolution and self-reliance ... clear-headed and direct in his ways of approaching a question ... and of

sound judgment.... The elevated railroads of New York would have been much more popular than they are if Colonel Hain could have had his way. He was loyal to his superiors and discreet in conversations, and he very seldom said things that revealed differences of opinion within the counsels of the company; but it must have been obvious to those who knew him well that, [if he had his way], many particulars [of] the elevated railroad service would have been made more agreeable to the public.

[However], he was not conciliatory and did not think it his duty to make it his policy to spend much time with the reporters of the daily newspapers. Probably, it would have been well for the elevated railroads to have had a diplomat to meet the newspaper men, [because] Colonel Hain was not made that way.

... No other railroad system in the world, great or small, carries so many passengers and probably none other carries them so safely.... In the 16 years that Colonel Hain [was in charge], the roads carried 2½ billion people, and not one passenger has ever been killed in a train on the system.

Why did this respected railroad executive end his life under the wheels of a freight car? Overwork ... inability or unwillingness to delegate authority ... leading to a "nervous breakdown" was the ostensible reason for his stay at the sanitarium. But an underlying motive brought him to end his life, and George Post could have spoken out because he knew Frank Hain better than any man.

"Nervous breakdown" is not a clinical term. It may relate to major depression or it can be a euphemism for an illness that nobody wants to talk about. An illness about which George Post and Annie Hain would be aware but keep from the public rather than jeopardize Frank Hain's reputation.

Social customs of the times played a major role in their thinking. People of means and social standing were extremely reluctant to reveal specifics of their illnesses, especially ones with life-threatening implications. Consumption — the terminal stage of tuberculosis — was one of them. In Jay Gould's case, it was apparent for at least three years prior to his death that he was suffering from a potentially terminal illness. "Consumption" was the rumored diagnosis amidst conflicting and confusing reports that included such vague discomfitures as "dyspepsia" and "nervousness." Russell Sage gave a "heads up" the year before Gould's death when he stated publicly that Gould suffered from "nervous prostration." The evasiveness went so far that Gould's personal physician, supposedly on prior instructions from the deceased, refused to reveal publicly the cause of his death. However, the *Times* determined that the official cause of death was *phthisis pulmonalis* or consumption.[19]

Frank Hain was in close contact with Jay Gould and exposed to his illness for at least three years. And, he worked in an "unhealthy" environment where he was in proximity to all categories of the population. By 1900, more than 80 percent of the U.S. population was infected with tuberculosis before the age of 20 and the disease was the single most common cause of death. The first effective antibiotic for tuberculosis was not discovered until the early 1940s. Gould's gradual deterioration included violent coughing fits, hemorrhages, and general physical debilitation. With those graphic images in his mind, Frank Hain must have concluded that a similar fate awaited him unless he took decisive action.

Again, Russell Sage's insight is revealing:

> We thought western Texas would be a good place for Colonel Hain to go — the air there is so dry at this season of the year, and he suffered somewhat from pulmonary trouble. Jay Gould prolonged his life a year and a half by living in that section of the country and traveling northward into Colorado as the summer advanced.[20]

In hindsight, the fresh air and wholesome climate of Colorado may have been the reason why Col. and Mrs. Hain and a group of the Goulds traveled to Colorado in July 1895. If so, the Goulds were along as "persuaders," because Frank Hain was not likely to make such a trip on his own volition because his track record shows a preference for the Catskills and the sea shore.

Suicide was another stigma that George Post downplayed to benefit the legacy of his long-time friend:

> Colonel Hain had everything to live for and there was nothing that happened or that could happen to induce my more than friend to commit so rash an act. It is true that his health was not fully recovered, but mentally he was quite sound, [and] cheerful enough in spirits.... Nobody saw him leave the house and nobody saw the accident and consequently it is a pure matter of conjecture to say that his death was caused in any way but accidentally.[21]

However, a reporter who covered the incident, and spoke with the local villagers, saw it differently. The villagers felt that Col. Hain went out of his way to crawl under a standing freight car when he could have passed around the end of the cars just as easily. While it was speculated that he might have fallen under the wheels while examining the couplers, the coroner's jury considered this possibility and concluded that Col. Hain was thoroughly familiar with the Janney coupler, and "would not have paid it a passing glance." The reporter also noted that when Col. Hain's body was found, "his eyes were calmly closed and not wide and staring, as seen in the usual cases of violent death." Moreover, "his hands and clothing were not soiled, nor was there any evidence that he had made a struggle for life."[22] In short, if the reporter's sources were correct, Frank Hain simply laid down on the tracks and waited for the freight car to roll over him.

Being in a depressed state of mind because of his health, Frank Hain would have given serious thought to contradictions in his career. On the public level, he was perceived as a highly competent and successful manager of an important business enterprise. But, for mostly a decade and a half, he had not taken a strong stand on the issue of steam versus electric. He had been in the railroad business for 35 years and could not fail to grasp that electric was riding a tidal wave that would not crest. But General Manager Hain was not entirely his own man. Not being an owner of the company, matters of extraordinary financial commitment were out of his hands. Furthermore, Gould, Sage, and the ubiquitous "anonymous" directors of the company spoke in such an unconvincing, contradictory fashion about electric that he could not fail to perceive their motive as deception that would maintain their profit-taking at the expense of the public for as long as possible. Against his professional judgment he joined in the ambiguities in order to keep his job. Thus, deep depression over his health was compounded by his concerns about the irresponsibility of senior management and the fact that he had little choice but to share in their insincerity.

IX. A Martyrdom to Duty

Failing health and career contradictions were not the only crosses that Frank Hain had to bear. His final three years on earth were lived while the nation was in the midst of a deep depression. His salary of about $15,000 may have been large enough to sustain him, but his social prominence and obligations were on the rise. In order to "keep up with the Joneses," he would have required additional liquid assets to maintain appearances. Stocks and bonds? Not very reliable safe havens in those depressed times, especially when seen in the light of the inventory and appraisement of his estate. His I and A was expected to mirror the man and reveal a shrewd and wealthy investor heavily loaded with top quality railroad issues. Not to be, for Frank K. Hain left an estate appraised at only $10,426 of which $4,683 was cash. Personal property amounted to an additional $15,000. Clearly, he "took a bath" on his investments, which totaled $102,720 and were valued at only $5,744 at the time of his death.[23]

INVENTORY AND APPRAISEMENT OF THE PERSONAL ESTATE OF FRANK K. HAIN

	Par Value	*Appraised Value*
Cash in Mercantile Trust Co.	$4,682.60	$4,682.60
175 shares Cons. Elec. Storage Co.	4,375.00	656.25
50 shares General Air Brake Co.	5,000.00	Nominal
7 shares Reading & So Wst Ry Co.	350.00	245.00
20 shares New Jersey Elec Ry Co.	2,000.00	Nominal
500 shares Ledyard Gold Mining Co.	5,000.00	Nominal
10 shares Iron Car Co.	1,000.00	Nominal
10 shares ... & Penn Ry Prefd	1,000.00	120.00
12 shares Mexican Telephone Co.	120.00	7.80
10 shares Mt. Penn Gravity (?) RR	500.00	200.00
56 shares Brooklyn Elec. RR	5,600.00	280.00
10 shares Gold St. Car Htg. Co.	500.00	450.00
100 shares Un Switch & Signal Co. Prefd	5,000.00	2,000.00
100 shares Un Switch & Signal Co.	5,000.00	250.00
10 shares Union P. Sw Gulf RR	1,000.00	200.00
55 shares U.S. Min Signal Mfg Co.	5,500.00	Nominal
90 shares West. Elec Mfg. Co.	4,500.00	360.00
3 shares Pine Forest Land Inv. Co.	1,500.00	No Value
1 share So. Brooklyn RR Ser. Co.	100.00	Nominal
33 shares Southern RR Prefd.	3,300.00	495.00
40 shares Florida Cen & Pen RR Co.	4,000.00	200.00
20 shares Cal & Hocking Valley Coal Co. Prefd	2,000.00	Nominal
Scrip N. J. Elec Ry Co, payable 11/1/97	25.00	10.00
Scrip N. J. Elec Ry Co, payable 5/1/98	50.00	20.00

Scrip West. Elect. Mfg. Co., payable 9/1/1900	200.00	200.00
Preferred Certf. Chaunay Property	6,000.00	Nominal
Comm. Certf. Chaunay Property	3,000.00	Nominal
10 Bonds Monterey & Mexican RR	10,000.00	Nominal
1 share N.Y. & So. Brooklyn Ferry Co.	100.00	No Value
500 shares Standard Metallic & Construction Co.	5,000.00	No Value
300 shares London Lanes Inspiratim Co.	15,000.00	No Value
200 shares Hallfind(?) Dist. Messenger Co.	2,000.00	No Value
200 shares New Haven Dist. Messenger Co.	2,000.00	No Value
200 shares Richmond Dist. Tel. Co.	2,000.00	No Value
1 gold watch & chain		50.00
... Apparel		Nominal

The last months of Frank Hain's life must have been agonizing. A health condition that had no cure promised a horrible death. However, during the months of April and May at the sanitarium, his intimates claimed that he was progressing well and they looked forward to the day when he could get back to work. But their hopes were based on sand. Because Frank Hain's improvement was not the result of a turn-around in his physical and mental health. It was because he had made peace with himself. Well before May 9, he looked into the mirror of life and decided on his course. Then, after an upbeat letter to Acting General Manager W. J. Fransioli, and a pleasant evening with family and friends, his time had come. On the fateful day, he arose from his nap and walked briskly to the freight yard and purposefully ended his life.

A coroner's jury convened at Clifton Springs, and after holding two or three sessions, the jury made its conclusion:

> Frank K. Hain came to his death by being run over by the front wheels of a box car attached to a freight train known as No. 289 on the track known as the passing branch, and according to the testimony given, no blame is attached to the New York Central and Hudson River Railroad Company or its employees.[24]

The Ontario County Archives has one box of coroner's records for the years from 1896 to 1899, but Frank Hain's file is not among them.[25] One might wonder whether the file contained details that the Hain family preferred to keep private and whether George Post, a former U.S. congressman, was influential in having the file removed.

Frank Hain's death was an unexpected and tragic incident. However, the outpouring of sorrow by his friends and fellow railroaders translated into a magnificent tribute. On June 6, 1896, the employees of the Manhattan Railway Company held a meeting and resolved to perpetuate the memory of their late chief by erecting a monument at his gravesite. John H. Constantine, a railroad engineer from New York City, was elected president of a 100-man dedicatory committee, of whom ten were appointed to select and place the monument on the ground.

The monument was funded by donations from 4,000 employees and resulted in gifts

Frank K. Hain monument, Fairview Cemetery, Danville, Pennsylvania: "ERECTED BY THE EMPLOYEES OF THE / MANHATTAN RAILWAY COMPANY OF THE CITY / OF NEW YORK IN MEMORY OF THEIR LATE / VICE PRESIDENT AND GENERAL MANAGER / F. K. HAIN / AS A TRIBUTE TO A TRUE AND CONSIDERATE FRIEND" (photograph by Cynthia Elder, 2008).

totaling $2,500. Forty meetings were held and as many original designs examined. The end result was a rectangular block of Vermont's famous Barre granite, designed by Cottrell & Hewes of Woodlawn, New York. The monument was 7 feet high, weighed 18 tons, and measured 9 feet long by 7 feet wide. The monument bears the simple inscription:

> Erected by the Employees of the Manhattan Elevated Railway Company of the City of New York, in memory of their late Vice-President and General Manager., F. K. Hain, as a tribute to a true and considerate friend.[26]

The dedication took place on May 26, 1897, at the Presbyterian Cemetery in Danville, Pennsylvania. "Thousands" of railroad men attended the unveiling, including about 200 employees of the Manhattan Company, among whom were Colonel Hain's successor, General Manager W. J. Fransioli, the heads of departments, engineers, conductors, dispatchers, and mechanics, as well as Annie R. Hain and George A. Post. They were transported to Danville by a special train of the Delaware, Lackawanna & Western Railroad.[27]

Elevated trainmen from New York City standing by the Delaware, Lackawanna & Western train that brought them to the Hain Memorial, Danville, Pennsylvania, May 26, 1897 (Montour County Historical Society).

The visiting delegation was welcomed at the Danville railway station by the mayor, common council and the honorary pall-bearers, after which a reception and luncheon was held at the Montour House. The program for the funeral was inscribed with the following citation:

> *None knew him but to love him.*
> *None named him but to praise.*

At one o'clock the procession began. The streets were decorated and a parade was organized into four divisions, each preceded by a band[28]:

First Division
Military companies and the Grand Army of the Republic

Second Division
Danville Common Council, participants in the ceremonies, invited guests, press representatives, and a color bearer

Third Division
Elevated railway committees, including the dedicatory committee of 100, in columns of fours. These participants wore the Hain Bronze Memorial Medal that had been specially struck for the occasion.

IX. A Martyrdom to Duty

Fourth Division
Danville civic organizations and citizens not otherwise assigned

When the procession reached the cemetery, a large crowd had assembled, including Annie Hain and her friends and relatives, George A. Post, and Thomas A. Mangin of New York, chairman of the Hain Monument Committee, who delivered a brief address, speaking of Frank Hain's generous treatment of the men under him:

> Ours is a heart tribute to that side of the General Manager's nature which made our days of work pleasanter, oiled the machinery of our prosaic existence, and removed many of the rocks and roots from the row which, under his supervision, it was our appointed task to hoe.

John H. Constantine, president of the Hain Memorial, delivered the dedicatory address saying:

> Colonel Hain was a born commander; he was a strict disciplinarian, but not a martinet; as the General Manager of a great corporation he was guided by the golden rule. He was dignified, but friendly, patient, and courteous always, and those who were subject to his orders were free from petty tyrannies. He knew how to be a boss over workingmen. He was a boss with a heart as well as a head. He had no favorites and believed in the merit system.

Considine went on to describe two events to illustrate his comments:

> During the Christmas holidays of 1895, he cleared up his affairs in New York City preparatory to a visit with his wife's family at Danville. "Sitting thoughtfully in his chair," [Col. Hain] called for his assistant and commented: "I shall enjoy my turkey better [on Christmas day] if I can feel that I have contributed something to the happiness of the boys [trainmen] who are in trouble." Whereupon he issued an order that cancelled suspensions and permitted all employees under disciplinary action to return to duty immediately. Here it will be noted that probably a hundred or so trainmen were under suspension at any one time for "breaches of discipline."

One day, two trainmen had an argument and came to blows after which Col. Hain discharged one of them. Several days later, he chanced upon a shop watchman in the neighborhood who had a little girl with him and they had the following exchange:

> "How do you do, William? Is that your little girl?"
> "No, sir," said William. "That is the little daughter of the man you discharged the other day."
> Col. Hain turned away and wiped a tear from his eye, and after a moment turned to William and said:
> "William, you know more about that case than I do; bring that man down to my office tomorrow morning."
> The following morning Col. Hain restored the discharged man to duty status.

Annie R. Hain was presented with a gold memorial medal, and George A. Post accepted the monument on behalf of the widow. The gold medal bore the profile of Col. Hain and a bas-relief of the monument with the inscription: "In memoriam, F. K. Hain, May 26, 1897."[29]

Annie R. Hain died on February 22, 1929, at age 92, of myocardial failure at her residence, 200 West 58th Street, Apt. 2A, Borough of Manhattan, New York City. She was buried at Fairview Cemetery, Danville, Pennsylvania, next to her husband and daughter in block D, lot 597. The funeral service was officiated by her personal friend, the Rev. S. G. Finney, pastor of the Mooresburg and Pottsgrove Presbyterian churches.[30] (Frank K. Hain's burial place in the old Presbyterian Cemetery was razed in 1907 to make way for a memorial park. The remains were removed to a new Presbyterian Cemetery, which was soon renamed Fairview Cemetery.)[31]

A Postscript — Admiral Piet Hein (1577–1629)

For reasons known only to him, Frank Hain maintained throughout his career that he was descended from Piet Hein, aka Pieter Pieterszoon Hein/Heyn, a famous Dutch Admiral (or pirate), who captured the Spanish "silver fleet" while in service of the Dutch West Indies Corporation. And he went to great lengths to prove it. However, despite extensive research by credible individuals, Frank Hain developed no proof of the connection. By all accounts, Piet Hein had no male heirs. Moreover, Frank Hain's obsession with Piet Hein flew in the face of logic and history because his ancestors were known to be Palatine Germans. It is not clear why Frank Hain pursued this fantasy, but if self-glorification was among his motives, he would not have been pleased with a statement attributed to Piet Hein's mother: "Ay. I thought that would be the end of him [his death in a battle at sea]. He was always a vagabond, but I did my best to correct him. He has got no more than he deserved."[32]

Pieter Pieterzoon Hein (1577–1629), admiral of the "Silver Fleet" (author's collection).

X

Electrification and the Subway

Frank K. Hain's premature death in 1896 deprived him of the opportunity to take part in the technological milestones that were achieved in the following decade. However, he was in charge of early experiments with electric traction, but he was more than five years in his grave when the Manhattan Railway converted to electric. He had no influence on development of the subway, which began service eight years after his death. Yet, this history of the Manhattan Railway would not be complete without a telling of the developments that unfolded shortly after Frank Hain's 16 years with the elevated system.

Frank Hain's successor, William J. Fransioli (1867–1949), was born in Brooklyn and entered service with the Manhattan Railway in 1880 (sic) as an agent and telegraph operator, and soon became chief telegrapher. He attracted the attention of Col. Hain who made him his secretary and then his assistant. During Col. Hain's disability, Fransioli stood in as acting general manager and was named full general manager in December 1896. In November of the same year, the board of directors sent him to examine Chicago's "third rail system." Upon his return, he submitted an "exhaustive report" and recommended installation of the Chicago system on the Manhattan roads with modifications to suit the New York situation.[1]

Electric Replaces Steam

On May 19, 1896, a few days after Frank Hain's death, a Johns Hopkins University professor addressed the American Institute of Electrical Engineers in New York City and spoke about the practicability of using electric motors on the Manhattan roads:

> It seems to me that the officers of the Manhattan elevated system are throwing away a valuable opportunity in delaying improvements of their system so long. There has been created an almost universal demand for further rapid transit facilities which must be a powerful competitor for their own road. It is a mistake to suppose that electric traction is still in the experimental stage. Almost every question connected with this subject has been already settled and the results have been in every case favorable to electricity so far as it has been tried.[2]

Meanwhile, Frank J. Sprague, despite being twice rebuffed by the Rapid Transit Commission, did not give up easily. In 1895, the commission was considering extensions of the Manhattan el as well as some "modifications" in motive power. Ten years earlier, Sprague had developed a concept of "distributive motive power," but had not successfully mastered a way to operate the system. However, by 1895, now referring to his development as "multiple unit control" (motors in each car), he contacted the commission once more. Sprague wrote: "I shall be glad to appear before your board to make in a definite manner a proposition either in connection with the Manhattan company, or entirely independent through myself and some associates, for a serious demonstration on the Ninth Avenue, or some other division."[3]

"The key part of Sprague's proposal was that each car would be provided with a special control to permit a car to be operated from either end at will, or for the operation at either end of a train composed of up to five cars in any required combination and without regard to their sequence." In other words, "with this invention, individually powered electric cars could be synchronized so they all accelerated and decelerated together, thus reducing station-to-station running times."[4] After listing the several advantages of multiple unit control, Sprague concluded with: "In short, a very large return on the capital required for a change of motive power." However, the commission had no interest in his proposal at this time.[5]

Sprague tried again in February 1897 when he addressed a letter to the Executive Committee of the Manhattan Railway. A month later, receiving no response, he wrote to George Gould directly. But, again, his proposals went unanswered. Sprague concluded: "… finding my philanthropic efforts unappreciated, I desisted from frontal attack, and busied myself with the elevator business to which I was financially deeply committed."[6]

The 14th Annual Report of the Board of Railroad Commissioners for the year 1896 (transmitted to the legislature January 6, 1897) reported on the progress of "Motive Power Experiments in New York City." After discussing trials on the city's surface roads, the report turned to the Manhattan Elevated's on-going experiments with compressed air and electricity.

The compressed air trials were to be made with a Hardie motor, which was being built by Rome and was "about the size of the engines at present in use on the elevated." The trials were planned for the Sixth Avenue Line, between Rector Street and 58th Street, with the compressor plant located at Rector Street. The engine under construction would "carry sufficient air to operate a train of five cars 13 miles without recharging" and be "ready for service some time in February [1897]." This motor, no. 400, was "a far more potent" engine than Hardie's earlier versions. "It had a cluster of thirty-six 9-inch diameter tubes packed inside a drum" that developed pressure "reported variously as being 2,000 or 2,400 psi, which was reduced to 150 psi before reaching the cylinders." However, despite the relative success of Hardie's most recent trials, the Manhattan Railway kept Hardie at arm's length.[7]

The electric trials, according to the Board, were conducted with a motor built on trucks of a dummy engine and successfully operated from October 5, 1896, on the 34th Street branch of the elevated lines from Third Avenue to the 34th Street ferry. A third rail was "placed on insulated chairs fastened to the guard timbers outside the track rail and standing about ten inches above the track rails." The connection was made by "two steel shoes which reach from the lower side of the motor and clasp the charged rail." Excess power generation was stored in accumulators located at the 34th Street ferry. The average power, including heat and light for the cars, was "45 amperes; voltage 450." No operational difficulties were experienced during snow storms, and the motor did all the work expected of it. However, regarding its economic efficiency, the line was too short and traffic too limited to draw meaningful comparisons with other electric motors.[8] (These are the same tests reported in the *Times* of February 5, 1896, and planned by the Electric Storage Company and General Electric. According to the *Times*: "after a protracted and careful investigation, the management of the Manhattan Railway Company came to the conclusion that a combined system of third rail and storage battery is best adapted to meet the requirements of the elevated roads" and it was decided to equip the 34th Street shuttle lines with the system. Moreover, the officers of the company were said to "feel sanguine that the test will demonstrate the practicability of equipping all of their lines the same way.")

A few months later, the *Times* reported that an unidentified Manhattan Elevated source "positively stated" that the company's board of directors had decided that the road would not be equipped with electricity and that all consideration of the matter had been dropped. This decision was in sharp contrast to earlier statements that the company was so impressed with the operation of General Electric's system on the Rock Island road (*sic*— probably the Chicago elevated) that it had commissioned General Electric to furnish the equipment for the Manhattan's Second Avenue Line. Now, a "prominent" director stated that owing to the poor showing of electrical companies in exhibitions and trials, the Manhattan Railway had decided not to spend the money on electricity until the system was better developed.[9]

However, in January 1898, a citizen, identified as "S," who, by the tone of the letter, may have been a set-up man for the *Times*, wrote to the editor of the newspaper, and said, among other things,

> I have read your editorial articles in reference to the Manhattan Elevated Railroad and the contemplated adoption of electricity as a motive power. If this is done, there will be nothing like it in the world.... I find that (the Manhattan Railroad) has had it under consideration for a long period, a year or more, having been examining every system both here and abroad through their best mechanical experts, with a view to obtaining the very best system....
>
> I like the tone of your two editorial articles, showing that you do not indiscriminately criticize and pitch into a great corporation like the Manhattan, hounding it, if I may use the expression, to take a step without the most careful consideration.

The *Times* took this opening to deliver a passionate response:

> The time has passed for hounding and pitching into the Manhattan company. Mr. George Gould has announced that [the company] will not only introduce electric motive power, but will extend its lines in full compliance with the Mayor's recommendations. The hounding and pitching in must now be reserved for anybody who obstructs the company in its attempts to perform its specific promises.

The situation is of the utmost seriousness for the Manhattan company, for the City Government, and for the public. The Mayor cannot wait, because the public will not. Good faith to the Mayor commands Mr. Gould to promptly make known his plans in their full extent.... Just now we have plans before us for a system of rapid transit that would carry passengers in large numbers and at great speed from one extremity of the city to another. Mr. Gould's promises have caused that plan to be thrown aside. He has the floor. His audience is impatient. He must speak at once, fully and frankly.... Let us know without any delay what and how much the Manhattan Elevated Railway Company proposes to do.[10]

Meanwhile, Chicago had been moving forward with construction of a steam-powered elevated system since 1890. The first line opened in May 1892 and a second began operation in November 1893. However, after the highly successful electric-powered "Intramural Railway" was exhibited at the Columbian Exposition from May to October 1893, Chicago's elevated railway managers were "quick to recognize the improved service and the more economic operation that electric power could provide."[11]

Chicago's third elevated line — the Metropolitan West Side Elevated Railway — had been under construction since April 1892, but based on the Intramural Railway's success, Metropolitan's managers rewrote their contract to provide for electric power instead of steam. Regular electric service began over the northwest branch from May through June 1895. By the end of the year, operating costs reportedly declined to 22½ cents per mile, while operating costs for the steam-powered South Side elevated were reportedly 48 cents per train mile.[12]

However, in 1897, the Chicago & South Side was reorganized to become the South Side Elevated Railroad, and a "progressive board of directors was ready to try an untested new electrical system." The president of the South Side called on Frank J. Sprague to comment on the specifications submitted for electrification of the line. Sprague's review was completed by April 1897 and essentially revolved around employing his "multiple unit control." Provisions of the contract required Sprague to equip 120 cars with the multiple unit system for the South Side elevated "provided it could be satisfactorily demonstrated first on 20 test cars." His tests were conducted successfully in July 1897, and "the multiple unit control ultimately became the standard for rapid transit railways all over the world."[13]

A comparison of the transportation expenses of the Southside Elevated Railway for July to September 1897, when steam locomotives were employed, were 2.8 cents per mile; whereas in the same months of 1898, when the line had converted to electric, the operating expenses were 1.9 cents per car mile — a savings of nearly .9 cent, or 33 percent.[14]

Soon after Sprague's South Side tests were completed, he tried again to convince the Manhattan Elevated to electrify. On December 13, 1897, he wrote to George Gould, highlighting his successful work in Chicago, and asked, "if, after investigation of what has been done, the Manhattan Co. will be inclined to entertain a proposition for the entire electrical equipment of its system, from power house to motors, for a price based in part upon a capitalization of the actual saving accomplished in coal and depreciation, or cost per passenger carried." Again, however, Sprague was left in limbo.[15]

In November 1898, Alfred Skitt was elected a director and vice president of the

Manhattan Railway. He was identified with the "Vanderbilt interests" and was general superintendent of the Fourth Avenue Street Railway until the Harlem Railroad Company sold the property to the Metropolitan Traction system. Later, Skitt was in charge of the New York Central's "lighterage" department and president of the Norfolk, Virginia Beach and Southern Railway. He was also a director of the American Safe Deposit Company.[16] Although W. J. Fransioli was to continue as general manager of the Manhattan Railway, Alfred Skitt would be "more or less identified with the direction of the operation of the road" and his "scope as Vice President" would be "similar to that of the late Col. F. K. Hain, with the exception that General Manager Fransioli [would] attend to the active mechanical management of the lines." Skitt's province would also include "look[ing] after the financial affairs of the system" and relieve R. M. Gallaway of these duties. President Gould stated that Skitt's role had "no other significance than that the board of directors desired an executive officer who combined the practical knowledge of a railroad man with the ability and experience of a financier."[17]

W. J. Fransioli evidently read a more sinister meaning into the goings on, because he resigned from the Manhattan Railway about six weeks later, in early January 1899. The executive committee met Fransioli's resignation with "proper and flattering terms" and Fransioli "spoke in eulogistic terms of his superiors." Moreover, Fransioli diplomatically "refuted several stories coined to explain his retirement ... [saying] it was purely voluntary and made for the purpose of accepting a position that had been offered to him by the Auto-Truck Company."

After their shameful squeeze on Fransioli, the executive committee turned to some honest work by discussing a plan to fit up a car for electric traction, "probably [on] the Ninth Avenue line, for experimental purposes." This plan prompted recollection of a flippant remark once uttered by Russell Sage when electric traction was seriously discussed in the "councils of the road": "Oh, just fit up a car and run it up and down one of the lines to show the public that the theory of progressiveness has not been ignored by us."[18]

In December 1898, the *Times* featured an article based on statistics compiled by the *Street Railway Journal*: *As to Motive Powers; New York and Chicago's Elevated Railway Operations—Comparison of their costs*. This study concluded that if the Manhattan Elevated's steam railroad and Chicago's electric elevated were run over the same 43,181,582 car miles, the steam railroad's operating costs would be 12.3 cents per car mile versus 10.9 cents for the electric railroad, or 1.4 cents per car mile higher than the operating expenses of the electric railroad.

Taking the analysis a step further, based on actual steam mileage in 1897 and 1898 of 43,181,582 versus estimated electric mileage of 50 million, the *Times* asserted: "Now suppose that the electrical equipment of [the Manhattan's] lines would have cost the [company] $10 million (a very large estimate) and that this sum would have been raised by an issue of 5 percent bonds, the stock remaining the same," the old and new statements would, therefore, [reflect] net income of 4.45 percent on the steam railroad versus 8.81 percent if the road was electrified.[19]

On February 28, 1899, more than 80 percent of the Manhattan Railway Company's stockholders (241,416 of 300,000) voted to increase the capital stock from $30 million to $48 million. The additional $18 million was earmarked for electrification of the system, to "betterments," and to settlement of claims and floating debt. About 40 persons attended the meeting, but the bulk of the stock voted was the holdings of a half dozen men or on proxies given to them.[20]

Meanwhile, the Manhattan company's inaction on Sprague's proposals continued for several months as he kept up a series of letters to the company and the Rapid Transit Commission. As Sprague advanced his case, the electric locomotives of Chicago's Metropolitan and Lake Street els were converted to multiple unit controls, followed by the Northwestern Elevated Railroad in May 1900, and the new Boston Elevated Railway Main Line in 1901.[21]

"Finally, in New York even the Manhattan Railway decided to proceed with electrification." In November 1900, Sprague's multiple unit controls were tested on a six-car train between 65th and 92nd streets on the Second Avenue Line. "The results were convincing, and by May 1901 contracts were awarded for an $18 million project that would be the largest electrification project yet started anywhere."[22]

However, while the executive committee of the Manhattan company awarded contracts to several firms to outfit the elevated road with electricity, "Frank Sprague lost the big contracts [because] General Electric would supply its own version of the multiple unit and power supply equipment" and, by early 1903, all four lines of the Manhattan Elevated operated with multiple unit control.[23] The Westinghouse Company received the contract for generators at the stationary central power plant to be built on East 74th Street. Babcock & Wilcox was awarded the contract for the boilers to supply the steam for the eight 8,000 hp engines which would drive the dynamos. Those engines were to be built by the Allis Company of Milwaukee, the constructors of the main driving engine at the Chicago World's Fair. Post & McCord was awarded the contract for the structural work on the new building. The first of

August Belmont, Jr. (1853–1924) (Library of Congress, Pach Brothers Photos).

the new engines were scheduled to arrive in September, and according to George Gould, "I see no reason why electric motor trains should not begin to run in February of next year [1901]."[24]

On January 9, 1902, "a six-car elevated train, propelled by electricity, with Edwin and Howard Gould and a large number of distinguished engineers and railroad men aboard, was run over the tracks of the Second Avenue Elevated Railroad from South Ferry to 129th Street." This event inaugurated the change to electric traction on the elevated roads. Conversion of the Second Avenue Line was followed by the Third Avenue, the Sixth Avenue and, finally, on February 18, 1903, the Ninth Avenue lines.[25]

In April 1902, August Belmont and his associates formed the Interborough Rapid Transit Company for the purpose of constructing and operating a municipally-owned rapid transit railroad. The company was capitalized with $25 million divided into 250,000 shares, par value $100 each, all in common stock. The certificate of incorporation with filed with the Secretary of State on May 6, 1902.[26]

August Belmont (1853–1924) was the son of August Schoenberg, a Jewish immigrant from the Rhineland-Palatinate who arrived in New York City in 1837, changed his family name to Belmont, and married the daughter of Commodore Matthew Perry. Young August Belmont was born to privilege, and, after joining the family's "banking empire," he developed close relationships with the city's most prominent business figures. He became well known for many successful enterprises associated with horse racing including building the luxurious Belmont Park racetrack.[27]

At the stroke of midnight on March 31, 1903, the Manhattan Railway Company leased all of its "railroads, properties, rights and franchises" for 999 years to the Belmont Syndicate, owners of the Interborough Rapid Transit Company (IRT). Thus, from April 1, 1903, the IRT Company gained control over all lines of the Manhattan company. This agreement enabled the IRT to "use the Manhattan system to break in the first subway cars and gain operating experience prior to the opening of the subway."[28]

The occasion took place at a private dinner for 12 and featured a symbolic transfer of the property. At five minutes to midnight, Alfred Skitt, vice president of the Manhattan Railway, recalled the ancient custom of transferring a piece of soil to the new proprietor of a property. This ceremony, he said, would not be practicable in the case of an urban railroad, but nevertheless, the former owners were prepared to hand over something to August Belmont that would be symbolic of their deed. As the clock struck midnight, Alfred Skitt produced a silver casket, about a foot long and as thick as a man's two hands. He gave it to August Belmont, who opened it and found that it contained an old, rusty railroad spike. The spike had been pulled from a cross-tie at the Battery station of the elevated lines, where all the different branches of the system came together. With that symbolic act, the storied Manhattan Elevated Railway was relegated to history.[29]

The lessee agreed to pay as rental seven percent on the capital stock of the lessor, which was $60 million. This transaction placed the IRT in control of "practically" all rapid transit lines in Manhattan and the Bronx.[30]

In anticipation of the takeover by the IRT, E. P. Bryan, long time chief of staff for August Belmont's transportation interests, and general manager of the IRT Company, elaborated on his plans in regard to the management of the Manhattan Elevated. He announced that the auditor, treasurer, and Vice President Skitt would continue their work for the company until 1906 in accordance with the terms of August Belmont's lease. However, Alfred Skitt's role would be "largely advisory," while Frank Hedley, secretary of the Interborough Company, would "direct operation of the road." Bryan and Hedley's office would be at the present headquarters of the Manhattan Railway, in the Western Union building. Bryan also had this to say about future operations:

> There is to be no radical change or general cleaning out of the men who have been working on the elevated roads. The clerical force in the main office, the trainmen, motor engineers, telegraphers, electricians, and the men in the mechanical departments are to be continued at their work. They are to have fair living wages and impartial hearing on all just claims.
>
> I mean to deal justly with the men, and expect in return just treatment. I hold at the same time that there are good and bad labor unions. I dealt with organized labor in connection with the Terminal Association of St. Louis, and I was always fairly treated by Chief Arthur of the Brotherhood of Locomotive Engineers. I have no fear of strike on the elevated roads.[31]

By now, February 18, 1903, the Manhattan Railways's conversion to electric was complete, but the *Times* could not refrain from lambasting the elevated roads despite the achievement: "No Device to Stop Third Rail Killings — Engineers Say Conditions Are Unavoidable on Elevated." At issue was "frequent accidents ... caused by workers coming in contact, directly or indirectly, with the current-carrying third rail." Officials connected with the Manhattan conversion project and the building of the subway were said to be investigating closely this "ever-present source of danger" and claimed that the subway appeared to be "amply protected against third-rail dangers," while on the elevated roads "no remedy is at present in sight."

William Barclay Parsons, chief engineer of the Rapid Transit Commission, explained the procedures for "guarding the third rail in the subway [construction began in 1900]," which he described as "adequate." The procedure involved placing a hood over the third rail in the form of an inverted "L" with the open side toward the tracks on which the train would run. The brush from the subway cars would run up under the L and connect with the third rail. This system would prevent anyone, workmen or passengers, who may walk along the tunnel [on the trackwalks] from getting an accidental shock.

This plan was decided upon because from time to time it may be necessary for passengers to make a short walk through the subway tunnel because of an outage in the power house. However, with the third rail protected, and an automatic shut off of power in the general system, "the third rail system, in the tunnel at least, is as nearly perfect as human ingenuity can devise." "Of course," workers repairing the third rail system might receive a shock if they removed the hood, but in such an event "the accident would be due solely to the carelessness of the workman."

On the elevated road, however, the same protection could not be employed on the third rail unless the tracks and cars were rearranged and reconstructed. The third rail on the el was too far removed from the car to work the same arrangement as on the subway. However, the third rail system on the elevated was said to be "without any especial element of danger to passengers, except, of course, should any of them try to walk along the tracks from station to station." With workmen, it would be "their own carelessness, and nothing more, that is responsible." General Superintendent Hedley of the Interborough Company went on to say that "no passengers have been killed by the third rail or by any other accidents on the elevated system since it has been in operation."

Another problem that was causing "a great deal of concern" on the elevated roads was the noise that came with the installation of heavier cars for electrical service. Shopkeepers and residents along the elevated lines, especially along Columbus Avenue, where the trains "now attain a high rate of speed" made many complaints. The noise was so bad that tradesmen stopped talking to their customers as trains passed by, because of "their inability to make themselves heard."

Superintendent Hedley attributed the noise to the heavier cars, the powerful motors in use, and the "old metal brakes that are attached to the cars, causing a creaking and squeaking sound as the trains are stopped at stations." Another official spoke to the matter:

> The people want rapid transit and have been demanding it in no unmeasured terms. We are giving them rapid transit [and with it comes] motor cars capable of hauling the passenger trains at a rate of forty miles an hour, and the cars hauled weigh two tons more than the old cars. All this makes greater noise, especially in view of the elevated structure, which seems to carry the noises along with it. As these noises are well-distributed, and not confined as in a subway, I do not see what can be done at this time to remedy the trouble.[32]

Origins of the Subway

The world's first subway opened in London on January 10, 1863, on a 3.7 mile track between Farringdon Street and Bishop's Rock, Paddington. The *London Times* described this steam-powered line as "the greatest engineering triumph of the day." And, it should be noted that the first subway in the United States was in Boston. On September 1, 1897, trolley cars of the West End Street Railway began operations into the Tremont Street subway.[33]

From 1880 to 1895, "the perpetual and gratuitous franchise was abolished and the right of the public to build, pay for, own and if necessary operate street railroads was successfully asserted." The Rapid Transit Act of 1891 was born during this time, and soon amended to permit cities to use public capital for construction. In 1894, the citizens of New York City passed a referendum in favor of public ownership. However, the change in public sentiment did not come without a struggle. It developed in this way.[34]

By the end of the 1880s, the elevated roads were congested and it was evident that additional rapid transit lines were required. In 1888, Mayor Abram S. Hewitt, regarded by many as the "father of modern rapid transit," urged common council to approve use of city credit for construction of a road to be owned by the city but leased to a private company for operation. However, Hewitt's plan was not approved and another bill introduced in 1888 also failed. Mayor Hewitt had this to say: "The prejudice against the scheme was so great ... that it was difficult to find any member of the Legislature who would be responsible for the introduction of a bill, which was opposed not only by the

Common Council of the City, but by the political organization which controlled the politics of the City" (i.e., Tammany Hall).[22]

Hugh J. Grant, "a Tammany man," became mayor of New York City in January 1889, and he urged construction of new lines that "must be built, equipped and operated by private capital." In his inaugural speech, he declared: "Private capital must ... furnish the means for the construction of the road, but the public authorities must be vigilant to guard the rights of the citizens to the enjoyment of a fair proportion of the benefits that will flow from its operation."[36]

In early 1891, a bill sponsored by Mayor Grant passed both houses and it was signed by Governor Hill on January 31, becoming the Rapid Transit Act of 1891. It created the Board of Rapid Transit Commissioners and "authorized the board to lay out routes and adopt plans for a rapid transit railroad, either supra- or subterranean, and to put up the franchise to build and operate at public auction. It also required the consents of the local authorities and of the abutting property owners to the extent of one half in the value of the property affected." The commission elected William Steinway president.[37]

While the law "contemplated" private ownership, advocates of public ownership soon stepped forward. One argument was that the city could borrow money at three percent—a much lower rate than private interests could obtain—and could, therefore, better afford such an investment. Another issue was the question of motive power. The interested parties desired an underground road, if practicable, and the method of motive power was an important consideration. The New York City environment was not conducive to steam power in an underground road; therefore, electricity was favored if a subway were built. During the summer, it was decided to build an underground road, preferably a route running up Broadway and the extension of Broadway, known as the Boulevard. Plans were drawn up, the commission adopted them, common council approved, and the mayor signed off on the plans on October 31. A decision on motive power was left open until a later date.[38]

Following the approvals, in the fall of 1892, the Commission solicited bids for the franchise. However, only one outrageously low bid was received, and it was rejected. Rumor had it that opposition by the elevated roads was responsible for the failure to sell the franchise. [Jay] "Gould of course, did not want a competitive transit line in the city, and certainly was powerful enough, financially and politically, to interpose obstacles." The Steinway Commission tried to get the Manhattan Railway Company to build extensions of its elevated roads, but they were refused.[39]

The failure of the Steinway Commission led to further efforts by Mayor Hewitt to bring about the construction of new rapid transit lines. He appealed to the legislature, which resulted in passage of the Rapid Transit Act of 1894 on May 22. The act created a new Rapid Transit Commission and made possible the use of the city's credit to bring the subway project to fruition. "The great object aimed at," said Mayor Hewitt, "was to secure the early completion of the work, its continued ownership by the city and its reversion at the end of fifty years to the city, free and clear of all encumbrances of every kind and nature whatever."[40]

The new board, known as the Board of Rapid Transit Railroad Commissioners, consisted of the mayor, the city controller, and several prominent businessmen, including William Steinway and Alexander Orr, the latter being president of the New York Chamber of Commerce. William Barclay Parsons was appointed chief engineer.[41]

"Early in its deliberations the new board reached the conclusion that the only way of meeting the transit situation was to build underground railroads and this decision ... met the approval of a public wearied with the inadequacy of the service supplied by the elevated railroads and the presence of their unsightly structures in the streets of the city." The new board was authorized to grant additional franchises to existing railroads (mostly the elevated lines) to lay out routes for rapid transit lines and cause lines to be constructed if consents of the abutting property owners were obtained. The citizens were to vote on "the question whether such railway or railways shall be constructed by the city and at the public expense."[42]

The referendum was held November 6, 1894, and the electorate voted overwhelmingly in favor of municipal construction (132,647 for; 42,916 against; 399 invalid). The board was now authorized to entertain proposals and enter into contract with persons or a corporation to build the road for the city at the city's expense. The contractor would be required "to operate the railroad as the lessee of the city for a term not less than 35 nor more than 50 years, and at an annual rental sufficient to pay the interest upon the bonds issued by the city for construction and one per cent in addition as a sinking fund to retire such bonds at maturity." However, after what appeared to be a future of extraordinary promise, numerous difficulties impeded progress. Among them were divergences of opinion over the best routes, legal obstacles, reluctant and hostile property owners, "diversions" by the Manhattan Railway Company, and municipal restraints. Nonetheless, by the end of 1899, "with all the legal difficulties cleared away, [and] all other obstacles surmounted ... the path open[ed] for the advertisement and award of the great contract."[43]

The board proceeded to seek out prominent railroad men with the "pioneer endeavor" to take on the venture "entailing as it did an expenditure of millions even though the cost of construction should be defrayed by the municipality." By January 15, 1900, three individuals stepped forward. But "fortune favored" August Belmont, who had the "nerve and immense financial resources" and John B. McDonald, a contractor with "capital and actual experience in underground construction."[44]

McDonald was almost as well known in the contracting field as was Belmont in finance. "Of powerful frame and much shrewd ability, he was well fitted for the arduous life of the contractor and had unusual success before he came to New York. He built the Baltimore & Ohio Railroad tunnels at Baltimore, a celebrated piece of work for those days." His plan for excavation consisted of a shallow "cut and cover" that allowed progressive sections to be completed and filled in before breaking ground on the next section.[45]

McDonald proposed to build the road for $35 million and he was awarded the contract, whereupon he arranged with August Belmont for financial backing. The latter entered into a contract with McDonald to organize a new company, which was later incorporated as the Rapid Transit Subway Construction Company. The appellate division approved the financial arrangements and the board executed the contract on February 21, 1900. The contract, known as Contract No. 1, among other things, positioned McDonald as both contractor and lessee, "but the city through the board was to exercise constant supervision over construction, even to the inspection and approval of materials and work." Motive power was to be either electricity or compressed air, unless a superior method became practicable, in which case the contractor had the right to adopt the method, if approved by the board.[46]

On March 24, 1900, ground was broken in front of City Hall for the new subway. The work was done by August Belmont's Rapid Transit Subway Construction Company under McDonald's supervision. The company was capitalized with $6 million, issued in common stock, to which Belmont and other investors subscribed.[47]

John B. McDonald (1844–1911) (Library of Congress, Pach Brothers Photos).

There was no turning back. Manhattan was "critically congested." "The city's population had increased by almost five fold during the last half of the nineteenth century and getting into town from the ... residential sections ... was a tedious and time-consuming task ... as business and commerce continued to grow. Streets were hopelessly clogged; horsedrawn buggies, foot traffic, pushcarts, wagons, and even an occasional horseless carriage, competed jealously and aggressively for maneuvering room."[48]

The first subway cars delivered to New York City were two experimental designs from Wason. They were the *August Belmont*, later designated no. 3340, and the *John B. McDonald*, becoming no. 3341. Neither car ran in regular passenger service, but they established design features for the earliest production-model subway cars and later orders numbering more than 2,500 cars. Wason also delivered the first regular cars to the Interborough Rapid Transit Company in the summer of 1903. On September 14, a five-car train of new subway cars conducted a demonstration run on the Second

X. Electrification and the Subway

IRT subway ground-breaking ceremonies, March 24, 1900 (MTA New York City Transit).

and Third Avenue elevated lines. By late fall, Wason and three other manufacturers delivered more than 200 of the original order of 500 cars.[49]

On October 27, 1904, after two years of excavation and construction, operation of the finished portion of the subway was to begin. The occasion was marked by a grand ceremony in the "packed" Aldermanic Chamber and was attended by about 600 people, headed by the new mayor, George B. McClellan, Jr., senior officials of the Interborough Rapid Transit Company, "famous engineers" and construction figures, political luminaries, and "cheering rows" of invited guests, including "a score of women and their escorts."

> The Chamber had been decorated hardly less elaborately than the exterior of the City Hall. From every window and corner hung National banners, and broad streamers fluttered from the balcony railing.
>
> Chief Engineer Parsons received a big ovation the moment he entered the door. Contractor McDonald's entrance was another signal for enthusiasm, and a moment later Mr. Belmont's name echoed through the room. It was hard to tell which was the more popular with the audience, the chief engineer or the contractor. Every time the name of either was mentioned there was a new demonstration, and when their turns came for speaking the din was deafening.

IRT subway construction work, Union Square, June 8, 1901 (Library of Congress).

At 1:04, the temporary chairman banged his gavel on the desk, marking the opening of the ceremony, and Mayor McClellan was introduced as the presiding officer. He made these remarks:

> Without rapid transit Greater New York would be little more than a geographical expression. It is no exaggeration to say that without interborough communication Greater New York would never have come into being.
>
> The present boundaries of our city included ten years ago a multitude of independent and heterogeneous communities which would have continued in all human probability to work out their own destinies independently had not modern genius and modern enterprise afforded their population the possibility of movement.
>
> When the Brooklyn Bridge was opened Greater New York was born. Every addition to transit facilities has stimulated her growth, which can only reach its full development when a complete system of rapid transit shall be rapid in fact as well as in name.
>
> We have met here today for the purpose of turning over a page in the history of our city; for the purpose of marking the advent of a new epoch in her development. If this new underground railroad which we are about to open proves as popular and as successful as I confidently expect it to be it will be only the first of many more which must ultimately result in giving us an almost perfect system of interborough communication.[50]

"At precisely 35½ minutes after two o'clock in the afternoon of Thursday, October 27, with Mayor George B. McClellan at the controls, a subway train pulled out of a terminal and carried passengers under the sidewalks of New York for the first time."[51]

The subway had four express and local service tracks as recommended by the Senate Committee of 1866. On the inaugural run, "Mayor McClellan was presented with an

X. Electrification and the Subway

IRT City Hall subway station under construction, 1900–1906 (Library of Congress).

inscribed, Tiffany-made solid silver control handle by the president of the Interborough Rapid Transit Company.... His Honor latched back the controller and fed 600 volts of direct current into the cars' traction motors. Subway service began."[52]

The eight-car train proceeded on a 9.1 mile, 26 minute trip that originated at City Hall, "ran up the east side under Fourth Avenue and Park Avenue South, then turned west just south of Grand Central. After running a few blocks under 42nd Street, it turned north again under Broadway, finally terminating at 145th Street."[53]

Not all went smoothly in the first weekend of its operation and the "heavy crowds" surfaced the inevitable complaints. "At several stations built on curves, a large gap developed between the platforms and the subway cars. This problem was eventually rectified by the installation of a mechanical 'sliding platform' which moved out to fill the gap as soon as the trains stopped." Also, the advertising signs, some complained, "defaced the beauty of the stations." And, a problem that never went away, was crowding in the trains and stations.[54]

Regardless of the complaints about the annoying advertisements, the stations were

IRT subway entrance and exit kiosks, E. 23rd Street, c. 1905 (Library of Congress).

"attractive in their design and appointments" and built in accordance with the construction contract: "The railway and its equipment as contemplated by the contract constitute a great public work. All parts of the structure where exposed to public sight shall therefore be designed, constructed, and maintained with a view to the beauty of their appearance, as well as to their efficiency." A trade journal described the subway stations as "dignified and artistic efforts of the highest order." A journalist pronounced them to be "architecturally superlative executions."[55]

The subway's "instant success provided Belmont his legacy and turned the mayor into a New York City folk hero." Mayor McClellan proved to be an organizational genius during his six-year term of office, including removal of the horsecars and adjusting the city's traffic grids to allow for the introduction of automobiles, and completion of the Queensborough and Manhattan Bridges, among other achievements. "Everything he accomplished, however, took a back seat among the citizens of the city to his being the mayor who 'gave' them a subway."[42] During the first year of operation, 1905, the subway carried 71 million passengers.[56]

X. Electrification and the Subway

IRT subway opening day, October 27, 1904 (MTA New York City Transit).

In June 1914, August Belmont outlined how the financial and legal challenges were overcome:

> With all due respect to McDonald ... and others, the subway would not have been built if I had not taken hold of the work. McDonald had a contract with the city, but he could not get the money to finance the work.... I went over the matter with McDonald [and] agreed to find the money necessary to carry out the contract.
>
> [After paying out well over $1,000,000 to the Controller on McDonald's behalf, Belmont went on to say], I paid that, knowing that I had no legal security to protect me. Counsel for the Rapid Transit Commission and my own lawyer tried to work out a plan which would absolutely protect me, but it could not be done. Finally, I told them I would take the risk. If I had not, the subway would not have been built — at least not at that time.
>
> The matter of getting an operating company caused me considerable annoyance.... At that time the old street car interests were all powerful with the Legislature, and when I tried to get a charter I found the door closed. Finally, I [went] straight to a man who was all powerful, or at least most influential with the powers that were. I told him just what I was trying to do, and what the project meant for New York and how certain influences were trying to prevent me from carrying it out. He promised his help and a short time later we got our charter. [The "influential man" was later determined to be William C. Whitney, one of the principal owners of the Metropolitan Street Railway system, operator of the surface car lines in Manhattan].[57]

On December 1, 1904, William B. Parsons resigned as chief engineer of the Rapid Transit Board. "The first New York subway stands as a monument to his skill and courage as an engineer." In July 1913, he reflected:

> I was thirty-five years of age when I became Chief Engineer ... When I look back now I am glad I was not older. I doubt if I could now undertake or would undertake such a work under similar conditions. But I had the enthusiasm of youth and inexperience. Had I fully realized all that was ahead of me, I do not think I could have attempted the work. As it was I was treated as a visionary.[58]

Other sections of the first subway were opened to traffic as follows:

- Broadway, 145th to 157th streets, November 5, 1904
- Lenox Avenue Branch, Broadway and 96th Street to 145th Street, November 20, 1904
- 149th Street and Third Avenue along Westchester Avenue and Boston Road to the terminus at 180th Street, November 26, 1904
- The intervening link from 145th Street under the Harlem River to Westchester Avenue was opened later and the remainder of the Broadway line, 157th Street to Kingsbridge, in March 1906.[59]

William Barclay Parsons (1859–1932) (Library of Congress, Pach Brothers Photos).

When the first subway began operation, the street railway systems in New York City were controlled by the Manhattan (Elevated) Railway Company and the Metropolitan Street Railway Company. The latter embraced most of the surface car lines in Manhattan and the Bronx by consolidating several surface car companies into one system that controlled all the main north and south and crosstown lines. However, once the subway was completed, it became apparent to the Metropolitan's management that its street surface lines would lose business, so they conceived a plan to petition the Rapid Transit Commission for a franchise to operate a competing subway. The crux of the plan was to enable the Metropolitan "not only to sell out to Belmont but to make him buy or merge."[47]

The Metropolitan proposed to build a line for the city and operate it under lease together with its surface lines and give free transfers for five cents a passenger. The plan would "practically bring rapid transit to the door of every citizen" and "relieve congestion on many overcrowded roads."

> [The Metropolitan's proposal stated that] by utilizing the surface lines for local traffic, and for carrying long-distance passengers to and from the nearest subway stations, it would be possible to very greatly reduce the number of railway stations which would otherwise be necessary, thus materially increasing the speed and efficiency of the underground service. [Moreover], the transfer system by which the underground lines and the surface lines would be operated as one system, would establish means of expeditious communication between all parts of Manhattan island for a five-cent fare. Such a comprehensive result is, of course, possible only with underground lines operated in connection with a complete network of surface lines.[60]

The proposal was taken under consideration by the Rapid Transit Commission and their deliberations progressed through various stages in 1904 and 1905 until "suddenly the community was electrified by the news that the Interborough Rapid Transit Company and the Metropolitan Street Railway Company had merged and the two immense transportation systems were hereafter to be controlled by one new company entitled the Interborough-Metropolitan Company." The new company was incorporated in January 1906 as a business instead of a railroad corporation, and it was capitalized with $155 million, 55 preferred, 100 common. It was to hold the stock of both the Interborough Rapid Transit and the Metropolitan Street Railway companies.[61]

In June 1914, August Belmont commented on the merger:

> You remember how the street car people talked about building a system of subways and giving transfers to the surface lines. Well, we couldn't stand that kind of competition, and so we combined with them. I admit that we didn't know the exact condition of the surface car system ... it took us some months to get to the bottom of it, but when we got down to the bottom of things they were worse than we expected. The old system has been reorganized, improved and put into shape where it ought to develop into a fine property. Everything will work out all right, I think.[62]

The final scenes in the play remained to be acted out. On May 12, 1955, the Third Avenue el, one of the last elevated lines to carry passengers in Manhattan, closed down. And, on February 16, 1956, the last steel column of the road that had "shut out the sunlight over Third Avenue for three-quarters of a century was uprooted." However, a short segment of the Sixth Avenue and Ninth Avenue lines, the so-called "Polo Grounds shuttle," continued in operation until 11:59 P.M. on August 31, 1958.[63] From that date on, the elevated railroads in Manhattan ceased to exist.

Appendix: A Brief Biography of Annie R. Hain (1836–1929)

Anna Rebecca McWilliams, was born April 14, 1836, at Liberty Township, Montour County. She was a daughter of Hugh McWilliams (1799–1877) and Rebecca Lemon (1803–1893).

Hugh McWilliams was a citizen-soldier in the Columbia Guards, a volunteer militia unit called to active duty during the Mexican War. The Guards were with General Winfield Scott when his forces landed near Vera Cruz on March 9, 1847, and captured the city. From there, Scott outmaneuvered the Mexicans, gaining several other victories, and despite being heavily outmanned, marched on Mexico City. However, the Mexicans chose not to defend their capital city, marking the effective defeat of Mexico.[1]

The McWilliams family emigrated from Scotland by way of County Armagh, Ireland, and settled near Danville, Montour County, Pennsylvania. The progenitors of the McWilliams family line in the U.S.—great-grandparents of Annie R. Hain—were (the first) Hugh McWilliams (1735–1778) and his wife, Rebecca Dunwoody, one of six children of John Dunwoody, of West Nantmeal, Chester County, Pennsylvania. (The first) Hugh McWilliams served as a lieutenant in the French and Indian War and died in an engagement called the "surpassing horror" of the Revolutionary War because of the brutal acts committed by the Iroquois and their loyalist allies.[2]

Robert McWilliams (1775–1823), a son of Hugh McWilliams and Rebecca Dunwoody, married Jane Curry (1773–1858), the first white child born between the north and west branches (the "forks") of the Susquehanna River. They were the parents of (the second) Hugh McWilliams, father of Annie R. Hain. Jane Curry's parents were Robert Curry (1741–1780) and Jane McWilliams (1750–1825), the latter being a sister of (the first) Hugh McWilliams.[3]

On March 25, 1776, Robert Curry was enrolled as a First Lieutenant in the Seventh Company (Capt. John Simpson's), First Battalion (Col. Hunter's), Northumberland Associators, and was killed by Indians in 1780.[4]

> In the Great Runaway the previous year they had fled on rafts down the river to Fort Augusta, that now had been erected midway between Danville and Northumberland,

and here Lt. Curry was doing military service and had his family with him for their safety. He and his wife, on horseback, were going over to their land on the north side of the mountain, when at a spring on the way up the southern slope, they were attacked by Indians and their horses were shot from under them. Mrs. Curry was seized by an Indian. She saw her husband tomahawked, scalped and killed, the blow of the weapon crushing his skull. She was taken captive, but somewhere in the Vincent Hollow they bivouacked. While it rained, she escaped from her captors, as they slept, and making her way back to the fort, she obtained assistance and brought back her husband's body, which was then buried with honors of war in the original burying ground at Danville. She had been bound with bark ropes to her captors, but she had a pair of scissors with her and used them to obtain release. The falling rain assisted her, and she hid a while in a hollow log, where the aroused savages came near finding her, as they paused nearby and called her, "Much pretty squaw, come."[5]

Annie Hain had a strong sense of patriotism. She was a member of the Daughters of the American Revolution (national number 12968) based on lineal descent from her great-grandfather, Lt. Robert Curry. She was a member of the New York Chapter of the Dames of the Loyal Legion of the United States, a heritage society open to lineal and collateral female descendants of commissioned officers of the regular and volunteer forces of the United States during the Civil War. And, in 1903, she became a member of the Pennsylvania Society of Colonial Dames of America based on lineal descent from another great-grandfather, Judge Thomas Lemon (1730–1775).[6]

On June 18, 1904, Annie R. Hain dedicated a monument at Fairview cemetery, Danville, Pennsylvania, in memory of her great-grandfather, Lt. Robert Curry, and "other pioneers of this section."[7] The monument was inscribed with a citation and the names of her honored relatives. Following preliminary ceremonies, she delivered a brief, but moving address.

> To honor the memory of those who were pioneers in blazing the path of civilization, or who yielded up their lives in defense of their country, is at once a duty and a pleasure. In erecting this modest monument in the memory of our kith and kin, whose bones have long since turned to dust, it is not the desire nor intention to exalt them above their compatriots, for whom no stone records their deeds and sacrifices. It is rather to show our loyal veneration for our dead, who in the long ago lived, labored and achieved amid privations and dangers to which their progeny are strangers.
>
> Others in the Colonial and Revolutionary days, doubtless, were more brilliant, more conspicuous and more highly honored by their fellows, but these are of our blood, who were earnest, true and patriotic, and their descendants do honor and revere them.
>
> Since the world began it has been for women to recount to the children the sturdy virtues and valor of their progenitors. This monument is simply a woman's story cut into granite, that it may endure when she who has caused these tablets to be inscribed, shall have been gathered to her fathers, and like them, shall be voiceless in the tomb.[8]

The Presbyterian Church of Mooresburg was constructed in 1830. In 1911, a bell tower was erected at the front entrance to the church. Annie R. Hain, presented a bell in memory of her father, Hugh McWilliams, and dedicated it in a ceremony on January 1, 1912. The bell was moved to the bell tower of the current building on September 5, 1958.[9]

Annie Hain received a U.S. Navy pension of $12.00 per month beginning August 18, 1908, increased to $50.00 per month beginning August 4, 1926.[10]

A Brief Biography of Annie R. Hain (1836–1929)

Annie R. Hain died on February 22, 1929, at age 92, of myocardial failure at her residence, 200 West 58th Street, Apt. 2A, Borough of Manhattan, New York City. She left an impressive estate, consisting of cash, stocks and bonds, and she was generous in bequeathing her wealth to relatives and a few friends. The total appraised value of her estate was $386,101.62 of which the net for distribution among twenty-five beneficiaries amounted to $366,474.94.

Twelve residuary legatees were bequeathed a total of $186,838.34 in cash, $150,573.50 in securities, and $8,055.10 in personal property. Thirteen general legatees, mostly her late husband's relatives, received a total of $20,500 in cash and $508 in personal property.[11]

George A. Post was an original co-executor of Annie R. Hain's estate, but he died in 1925 and his son, George A. Post, Jr., was appointed co-executor in his father's stead. Annie Hain stated in her Will: "For over fifty years he [George A. Post] has been like a brother to me and ever since the death of my husband he has given freely and generously of his time and efforts in aiding me in my personal and business affairs. No relative of mine has been so situated as to do as much for my comfort and welfare as he."[12]

Anna R. Hain's personal property was distributed according to a list that was included among her papers. The complete list of personal property indicates a very well-appointed, if not lavish, household suitable for entertaining at a high level of sophistication. Following are some of the more interesting items among the total personal property ($8,055.10) bequeathed mostly to grandnieces and grandnephews:

Persian rug, 8.9' × 8.8', $140
Hudson seal coat, $100
Solitaire ring, gold, diamond of 1¼ kt, $310
Solitaire diamond ring, 3 kt, gold, $900
Solitaire ring, diamond, ¾ kt, gold, $160
Kirmen rug, 9.6' × 16.9', pink, all-over design, $300
Mahogany sofa, upholstered, silk damask, $125
Sterling fruit dish, large 3" × 14", monographed "From Helen and Frank Jay Gould," $150
Sterling fruit bowl, 8½" × 4", #1893-A, $75
Gorham Sterling tea and coffee service, #1621, $125
Old fashioned gold brooch, set with various stones, $200
Broken necklace of oriental baroque pearls comprising 80 pearls and having amethyst and diamond clasp containing 10 diamond chips, $900
Silver water pitcher, marked F.K.H. A.R.McW.
Steinway upright piano and stool, $350
Diamond pendant with large cabochon amethyst set in platinum, tiny platinum chain with 125 chips and 3 diamonds, 1 point each, $325
Solitaire ring, gold, diamond of 1⅜ carats, $350.[13]

Notes

Chapter I

1. James Blaine Walker, *Fifty Years of Rapid Transit, 1864–1917* (reprint by Arno Press and *New York Times*, 1916), Chapter I.
2. New York City Subway History, Photos & More, Chapter 6, "The Elevated Railroads" (www.nycsubway.org); New York City Transit (www.mta.info/nyct-MTA); New York Transit Museum, "History of Public Transportation in New York City."
3. Gene Sansone, *New York Subways: An Illustrated History of New York City's Transit Cars* (Baltimore: Johns Hopkins University Press in association with the New York Transit Museum, 1997), 1.
4. Walker, *Fifty Years of Rapid Transit, 1864–1917*, Chapter I.
5. *Ibid.*, Chapter II.
6. William Fullerton Reeves, *The First Elevated Railroads in Manhattan and the Bronx of the City of New York* (New York: New York Historical Society, 1936), 1–3.
7. Joseph Brennan, *The Beach Pneumatic Transit Company*, Chapter 7, "An Extraordinary Pneumatic Tunnel Bill, 1870," original web publication, 2004–2005.
8. Sansone, *New York Subways*, 2.
9. Brennan, *Beach Pneumatic Transit Company*, Chapter 7.
10. *Ibid.*
11. "Alfred Ely Beach: Beach's Bizarre Broadway Subway" (www.klaatu.org).
12. Reeves, *First Elevated Railways*, 4–6.
13. Robert C. Reed, *The New York Elevated* (New York: A. S. Barnes, 1978), 36.
14. Reeves, *First Elevated Railways*, 6.
15. *Ibid.*, 7.
16. *Ibid.*, 9.
17. *Ibid.*, 11.
18. *Ibid.*, 12–13; Annual Report of the Board of Railroad Commissioners, FY 1885, Vol. II, 1159.
19. Reeves, 28.
20. *New York Times*, September 3, 1881, and April 3, 1880; Annual Report of the Board of Railroad Commissioners, FY 1883, Vol. II, 883, and 1895, Vol. II, 719; Official Map and Guide to All the Elevated Railways in New York City, 1881.
21. Annual Report of the Board of Railroad Commissioners, FY 1885, Vol. II, 1153.
22. *Ibid.*, 1159.
23. *Ibid.*
24. Reeves, *First Elevated Railroads*, 19; Annual Report of the Board of Railroad Commissioners, FY 1885, Vol. II, 1153.
25. Reeves, *First Elevated Railways*, 22.
26. *Ibid.*
27. *Ibid.*, 30.
28. *Ibid.*, 31–32.
29. *New York Times*, September 3, 1881, and April 3, 1880; Annual Report of the Board of Railroad Commissioners, FY 1883, Vol. II, 883, and 1895, Vol. II, 719; Official Map and Guide to All the Elevated Railways in New York City, 1881.
30. Annual Report of the Board of Railroad Commissioners, FY 1885, Vol. II, 1153.
31. "The Progress of Elevated Railways," *Scientific American*, Vol. XLI, No. 17, October 25, 1879.
32. Reed, *The New York Elevated*, 72–73.
33. *Ibid.*, 74.
34. *Ibid.*, 75.
35. *Ibid.*, 76.
36. *Ibid.*, 77.
37. *Ibid.*
38. *Ibid.*
39. *Ibid.*
40. *Ibid.*, 78–80.
41. *Ibid.*, 52.
42. John H. White, Jr., "Spunky Little Devils: Locomotives of the New York Elevated," *Railroad History*, Spring 1990, 23–27; William D. Edson, "Locomotive Roster, New York Elevated," 59–79.
43. White, Jr., "Spunky Little Devils," 28–29; Reed, *The New York Elevated*, 83.
44. Brennan, *The Beach Pneumatic Transit Company*, Chapter 17, "Moving in Mid-Air Upon Nothing 1878."

45. White, Jr., *Spunky Little Devils*, 30–31; Edson, "Locomotive Roster," 61, 68–70; Reed, 82.
46. Edson, "Locomotive Roster," 60, 63–67.
47. *Ibid.*, 60, 71–72.
48. Sansone, *New York Subways*, 28, 18.
49. Reed, *The New York Elevated*, 85.
50. Brian J. Cudahy, *Under the Sidewalks of New York: The Story of the Greatest Subway System in the World* (Brattleboro, VT: The Stephen Greene Press, 1979), 19.
51. Reed, *The New York Elevated*, 85; Reeves, 46.
52. White, Jr., "Spunky Little Devils," 39.
53. Reed, *The New York Elevated*, 93.
54. *Ibid.*, 88–93.
55. *Ibid.*, 94.
56. Reed, *The New York Elevated*, 95; John H. White, Jr., "A Perfect Light is a Luxury: Pintsch Gas Car Lighting," *Technology and Culture*, Vol. 18, No. 1, January 1977, 64–69; "The Manufacture of Pintsch Gas," *Scientific American*, July 9, 1898.
57. Reed, *The New York Elevated*, 95; *New York Times*, March 7, 1886.
58. Reed, *The New York Elevated*, 95; White, Jr., "Spunky Little Devils," 34.
59. Sansone, *New York Subways*, 30–31, 332.
60. *Ibid.*, 32, 333.
61. Reed, *The New York Elevated*, 49–50.
62. Sansone, *New York Subways*, 3–34, 334–335.
63. *Ibid.*, 35, 336–338.
64. *Ibid.*, 35, 336–337, 342.
65. *Ibid.*, 38, 40, 345–348.
66. *Ibid.*, 41, 343, 344, 349–351.
67. *Ibid.*, 104.
68. *Ibid.*, 101.
69. *Ibid.*, 99.
70. *Ibid.*, 101.
71. Jackie Craven, "No Two Alike—Victorian Character," *RealtorMag*, August 1, 2004.

Chapter II

1. Annual Report of the Board of Railroad Commissioners, FY 1883, Vol. I, 123; Maury Klein, *The Life and Legend of Jay Gould* (Baltimore: Johns Hopkins University Press, 1986), 283.
2. Julius Grodinsky, *Jay Gould, His Business Career 1867–1892* (Philadelphia: University of Pennsylvania Press, 1957), 289; Annual Report of the Board of Railroad Commissioners, FY 1883, Vol. I, 124–125.
3. Annual Report of the Board of Railroad Commissioners, FY 1883, Vol. I, 124–125; *Times*, May 24, 1879, May 29, 1879, June 18, 1879.
4. Annual Report of the Railroad Commissioners, FY 1883, Vol. I., 124–125.
5. www.famousamericans.net.
6. William W. Withuhn, *Rails Across America: A History of Railroads in North America* (New York: Smithmark Publishers, 1993).
7. *Ibid.*

8. Census of the U. S., Department of the Interior, Bureau of the Census, Report on the Agencies of Transportation in the U. S. (Washington, DC: Government Printing Office, 1883).
9. *Elevated Railway Journal*, Vol. II, No. 10, December 4, 1880, New York, 1. (Author's files).
10. *Times*, September 3, 1881; Annual Report of the Board of Railroad Commissioners, FY 1883, Vol. II, 883–885.
11. *New York Times*, September 3, 1881, October 9, 1881, and December 27, 1881.
12. *New York Times*, December 27, 1881.
13. Grodinsky, *Jay Gould*, 308–310; Annual Report of the Board of Railroad Commissioners, FY 1885, Vol. II, 1145.
14. Klein, *Life and Legend of Jay Gould*, 331.
15. Grodinsky, *Jay Gould*, 308–310; Annual Report of the Board of Railroad Commissioners, FY 1885, Vol. II, 1145.
16. *New York Times*, December 7, 1884.
17. *Ibid.*
18. Klein, *Life and Legend of Jay Gould*, 45–51.
19. *Ibid.*, 67, 73–75.
20. *Ibid.*, 86, 291.
21. Paul Sarnoff, *Russell Sage: The Money King* (New York: Ivan Obolensky, 1965), 215–218.
22. *Ibid.*, 220–221.
23. *Ibid.*, 322–324.
24. *New York Times*, December 5, 1891.
25. Sarnoff, *Russell Sage*, 327.
26. Cyrus W. Field (www.nndb.com/people); Cyrus West Field (www.all-biographies.com/business).
27. Samuel Carter III, *Cyrus Field: Man of Two Worlds* (New York: G. P. Putnam's Sons, 1968), 317.
28. *Ibid.*, 341–343.
29. Grodinsky, *Jay Gould*, 314.
30. *New York Times*, July 13, 1892, and July 14, 1892.

Chapter III

1. *Hain Family* (Reading, PA: *Reading Eagle Press*), 87.
2. The Story of Berks County, PA (www.archives.org); Living Places (www.livingplaces.com/PA/Berks).
3. History of Greater Reading, Berks County, PA (www.readingberkspa.com).
4. Berks County Recorder of Deeds, Deed Book 62, p. 549; Deed Book 1183, p. 524. According to Frederick C. Sheeler, Berks County Recorder of Deeds, property was customarily purchased by a wife when the husband was somehow disabled or incapacitated.
5. *Times*, May 10, 1896.
6. Historical Society of Berks County, PA.
7. *Ibid.*
8. NARA, Military Pension File. The *Colorado* was a three-masted, wood-hulled, steam screw frigate displacing 3,425 tons and armed with 40 guns (2–

10", 24–9", and 14–8"). She was 264 feet in length, beam 53 feet, draft 22 feet, speed 9 knots. The ship was commissioned on March 13, 1856, and commanded by Captain William. H. Gardner. She put to sea from Norfolk on May 12, 1856. The *Colorado* was re-re-commissioned in 1861 and saw extensive action in the Civil War and afterward in the Mediterranean and Adriatic, and still later in the Far East. The ship was scrapped in 1885, but the ship's memory lived on in the form of its bell, which was resurrected from the Navy Archives in 1896 and attached to the bridge of the USS *Puritan*, a Monitor that saw action in the Spanish-American War. After *Puritan* was decommissioned, the bell was attached to the bridge of the second *Colorado* in 1905. In the evolution of ship naming, the second *Colorado* was eventually designated the USS *Pueblo*, and it will be remembered as the electronic intelligence ship that was seized by the North Koreans in 1968. *Dictionary of American Naval Fighting Ships* (Washington, DC: Dept. of the Navy, Naval Historical Center, 1959–1981.

9. Frank M. Bennett, *Steam Navy of the United States* (Westport, CT: Greenwood Press, 1896), 4.

10. *Ibid.*, 197.

11. *Dictionary of American Naval Fighting Ships*.

12. *Ibid.*

13. NARA, Military Pension File.

14. *Danville Intelligencer*, May 15, 1896.

15. *Hain Family*, 87; D. H. B. Brower, *Danville, Montour County, Pennsylvania: A Collection of Historical and Biographical Sketches* (Harrisburg, PA: Lane S. Hart, printer and binder, Montour County Genealogical Society, 1881).

16. NARA, Military Pension File.

17. ORN, Series I, Vol. I, 40.

18. NARA. Military Pension File.

19. ORN, Series I, Vol. 1, 96, 118.

20. Virgil C. Jones, *Civil War at Sea* (New York: Holt, Rinehart, Winston, 1961), 167; *Dictionary of American Naval Fighting Ships*.

21. *Dictionary of American Naval Fighting Ships*.

22. J. Rickard, "Capture of New Orleans, 18–29 April 1862" (www.historyofwar.org/articles), June 15, 2007.

23. Bennett, *Steam Navy of the United States*, 321.

24. Chester G. Hearn, *The Capture of New Orleans 1862* (Baton Rouge: Louisiana State University Press, 1995), 232, 233.

25. www.Hazegray.org.

26. ORN Series I, Vol. 18, 118.

27. Charles L. Dufour, *The Night the War Was Lost* (New York: Doubleday, 1960), 234.

28. Jones, *Civil War at Sea*, 167.

29. *Ibid.*

30. NARA, Military pension file.

31. *Ibid.*

32. ORN Series I, Vol. XIX, 174, 175, 211, 236.

33. Rickard, *Capture of New Orleans*.

34. NARA, Military pension file.

35. *Times*, May 10, 1896.

36. Graham R. Lobb, "Remember the D&H," *Bridge Line Historical Society Bulletin*, Vol. 5, No. 9, 1995.

37. Samuel P. Bates, *Pennsylvania in the Civil War: Militia Troops of 1863* (Harrisburg, PA: B. Singerly, State Printer, 1869–1871; *History of the PA Volunteers, 1861–1865*, Harrisburg, 1868–1871; www.campcurtin.org; ORN Series I, Vol. 27, Part 3, 812.

38. *Biographical Directory of the Railway Officials of America*, 1893.

39. J. P. Ashcom, *History of Renovo*, from the 1871 *Renovo Record*, transcribed by Stephen F. Miller, Jr.

40. *Times*, May 10, 1896.

41. The majority of Baldwin's records and drawings were destroyed when the firm's locomotive production ceased in the mid-1950s. What remains is widely scattered among private collectors and the Railroad Museum of Pennsylvania, Historical Society of Pennsylvania, the DeGolyer Library of Southern Methodist University, the Smithsonian's National Museum of American History, and others.

42. Philadelphia city directories, 1868, 1869.

43. Steam Locomotive Builders (www.steamlocomotive.com).

44. John K. Brown, *The Baldwin Locomotive Works 1831–1915* (Baltimore: Johns Hopkins University Press, 1995), 85.

45. *Ibid.*, 75, 85.

46. *Ibid.*, 109–111.

47. *Ibid.*, 45.

48. *Ibid.*, 83.

49. "Passengers Arrived; Passengers Sailed," *Times*, July 2, 1871, and November 10, 1871; Passport applications (www.ancestry.com). The SS *Atlantic* was a single screw, four-masted vessel of the White Star Line. On April 1, 1873, on its 19th voyage, the *Atlantic* struck an underwater rock off Nova Scotia and 562 of the 957 people on board perished.

50. *New York Times*, August 31, 1875.

51. *Biographical Directory of the Railway Officials of America*, 1893.

52. *History of the Baldwin Locomotive Works, 1832–1913* (Philadelphia, 1913), 68.

53. Baldwin Locomotive Works files, *Register of Engines Made by Burnham, Parry, Williams, 1874* (Washington, DC: Smithsonian Institution, National Museum of American History, 1874), 51, 182.

54. *Ibid.*

55. DeGolyer Library, Baldwin Locomotive Collection, Southern Methodist University, University Park, Texas.

56. "The Manufacture of Locomotives," *Scientific American*, May 31, 1884.

57. www.u-s-history.com; www.publicbookshelf.com; *Times* from the *Philadelphia Ledger*, November 6, 1873.

58. *Biographical Directory of the Railway Officials of America*, 1893.

59. *Ibid.*

60. Edward Hungerford, *Men of the Erie: A Story*

of Human Effort (New York: Random House, 1946), 104.

60. *Erie Railroad Magazine*, Employee Master Index (www.rootsweb.ancestry.com).
61. *New York Times*, May 5, 1876.
62. *Biographical Directory of the Railway Officials of America*, 1893.
63. Keokuk City Directories, 1877–1880.
64. William Edward Hayes, *Iron Road to Empire: The History of 100 years of the Progress and Achievements of the Rock Island Lines* (New York : Simmons-Boardman,1953), 98, 100–101.
65. *Biographical Directory of the Railway Officials of America*, 1893.
66. Hayes, *Iron Road to Empire*, 101.

Chapter IV

1. *New York Times*, April 3, 1880.
2 *New York Times*, November 20, 1880.
3. Hal R. Varian, "Dealing with Inflation," Nytimes.com, June 5, 2003.
4. *New York Times*, February 21, 1882.
5. *New York Times*, March 29, 1882.
6. *New York Times*, March 30, 1882.
7. *New York Times*, March 31, 1882.
8. *New York Times*, April 1, 1882.
9. *New York Times*, April 3, 1882.
10. Annual Report of the Board of Railroad Commissioners, FY 1885, Vol. II, 1151.
11. *New York Times*, September 27, 1882, and October 13, 1882.
12. *New York Times*, December 31, 1882.
13. *New York Times*, January 6, 1883.
14. *Ibid*.
15. *New York Times*, January 9, 1883.
16. *New York Times*, January 12, 1883.
17. *New York Times*, January 30, 1883.
18. *New York Times*, August 2, 1880.
19 Annual Report of the Board of Railroad Commissioners, FY 1884, Vol. I, 93.
20. *New York Times*, December 5, 1885.
21. *New York Times*, January 13, 1882.
22. John H. White, Jr., "Spunky Little Devils: Locomotives of the New York Elevated," *Railroad History* 162, Spring 1990, 52.
23. *New York Times*, December 28, 1881.
24. *New York Times*, November 19, 1884, and November 26, 1884.
25. John R. Stevens, ed., *Pioneers of Electric Railroading* (Electric Railroaders' ' Association, 1991), 42.
26. *New York Times*, November 19, 1884, and November 26, 1884.
27. Samuel Carter, III, *Cyrus Field: Man of Two Worlds* (New York: G. P. Putnam's Sons, 1968), 339.
28. Stevens, *Pioneers of Electric Railroading*, 42.
29. *Ibid*.
30. *New York Times*, November 13, 1885, and November 14, 1885.
31. *Ibid.*, 43.

32. *Ibid.*, 44.
33. *Ibid*.
34. William D. Middleton and William D. Middleton, III, *Frank Julian Sprague, Electrical Inventor & Engineer* (Bloomington: Indiana University Press, 2009), 51.
35. *Ibid.*, 52.
36. *New York Times*, May 14, 1880.
37. *New York Times*, December 21, 1881.
38. *New York Times*, September 20, 1880.
39. *New York Times*, May 12, 1896.
40. *New York Times*, October 24, 1880.
41. *The Sun*, January 22, 1881.
42. *New York Times*, February 6, 1881.
43. Annual Report of the Board of Railroad Commissioners, FY 1885, Vol. I, 238–240.
44. *New York Tribune*, January 17, 1888.
45. *New York Times*, April 8, 1882.
46. *The Sun*, May 10, 1883.
47. *New York Times*, January 11, 1888, January 12, 1888, and November 10, 1888.
48. *New York Times*, April 14, 1885.
49. *New York Times*, July 16, 1881.
50. *New York Times*, February 10, 1881.
51. *New York Times*, March 11, 1884.
52. Annual Report of the Board of Railroad Commissioners, FY 1885, Vol. II, 1149, 1152, 1158, 1164.
53. Annual Report of the Board of Railroad Commissioners, FY 1885, Vol. II, 1146.

Chapter V

1. Gene Sansone, *New York Subways, An Illustrated History of New York City's Transit Cars,* (Baltimore: Johns Hopkins University Press in association with the New York Transit Museum, 1997), 28.
2. www.nyc.architecture.com; Elizabeth Hawes, *New York, New York, How the Apartment House Transformed the Life of the City (1869–1930)* (New York: Henry Holt, 1993). The Navarro Apartments were razed in 1930 and the site is currently the home of the New York Athletic Club.
3. *New York Times*, January 4, 1886.
4. *New York Times*, January 5, 1886.
5. *New York Times*, January 6, 1886.
6. *Brooklyn Eagle*, January 6, 1886.
7. *New York Times*, January 6, 1886.
8. *New York Times*, January 8, 1886.
9. *New York Times*, January 9, 1886.
10. William Fullerton Reeves, *The First Elevated Railroads in Manhattan and the Bronx of the City of New York* (New York: The New York Historical Society, 1936), 34–35.
11. *Ibid.*, 35–36.
12. *Ibid.*, 36–39; Sansone, *New York Subways*, 27.
13. *Ibid.*, 41.
14. Annual Report of the Board of Railroad Commissioners, FY 1895, Vol. II, 719; *Times*, November 10, 1892, November 9, 1893, November 14, 1895.
15. *New York Times*, June 5, 1886.

16. *New York Times*, June 6, 1886.
17. *New York Times*, July 3, 1886.
18. *New York Times*, October 21, 1886.
19. *New York Times*, October 25, 1886, and October 26, 1886.
20. *New York Tribune*, May 8, 1886.
21. *New York Times*, April 11, 1887.
22. *New York Times*, June 10, 1887.
23. Annual Report of the Board of Railroad Commissioners, FY 1886, Vol. I, xix; *Times*, June 3, 1886; *The Sun*, October 13, 1886.
24. *The Sun*, October 26, 1886.
25. *New York Times*, December 4, 1887.
26. *New York Times*, October 1, 1888.
27. John R. Stevens, ed., *Pioneers of Electric Railroading* (Electric Railroaders, Association, 1991), 45; William D. Middleton and William D. Middleton, III, *Frank Julian Sprague, Electrical Inventor and Engineer* (Bloomington: Indiana University Press, 2009), 50.
28. *Ibid.*, 55.
29. *Ibid.*, 56.
30. *Ibid.*, 58.
31. *Ibid.*
32. Stevens, *Pioneers of Electric Railroading*, 46.
33. Middleton and Middleton, III, *Frank Julian Sprague*, 112.
34. *Ibid.*, 43.
35. *Ibid.*
36. *New York Times*, April 21, 1886.
37. *New York Times*, June 6, 1886.
38. *Times*, March 3, 1887.
39. *New York Times*, October 20, 1886; *New York Tribune*, October 30, 1886.
40. *New York Times*, June 29, 1887.
41. www.nycsubway.org/articles.
42. *New York Times*, March 13, 1888.
43. *The Sun*, March 13, 1888.
44. *New York Daily Graphic*, March 15, 1888.
45. www.newyorkhistory.info.
46. Author's family files. Reference to FKH's birth "some fifty years ago" suggests the article is dated 1886. However, reference to his service with the Manhattan company, "the last thirteen years," suggests 1893; *Reading Press*, March 4, 1886.
47. *Railroad Gazette*, March 19, 1886.
48. *New York Tribune*, January 14, 1887.
49. *New York Times*, January 11, 1888, and January 12, 1888.
50. *New York Tribune*, January 12, 1888.
51. *New York Times*, November 10, 1888.
52. *New York Tribune*, November 11, 1888.
53. *Ibid.*
54. Annual Report of the Board of Railroad Commissioners, FY 1886, Vol. I, 158–159.
55. *New York Times*, December 12, 1886.
56. *New York Times*, January 20, 1887.
57. *New York Times*, February 24, 1884.
58. *New York Times*, February 9, 1887.
59. Annual Report to the Board of Railroad Commissioners, FY 1887, Vol. I, 111.
60. *New York Times*, May 5, 1887.
61. *New York Times*, October 19, 1887.
62. Annual Report of the Board of Railroad Commissioners, FY 1888, Vol. I, 197–198.
63. *New York Times*, May 10, 1888.
64. John H. White, Jr., "Spunky Little Devils: Locomotives of the New York Elevated," *Railroad History*, Spring 1990, 43.
65. Annual Report of the Board of Railroad Commissioners, FY 1889, Vol. 1, 189–190.
66. *New York Times*, October 23, 1888.
67. *New York Times*, April 3, 1887.
68. *New York Times*, March 7, 1886.
69. *New York Tribune*, June 25, 1888.
70. *New York Times*, May 13, 1887.
71. *Times*, July 29, 1888; "Newport History—Class and Leisure at America's First Resort, 1870–1914" (xroads.virginia.edu).

Chapter VI

1. *New York Times*, August 22, 1922; *Brooklyn Eagle*, August 23, 1892.
2. Annual Report of the Board of Railroad Commissioners, FY 1890, Vol. II, 677.
3. *New York Times*, July 13, 1892, and July 14, 1892.
4. *New York Times*, December 3, 1892, and *New York Tribune*, December 3, 1892.
5. Maury Klein, *The Life and Legend of Jay Gould* (Baltimore: Johns Hopkins University Press, 1986), 484–485.
6. *Ibid.*, 486, 489.
7. *New York Times*, May 24, 1891.
8. Alfred Price, *Rail Life, A Book of Yarns* (Toronto: Thomas Allen, 1925), 237–238.
9. *New York Times*, December 23, 1889.
10. William D. Middleton and William D. Middleton, III, *Frank Julian Sprague, Electrical Inventor and Engineer* (Bloomington: Indiana University Press, 2009), 112–113.
11. *New York Times*, October 12, 1892.
12. *New York Times*, October 13, 1892.
13. *New York Times*, December 31, 1892.
14. *New York Times*, March 8, 1889.
15. *New York Times*, October 3, 1890.
16. *New York Times*, December 13, 1890.
17. *New York Times*, June 26, 1891.
18. *New York Times*, January 10, 1892.
19. *New York Times*, September 28, 1890.
20. *New York Times*, April 17, 1892.
21. *New York Times*, December 4, 1892.
22. *New York Tribune*, May 17, 1892.
23. *New York Tribune*, May 19, 1892.
24. *New York Times*, May 24, 1891.
25. *Brooklyn Eagle*, November 1, 1889.
26. *New York Times*, February 13, 1891.
27. *New York Times*, January 3, 1891.
28. Annual Report of the Board of Railroad Commissioners, FY 1891, Vol. 1, 231.

29. *New York Times*, January 11, 1888, January 12, 1888, and November 10, 1888.
30. *New York Times*, December 7, 1891.
31. *New York Times*, December 29, 1891.
32. *New York Times*, January 12, 1891.
33. Annual Report of the Board of Railroad Commissioners, FY 1891, Vol. 1, 230.
34. *New York Times*, May 30, 1890.
35. *New York Times*, June 7, 1890.
36. *New York Times*, August 9, 1890.
37. *New York Times*, July 24, 1891.
38. *New York Times*, July 13, 1890, and January 18, 1891.
39. *The Sun*, May 17, 1891.
40. *New York Times*, March 30, 1889.
41. *New York Times*, January 14, 1891.
42. *New York Times*, November 26, 1892.
43. *Times*, July 21, 1889, and July 30, 1889; Frank K. Hain's cousin, Mary Ellen (Kintzel) Wallace, music teacher, born October 1865 in Pennsylvania, daughter of Mary A. Thomas and Christian Kintzel.
44. *New York Times*, December 27, 1891.
45. *New York Times*, May 25, 1892.
46. *Brooklyn Eagle*, July 22, 1892.
47. *New York Times*, November 13, 1890, November 11, 1891, and November 10, 1892.

Chapter VII

1. Minnesota Public Radio, News & Features, December 3, 2009; www.historycentral.com/Industrialage; www.u-s-history.com; www.usgennet.org.
2. *Times*, November 9, 1893, November 15, 1894, December 6, 1895; Annual Report of the Board of Railroad Commissioners, FY 1895, Vol. II, 717.
3. *New York Times*, December 29, 1893.
4. *New York Times*, November 17, 1894.
5. *New York Times*, January 18, 1893.
6. *New York Times*, May 27, 1893.
7. *New York Times*, June 4, 1893.
8. Lelia Robinson (1850–1891), the first woman admitted to the Massachusetts Bar; Law Library of Congress: *Women Lawyers and State Bar Admission*. Annie R. Hain graduated from the Women's Law Class (WLC) of New York University on April 29, 1896. The WLC opened for women on October 30, 1890, and did not lead to a professional law degree, but was akin to a continuing education program for women interested in the law. Although some women went on to obtain law degrees, the program was founded to provide women with legal knowledge. The WLC was administered by the Women's Legal Education Society (WLES) under the auspices of the university. Miss Helen Gould, daughter of Jay Gould, completed the course a year earlier than Annie R. Hain and was a benefactor of the WLC as well as a president of the WLES. (*Times*, April 30, 1896; Gretchen Feltes, Reference Librarian, New York University Law Library, August 11, 2008; NYU Archives, Select Guide to Women's History Collection, Emilyn L. Brown).
9. *New York Times*, September 25, 1893.
10. *New York Times*, September 28, 1893.
11. *New York Times*, September 29, 1893.
12. *New York Times*, October 4, 1893.
13. *Ibid*.
14. *New York Tribune*, January 14, 1887.
15. John H. White, Jr., "Spunky Little Devils: Locomotives of the New York Elevated," *Railroad History*, Spring 1990, 41–44.
16. Author's family files.
17. *New York Times*, April 26, 1894.
18. *New York Times*, June 16, 1894.
19. *New York Times*, June 21, 1895.
20. *New York Times*, August 14, 1895.
21. *New York Times*, December 6, 1893.
22. *New York Times*, February 18. 1894.
23. *New York Times*, April 1, 1894.
24. *New York Times*, April 25, 1894.
25. *New York Times*, May 10, 1896.
26. *Times,* December 6, 1895; Annual Report of the Board of Railroad Commissioners, FY 1895, 715–721.

Chapter VIII

1. Steamtown Special History Study, American Electric Locomotives, based on William D. Middleton, *When the Steam Railroads Electrified* (Milwaukee: Kalmbach Books, 1974).
2. Randy Alfred (www.wired.com/science/discoveries), June 2, 2008.
3. *New York Times*, May 21, 1893.
4. *New York Times*, December 6, 1894.
5. *New York Times*, April 11, 1895.
6. *New York Times*, June 1, 1895.
7. *New York Times*, June 14, 1895.
8. *New York Times*, June 15, 1895.
9. *New York Tribune*, June 25, 1895.
10. *New York Times*, August 25, 1895.
11. *Wall Street Journal*, October 13, 1895.
12. *Wall Street Journal*, October 23, 1895.
13. *Wall Street Journal*, December 6, 1895.
14. *New York Times*, February 2, 1896.

Chapter IX

1. *Montour American*, Danville, PA, May 14, 1896; *New York Tribune*, June 7, 1896.
2. *New York Times*, August 19, 1894.
3. *New York Times*, October 14, 1894.
4. *New York Times*, December 23, 1894.
5. *Times*, January 23, 1895; William Fullerton Reeves, *The First Elevated Railroads in Manhattan and the Bronx of the City of New York* (New York: New York Historical Society, 1936), 47; Robert C. Reed, *The New York Elevated* (New York: A. S. Barnes, 1978), 95.

6. *New York Times*, March 5, 1895.
7. *New York Times*, June 30, 1895.
8. *Brooklyn Eagle*, July 8, 1895.
9. *New York Times*, August 18, 1895.
10. *New York Tribune*, December 1, 1895.
11. *New York Times*, December 15, 1895.
12. *New York Times*, May 10, 1896; *New York Sun*, May 14, 1896.
13. *New York Times*, May 10, 1896.
14. *Ibid.*
15. Clifton Springs Hospital and Clinic (www.cshosp.com/history).
16. *Brooklyn Eagle*, May 10, 1896.
17. *New York Daily Tribune*, May 13, 1896.
18. *New York Daily Tribune*, May 11, 1896.
19. Maury Klein, *The Life and Legend of Jay Gould* (Baltimore: Johns Hopkins University Press, 1986), 472; *Times*, December 3, 1892.
20. *New York Times*, May 10, 1896.
21. *New York Daily Tribune*, May 11, 1896.
22. *New York Sun*, May 14, 1896.
23 Frank K. Hain, Proving Last Will and Testament, Surrogate's Court, City and County of New York, July 31, 1896; Inventory & Appraisement, September 1, 1896, New York County, New York.
24. *Clifton Springs Press*, May 10, 1896.
25. Ontario County Archives, April 21, 2008. Neither the Ontario County Historical Society nor the Clifton Springs Historical Society have medical records from the sanitarium. Furthermore, the sanitarium's medical records department was not established until 1908, and in any case, records are not retained longer than ten years.
26. *Times*, May 27, 1897; *The Gem*, Danville, PA, May 27, 1897.
27. *Ibid.*
28. *Ibid.*
29. *Times*, May 27, 1897, and April 4, 1897; *New York Daily Tribune*, May 27, 1897; *New York Evening Telegram*, May 26, 1897.
30. *Morning News*, Danville, PA, February 25, 1929.
31. Cynthia Elder, Montour County Genealogical Society, e-mail, February 18, 2008.
32. C. M. Davies, *History of Holland from the Beginning of the Tenth to the Eighteenth Century* (London: John W. Parker West Strand, 1842), Vol. 2, 571.

Chapter X

1. *New York Times*, January 18, 1899.
2. *New York Times*, May 20, 1896.
3. William D. Middleton and William D. Middleton, III, *Frank Julian Sprague, Electrical Inventor & Engineer* (Bloomington: Indiana University Press), 2009, 113.
4. Gene Sansone, *New York Subways, An Illustrated History of New York City's Transit Cars* (Baltimore: Johns Hopkins University Press in association with the New York Transit Museum, 1997), 5.

5. Middleton and Middleton, III, *Frank Julian Sprague*, 114.
6. *Ibid.*
7. John H. White, Jr., "Spunky Little Devils: Locomotives of the New York Elevated," *Railroad History* 162, Spring 1990, 53.
8. Annual Report of the Board of Railroad Commissioners for the Year 1896, Vol. I, xi-xii.
9. *New York Times*, May 2, 1897.
10. *New York Times*, January 16, 1898.
11. Middleton and Middleton, III, *Frank Julian Sprague*, 115–116.
12. *Ibid.*, 117.
13. Middleton and Middleton, III, *Frank Julian Sprague*, 118, 121, 126.
14. *New York Times*, December 5, 1898.
15. Middleton and Middleton, III, *Frank Julian Sprague*, 132.
16. Alfred Skitt was born August 4, 1850, in London. He emigrated to the United States on May 1, 1871, and he was naturalized on May 31, 1898 (ancestry.com).
17. *New York Times*, November 23, 1898.
18. *New York Times*, January 18, 1899.
19. *New York Times*, December 5, 1898.
20. *New York Times*, March 1, 1899.
21. Middleton and Middleton, III, *Frank Julian Sprague*, 1134.
22. *Ibid.*
23. *Ibid.*; Brian J. Cudahy, *Under the Sidewalks of New York* (Brattleboro, VT: The Stephen Greene Press, 1979), 22.
24. *New York Times*, June 13, 1900.
25. *Times*, January 10, 1902; Sansone, *New York Subways*, 19.
26. James Blaine Walker, *Fifty Years of Rapid Transit, 1864–1917* (copyright 1916, reprint by Arno Press and *The New York Times*, 1970), 183.
27. www.newyorkhistory.info.
28. Sansone, *New York Subways*, 27; *Times*, April 4, 1903.
29. *New York Times*, April 4, 1903.
30. Walker, *Fifty Years of Rapid Transit*, 186.
31. *New York Times*, March 28, 1903.
32. *New York Times*, August 28, 1903.
33. Cudahy, *Under the Sidewalks*, 18.
34. Walker, *Fifty Years of Rapid Transit*, 123.
35. *Ibid.*, 129–130.
36. *Ibid.*, 130.
37. *Ibid.*, 132–133.
38. *Ibid.*, 134–135.
39. *Ibid.*, 136.
40. *Ibid.*, 139.
41. *Ibid.*, 140.
42. *Ibid.*, 141.
43. *Ibid.*, 141–161.
44. *Ibid.*, 163.
45. *Ibid.*, 171.
46. *Ibid.*, 164–166.
47. *Ibid.*, 172.
48. Cudahy, *Under the Sidewalks*, 12.

49. *Ibid.*, 28–29.
50. *New York Times*, October 28, 1904.
51. Cudahy, *Under the Sidewalks*, 12.
52. *Ibid.*, 13.
53. Joseph Brennan, *The Beach Pneumatic Transit Company* (an original web publication, copyright 2004–2005), Chapter 20, "It is Contemplated to Amalgamate"; Sansone, *New York Subways*, 5–6.
54. Cudahy, *Under the Sidewalks*, 17.
55. *Ibid.*
56. www.mta.info/nyct, MTA New York City Transit — History and Chronology.
57. www.nycsubway.org/articles.
58. Walker, *Fifty Years of Rapid Transit*, 167–171.
59. *Ibid.*, 188.
60. *Ibid.*, 190.
61. *Ibid.*, 192–193.
62. *Ibid.*, 198.
63. www.nycsubway.org/articles.

Appendix

1. D. H. B. Brower, *Danville, Montour County, Pennsylvania: A Collection of Historical and Biographical Sketches* (Harrisburg, PA: Lane S. Hart, printer and binder, Montour County Genealogical Society, 1881), 85–87.
2. *Ibid.*
3. *Ibid.*
4. *Pennsylvania Archives*, Series 5, Vol. III, 636, and Series 2, Vol. XIV, 317 and 343.
5. William Gardner Finney, *History of the Chillisquaque Church* (Montour County Genealogical Society, 1926), 11.
6. DAR membership rolls; *Morning News*, Danville, PA, February 23, 1929; Register of the Pennsylvania Society of Colonial Dames of America, 1903, Wickersham Co., PA.
7. *Montour American*, June 23, 1904, Danville, PA (MCGS). The inscription and relatives honored: "These bodies were removed from the Presbyterian grave yard and the Lemon homestead and this monument erected in their honor by their granddaughter, Anna R. McWilliams Hain, 1903." Lt. Robert Curry (1741–1780) and his wife, Jane McWilliams (1750–1825), [Annie R. Hain's great-grandparents]; Thomas Lemon (1730–1775), a judge of the First Court of Common Pleas, Northumberland County, appointed by George III, 1772, and his wife, Margaret Slough (1735–1824), [maternal great-grandparents]; James Lemon (1757–1842) and his wife, Rachel Fleming (1765–1840), [maternal grandparents]; Robert McWilliams (1775–1823) and his wife, Jane Curry (1773–1858), [grandparents].
8. *Ibid.*
9. Paul F. Kostenbauder, *Mooresburg Presbyterian Church History*, 1976, 7 (MCGS).
10. NARA, Frank K. Hain pension file.
11. Annie R. Hain, Probate File 694–1929, Surrogate's Court, New York County, NY.
12. George Adams Post was born at Cuba, Allegany County, NY, on September 1, 1854, and died on October 31, 1925, at Somerset, NJ, where flags were flown at half mast and businesses closed on the afternoon of his funeral. He was buried at Evergreen Cemetery, Oswego, NY. He was married to Minnie C. Munson of Susquehanna, PA. His father, Ira A. Post, was an employee of the Erie Railroad for 50 years and was station agent at Susquehanna Depot in 1880. George A. Post began his business career at age 18 when he entered the freight department of the Erie and advanced to assistant to Frank K. Hain, superintendent of motive power at Susquehanna Depot. At age 22, he was elected mayor of Susquehanna Depot. He studied law while clerking with the Erie, was admitted to the Bar in 1881, and began his practice in Montrose, PA. From 1883–1889 he was one of the owners and editors of the *Montrose Democrat*. He was elected as a Democrat to the 48th Congress, 1883–1885, where he was the youngest member of the House. George A. Post moved to NYC in 1889 and became a writer for the *New York World*. He returned to his railroad roots and entered into the manufacture of railway equipment, serving as vice president and later president of the Standard Coupler Company. He was founder and president of the Railway Business Association and chairman of the railroad committee of the U. S. Chamber of Commerce. He had many influential friends, among whom were former U. S. Senator Joseph S. Freylinghuysen (R-NJ); Julius S. Barnes, president of the U. S. Chamber of Commerce; Emory R. Johnson, dean of the Wharton School of Finance; University of Pennsylvania, R. W. Green of the NYSE firm Green, Elling & Anderson; and Thomas A. Flockhart, mayor of Somerset, NJ (*Unionist Gazette*, Somerville, NJ, November 25, 1925).
13. Annie R. Hain, Probate File, Schedule F.

Bibliography

Annual Report of the Board of Railroad Commissioners of the State of New York, FY 1883, 1885, 1886, 1887, 1888, 1889, 1891, 1895.

Baldwin Locomotive Works Collection. DeGolyer Library, Southern Methodist University, University Park, Texas.

Baldwin Locomotive Works Collection. *Register of Engines Made by Burnham, Parry, Williams, 1874.* Washington, DC: Smithsonian Institution, National Museum of American History, 1874.

Bates, Samuel P. *Pennsylvania in the Civil War: Militia Troops of 1863, History of the Pennsylvania Volunteers 1861–1865.* Harrisburg, PA: B. Singerly, State Printer, 1869–1871.

Bennett, Frank M. *Steam Navy of the United States.* Westport, CT: Greenwood Press, 1896.

Biographical Directory of the Railway Officials of America for 1887. Chicago: Railway Age, 1887.

Boston Globe.

Brennan, Joseph. *The Beach Pneumatic Transit Company*, 2004–2005. www.columbia.edu/~brennan/beach/.

Brooklyn Eagle.

Brower, D. H. B. *Danville, Montour County, Pennsylvania: A Collection of Historical and Biographical Sketches.* Harrisburg, PA: Lane S. Hart, printer and binder, Montour County Genealogical Society, 1881.

Brown, John K. *Baldwin Locomotive Works, 1831–1915.* Baltimore: Johns Hopkins University Press, 1995.

Carter III, Samuel. *Cyrus Field: Man of Two Worlds.* New York: G. P. Putnam and Sons, 1968.

Census of the U. S. Department of the Interior. *Report on the Agencies of Transportation in the United States.* Washington, DC: Government Printing Office, 1883.

City Directories, Keokuk, IA, 1877–1880.

City Directories, New York City, 1880–1920.

City Directories, Philadelphia, PA, 1868, 1869.

Cobb, Graham R. "Remember the D & H." *Bridge Line Historical Society Bulletin*, Vol. 5, No. 9, 1995.

Daily Graphic. New York.

Death Registers, City of Reading, PA.

Dictionary of American Naval Fighting Ships. Washington, DC: Department of the Navy, 1959–1981.

Dufour, Charles L. *The Night the War Was Lost.* Garden City, NY: Doubleday, 1960.

Elevated Railway Journal, Vol. II, No. 10, December 4, 1880.

Erie Railroad Magazine, Employee Master Index, rootsweb/ancestry.com.

Finney, Rev. William Gardner. *History of the Chillisquaque Church.* Montour County (PA) Genealogical Society, 1926.

Gate City. Keokuk, IA.

Gem. Danville, PA.

Goebel, Lt. Col. Peter. "Evacuation Day." *SAR Magazine*, Vol. 103, No. 3, Winter 2009.

Grodinsky, Julius. *Jay Gould, His Business Career, 1867–1892.* Philadelphia: University of Pennsylvania Press, 1957.

Hain Family. Reading, PA: *Reading Eagle* Press, 1941.

Hayes, William Edward. *Iron Road to Empire: The History of 100 Years of the Progress and Achievements of the Rock Island Lines.* New York: Simmons-Boardman, 1953.

Hearn, Chester G. *The Capture of New Orleans, 1862.* Baton Rouge: Louisiana State University Press, 1995.

Historical Society of Berks County, PA.

History of the Baldwin Locomotive Works, 1832–

1913. Philadelphia: BalwdinBaldwin-Lima-Hamilton Corp., 1913.

"History of Public Transportation in New York City." New York Transit Museum.

Hungerford, Edward. *Men of the Erie: A Story of Human Effort*. New York: Random House, 1946.

Intelligencer. Danville, PA.

Jones, Virgil C. *Civil War at Sea*. Winston, NY: Holt, Rinehart, Winston, 1961.

Klein, Maury. *The Life and Legend of Jay Gould*. Baltimore: Johns Hopkins University Press, 1986.

Kostenbauder, Paul F. *Mooresburg Presbyterian Church History*. 1976.

Langley, Harold D. "Fighting Fortune." William C. Davis, ed., *The Civil War Sailor's Life: The Images of War, 1861–1865, Vol. IV*. 6 vols. New York: Doubleday, 1981–1984.

Law Library of Congress, Women Lawyers and State Bar Admission.

Middleton, William D. *Steamtown Special History Study, American Electric Locomotives* (based on "When the Steam Railroads Electrified"). Milwaukee: Kalmbach Books, 1974.

Middleton, William D., and William D. Middleton, III, *Frank Julian Sprague, Electrical Inventor and Engineer*. Bloomington: Indiana University Press, 2009.

Minnesota Public Radio, News and Features, December 3, 2009.

Montour American. Danville, PA.

Montour County, PA, Genealogical Society.

Montour County, PA, Historical Society.

Morning News. Danville, PA.

New York Sun.

New York Times.

New York Tribune.

New York World.

New York University Archives, Select Guide to Women's History Collections.

New York University Law Library.

Official Map and Guide to all the Elevated Railways in New York City. Manhattan Railway Company, 1881.

Official Record, Navy (ORN) — Military Pension File (1857–1926), Deck Logs (1858 and 1861–1862). Washington, DC: National Archives and Records Administration,

Ontario County, NY, Archives.

Pennsylvania Archives.

Price, Alfred. *Rail Life, A Book of Yarns*. Toronto: Thomas Allen, 1925.

Probate Records, New York County.

Recorder of Deeds, Berks County, PA.

Reed, Robert C. *The New York Elevated*. New York: A. S. Barnes, 1978.

Reeves, William Fullerton. *The First Elevated Railroads in Manhattan and the Bronx of the City of New York*. New York: New York Historical Society, 1936.

Sansone, Gene. *New York Subways: An Illustrated History of New York City's Transit Cars*. Baltimore: Johns Hopkins University Press, 1997.

Sarnoff, Paul. *Russell Sage: The Money King*. New York: Ivan Oblensky, Inc., 1965.

Stevens, John R. *Pioneers of Electric Railroading*. New York: Electric Railroaders Association, 1991.

"The Manufacture of Locomotives." *Scientific American*, May 31, 1884.

"The Progress of Elevated Railways." *Scientific American*, Vol. XLI, No.17, October 25, 1879.

Unionist Gazette. Somerville, NJ.

Walker, James Blaine. *Fifty Years of Rapid Transit*. New York: Arno Press and the *New York Times*, 1916.

White, Jr., John H. "Spunky Little Devils: Locomotives of the New York Elevated." *Railroad History* 162, Spring 1990.

Withuhn, William L., *Rails Across America: A History of Railroads in North America*. New York: Smithmark Publishers, 1993.

Index

Numbers in ***bold italics*** indicate pages with photographs.

accidents 61–64, 81–86, 96, 103–106, 118
Accommodation 5
Albany Street Iron Works 16
Allis 146
A.R. Whitney Company 14
Arcade Railroad *6*, 7–8
Arthur, P.M. *see* Brotherhood of Locomotive Engineers

Babcock & Wilcox 146
Baldwin engines *17*, *19*, *45–46*, 57
Baldwin Locomotive Works 44
Beach, Alfred Ely *7–8*
Belmont, August *146*–147, 151, 153, 157
Benjamin Franklin 58–59, 77
block system 62–63
Board of Rapid Transit Commissioners 96, 142, 146, 149–150
Boston Elevated Railway 146
Boston West End Street Railway 149
Bowers, Dure 23
Bowery, 1900 *85*
Brooks *16*
Brotherhood of Locomotive Engineers 52–54, 67–68, 70–71, 73, 117–118, 148
Brower, Abraham *see* *Accommodation*
Brush motor 58
Bryan, E.P. 147–148
Burnham, George 44, *45*

Chauncey real estate syndicate 107
Chicago & South Side 144
Chicago elevated railways 122–124, 144
Chicago Railway Exhibition 121
Chicago, Rock Island and Pacific Railroad 49

Chicago World's Fair 121–123
Clark, Reeves 14
coal burning stoves 20
color blindness in employees 104–105
Colorado 39nn8–13
Columbian Intramural Railroad 122, 124
Constantine, John H. 139
construction 11, 13–15
Corbin, Austin 78
Cropsey, Jasper 25

Daft, Dr. Leo 58–59, 77
Delaware, Lackawanna & Western 42
Dillon, Sidney 71
distributive motive power *see* Sprague, Frank J.
Dows, David 16
Drexel, Morgan & Company 58
dummy engines *16*–17

Eames vacuum brake 20
Eastlake, Charles L. 25
Edge Moor Iron 14
Edison-Field motor *see* Field, Stephen D.
Eickemeyer-Field Company *see* Field, Stephen D.
Electric Storage Company 126, 143
elevated road near 116th Street *98*
elevated stations *24*, *84*
engine no. 10 *19*
Erie Railroad 48
Ewing, Dr. William A. 131

Farragut, Adm. David G. 41
Field, Cyrus W. 30–31, 33–36, 58, 71, 76–77, 93
Field, Dr. 81

Field, Edward M. 93
Field, Stephen D. 57–59, 76, 121
Forney, Matthias 16
Forney locomotives 16, *17*, 18, 86, 115
41st Regiment, Pennsylvania Infantry Militia 42–43
Foster, Dr. Henry 131
Fransioli, W.J. 103, 109, 119, 136–137, 141, 145

Gallaway, R.M. 31, 56, 59, 63, 70–71, 145
General Electric 124, 126, 143, 146
Gilbert, Rufus H. 11, *12*
Gilbert & Bush 23–24
Gilbert Elevated Railroad Company 11, *12*, 13
Gold, Stephen J. 20
Gould, Edwin 32, 147
Gould, Frank 32, 124
Gould, George Jay 93, *94*, 95 125–126, 143–144, 147
Gould, Howard 32, 147
Gould, Jason "Jay" 30–*31*, 32–34, 39–40, 48–49, 59, 78–79, 93, 133
Grant, May. Hugh J. 150
Grant Locomotive Works 17
Green, Andrew H. 106
Green, Charles L. 53

Hain, Annie R. 39–40, 112–113n8, 119, 131, 139, 161–163
Hain, Charles H. 37, 48
Hain, Frank K.: association with Jay Gould 32, 39, 48, 49; Baldwin in Russia 44, *45–46*, 47; character 80, 119, 127–128; civic positions 87, 106–107, 118–119; death 131–139; early life 37; elec-

175

Index

tric and pneumatic power 57–60, 123–126; health 40, 42–43, 79, 129, 132–134; management style 30, 81–82, 88, 101–102, 104–105, 115–116, 118; marriage 40–41; military service 39–**40**, 43; operations 28–30, 51, 54–55, 60, 62–63, 65, 67, 76–77, 79–80, 83–88, 105; railroad career **38**, 42–49; society 65, 67–**69**, 88, 108, 112, 129–130; union relations 52–54, 68–71, 73
Hain, George Meily 37, 44
Hain, Lydena 37
Hain, Margaret F. Kintzel 37
Hain, Rebecca McWilliams 41, 43
Hain, Samuel 37
Hain Club 119
Hardie, Robert 57, 142
Harvey, Charles T. **8**, 9, 16
Hedley, Frank 148, 149
Hein, Adm. Piet **140**
Hewitt, May. Abram S. 149–151
Hoffman, Gov. John 8

integrated rapid transit 91–92
Interborough Rapid Transit Company (IRT) 19, 147, 159
Intramural Railway 144
Iroquois **40**–42

Jackson & Sharp 21
Janney, Eli 29, 134
Johnson, E.H. *see* Field, Stephen D.
Julien Electric Traction Company 87

Keokuk & Des Moines 48–49
Keystone Bridge 14

Lake Street Elevated Railroad 146
Lighting *see* Pintsch, Julius

Mangin, Thomas A. 139
Manhattan Railway Company: accidents 62–64, 79, 81–86, 96, 103–106, 118; complaints 20, 55–56, 61, 87, 97, 99–102, 111, 113–115; conversion to electric 57, 59–60, 76–77, 121, 124–126, 141–149; earnings 65–66, 74–76, 88, 92, 96, 108–110, 119–120; five cent fare 72, 75; lease to Belmont Syndicate 147; locomotives *see* rolling stock; passenger cars *see* rolling stock; receivership 30, 51; Tripartite Agreement 27–36
Mason, John 5
McClellan, May. George B., Jr. 153–156
McDonald, John B. 150–**152**, 153, 157
McWilliams, Annie Rebecca *see* Hain, Annie R.
mechanical block system 62–63

Metropolitan Elevated Railway: articles of association 11–13; construction 14; New York Loan and Improvement Company 11; *see also* rolling stock
Metropolitan Street Railway Company 158–159
Metropolitan West Side Elevated Railroad 122–124, 144, 146
Mills & Ambrose 14
Morgan, J. Pierpont 97
multiple unit control *see* Sprague, Frank J.

National Cordage Company 109
Navarro, Jose de 68
Navarro Apartments aka Spanish flats 67–68, **69**
New York Elevated Railroad 9–11; *see also* rolling stock
New York Loan and Improvement Company 11
New York–New Jersey Bridge Act 106
Ninth Avenue Line *see* New York Elevated Railroad
Northwestern Elevated Railroad 146

Panic of 1873 11
Panic of 1893 109
Parsons, William Barclay 148, 151, 153, **158**
Passaic Rolling Mill 14
Peeples, Thomas Whitson 68
Philadelphia & Erie 43
Philadelphia & Reading 38, 67, 109
Pintsch, Julius 20
Pneumatic Tramway Engine Company 57
Post, George Adams 48, 129, 131, 133–134, 136–137, 163, 172n12
Post & McCord 146
Pullman 18, 23–24

Rapid Transit Act of 1891 and 1894 150–151
Rapid Transit Commission 10, 11, 25, 72, 96–97, 142, 158–159
Rapid Transit Subway Construction Company 151–152
Rhode Island 17
rolling stock 15–**16**, **17**–23
Rome 142

Sage, Russell 15, 30, 33–34, 58, 78–79, 110, 118, 123, 131, 134, 145
Sargent, Henry 6
School of Telegraphy 76
Second Avenue Line *see* Metropolitan Elevated Railway
shad belly 21–**22**; *see also* rolling stock
Siemens electric motor 58, 121–**122**

Sixth Avenue Line *see* Metropolitan Elevated Railway
Skitt, Alfred 144–145, 147, 171n16
South Side Elevated Railroad 144
Sprague, Frank J. 59–60, 76, 96, 142, 144, 146
stations 24–25
steam-heated cars *see* Gold, Stephen J.
steeple cab locomotive 76
Steinway, William 96, 150
Steinway Commission 96, 150
Stewart, A.T. 8
stock jobbing 29–30, 35, 132
strikes *see* Brotherhood of Locomotive Engineers
Suburban Rapid Transit Company 24, 67, 71–72
Subway (IRT): August Belmont **146**, 151, 152; Board of Rapid Transit Commissioners 150; first lines 158; ground breaking 153; Interborough-Metropolitan Company 159; John B. McDonald 151–**152**; Maj. Abram S. Hewitt 149; May. George B. McClelland, Jr. 153, 156; May. Hugh J. Grant 151; Rapid Transit Act of 1891 149; Rapid Transit Act of 1894 150; Rapid Transit Subway Construction Company 151; service begins 154; stations 155–156; Steinway Commission 150; William Barclay Parsons **158**
Swan, Charles H. 106

Third Avenue Line *see* New York Elevated Railroad
third rail 142–143
Tows, Francis H. 10
Tweed, William M. "Boss" 8–9

Vail, Charles M. 106
Viaduct Plan 8–9

Wason 22–24, 152–153
Westbrook, Judge Theodoric R. 30, 34
Westinghouse, George 29, 131
Westinghouse Electric 20, 121, 124, 146
Westside and Yonkers Patented Railway *see* Metropolitan Elevated Railway
Westside Patented Elevated Railway *see* Metropolitan Elevated Railway
Whitney, William C. 157
Willson, Hugh B. 6
Winslow, Edward F. 28
Wyman, David W. 16

YMCA Railroad Department 119

www.ingramcontent.com/pod-product-compliance
Lightning Source LLC
Chambersburg PA
CBHW081600300426
44116CB00015B/2943